Gotcha Back

L.A. Lane

www.lalanebooks.com

Gotcha Back

Published by:
L.A. Lane Books LLC
L.A. Lane
P.O. Box 6911
Columbia, MO 65205
www.lalanebooks.com

Library of Congress Cataloging -in-Publication Data
Gotcha Back
ISBN 978-0-6923-5149-9

Library of Congress Control Number: 2014922435
Printed in the United States

Publisher's Note:
This is a work of fiction, names, characters, places and incidents either are the product of the author's imagination or are used fictitiously, and any resemblance to actual persons, living or dead, business establishments, events or locales is entirely coincidental.

DEDICATION

Mary "Ms. Wee Wee" Lane

ACKNOWLEDGMENTS

I would like to acknowledge the following people with the help of publishing my first novel: First and foremost I would like to give thanks to God. Without Him I don't know where I would be. Secondly I would like to thank my husband and son for always having faith in me. Even when I wanted to give up on the book and many other things in my life you both stood in my corner and pushed me forward. I am truly thankful. I also would like to thank my Momma for being so supportive and understanding throughout my entire life. No matter what choices I made you always had my back. I would also like to thank my awesome team for helping me. You ladies are the glue that held this journey together. I am so thankful for you. Tiffany Lane, Marshanna Gresham, Sonya Collier and Ida Hatton thanks a bunch. To all my family and friends who were also supportive thanks. I am truly appreciative. I would like to thank LaTia Glasgow for the awesome book cover.

Prologue

June 7, 1999

It had been nine years since the Davis-Williams family moved from St. Louis to Columbia, Missouri. The Davis-Williams family was an ideal family. They were a family who actually behaved like a family. They cared, loved, honored and respected each other. Dena, a devoted mother of two worked as a paralegal for the Boyd & Boyd Law Firm. She only worked to buy designer clothes and to keep busy. She had three children from a previous marriage. However, she only raised two of them. Shanae and Victor were amazing children. After her divorce from their father Dena married Bernard. Bernard was the lead surgeon over the neurology unit at a local hospital. Besides making enough money from his profession and research projects to put him in the top 2% of highest paid neurologists in the country, Bernard was left a hefty amount of inheritance from his paternal grandparents who were also consistently and reliably involved in his life. This was one of the major reasons Dena was head over heels for Bernard.

The family lived in a mansion worth over $4.5 million. The breathtaking stately home was positioned on 75 acres. The home had an immense number of quarters. The interior of the house is focused around a large central hallway serving as the main avenue of traffic and entrance area to the adjacent rooms. None of the rooms was too busy, too stark or too contemporary. Each room had the perfect art chosen for its own décor. Dena had spent the greater part of her time with interior designers to perfect the mansion. There were four living rooms, two dining rooms and six bedrooms. Each room had a personal sitting area. The en suite in the bedrooms have Jacuzzis, as well as a shower and oversized jetted tubs. Her favorite was her master bedroom a single beam of daylight entered through a break between the curtains. None of the others compared to the sanctuary of hers. The bedroom held so many secrets that it never told anyone. It is unimaginable.

Dena coming from the old school worked hard for everything she had. No matter if it was working hard to get a rich man or working a nine to five job. Dena always handled her business. She wanted her children to understand that life wasn't easy. She didn't want to raise rich snobs. She wanted her children to be well rounded, diverse and aware of their heritage and ethnicity. Those were the main reasons she insisted her children go to a public high school. Her children had gone to Town and Country private school from kindergarten through eighth grade. She was particularly impressed with it because of the advanced technology available for her children. Shanae acquired her expensive tastes beginning in kindergarten.

During Shanae's first year of high school, Dena did the unthinkable. She enrolled Shanae in a public school. Bernard was totally against the drastic change, but he never voiced his opinion to Dena. Bernard was against this because he thought in public schools children learned all the wrong things. Dena sent her children to Hickman High School even though she knew it wasn't the best education her money could buy. She didn't want to shelter her kids from the truths of the world.

Hickman was a great learning experience for both Shanae and Victor. Over the years, they both fit in well with the majority of the students. Their time at Hickman High flew by. Dena couldn't believe Shanae was already graduating.

"Shanae, do you have everything you need?" Dena screamed upstairs.

"Yes, Momma, I do," replied Shanae.

Her momma was more thrilled than she was. Shanae was given early acceptance to Harvard, University of Virginia and Stanford. She chose to go to the University of Missouri-Saint Louis. It was closer to home. Shanae was very intelligent. She was able to learn easily, understand things quickly and could deal with new or difficult situations. She was also an attractive young lady. Dena's worst nightmare was sending her beautiful daughter off to college. They would both be in the same state just not under the same roof. The idea of Dena and Shanae not being under the same roof frustrated Dena. She could remember the activities that she participated in during college. Dena loved her daughter more than life itself, and nothing could ever change the love they shared. Dena was very proud of her daughter and everyone knew it.

Shanae was so gorgeous that people would hesitate to look at her a while longer because her beauty was intriguing. Shanae reminded Dena of herself in her younger days. The only thing Dena didn't particularly like about Shanae was how serious she was about her boyfriend. Don't get her wrong; Dena loved Hasaun because he treated her daughter with the utmost respect. On the other hand, Dena thought Shanae was too young to be so serious. Hasaun and Shanae have been dating since the summer before ninth grade. They are happy together. He played basketball and she was the captain of the cheerleading squad. Dena never had many objections towards Shanae's friends or acquaintances. Except, Dena couldn't stand her daughter's best friend Keya. Dena thought Keya was the most ill mannered child God had ever put a breath into.

Dena always told Shanae, "You betta watch that girl. She's not of our class. She ain't right." Despite Dena's objections,

Keya and Shanae remained friends throughout the years.

The evening when Dena saw her daughter walk across the stage and receive her diploma, she almost cried because she was so ecstatic. Dena was both happy and sad that night. Happy because Shanae was outstanding and sad because she knew in some other city she had another little girl graduating from high school also.

She would miss her graduation just like she had missed everything else in her life. Dena hated herself for not keeping her daughter. Dena grabbed Bernard's hand and held it tight. They were very proud of both Shanae and Victor. They had raised them to be well-thought of individuals. Shanae was graduating, and Victor would be doing the same in two years.

Later that evening before the senior all night party Dena had a brief talk with Shanae.

"Shanae, I am so proud of you."

Looking at her momma with a smile on her face Shanae replied. "I know you are, Momma." Walking over to hug her Shanae said, "Momma tonight is a joyous occasion so please put a smile on your face. It is not the end of the world. I am only going to college."

Dena knew her daughter was right and gave her vivid smile

she always gave. Shanae thought the conversation was over and began to walk away.

Her momma touched her arm and told her, "I love you so much and so does Bernard. If there is ever anything and I do mean anything you need, Bernard and I gotcha back."

Silently laughing Shanae replied, "Momma, I know you guys got my back so stop trippin' aight."

"Foo sho," Dena replied.

"Momma, you really need to stop letting Victor influence you so much because I don't think I can handle all this slang."

For the first time that evening, Shanae and Dena were laughing together.

"Shanae—" Before Dena could get her daughter's name out she was rudely interrupted.

"Shanae, come on girl." Keya yelled.

When Dena heard her voice she abruptly turned around. If looks could kill, Keya would have been dead. Dena was furious. She wanted to know how the little heifer got in her house and why she was so rude. Then she remembered Keya's family life. Father in prison, mother an alcoholic and who knew what else. Dena decided to let it slide. She gave her daughter a kiss on the cheek and gave Keya a shitty grin, which Keya knew wasn't sincere.

Keya didn't care and continued talking. "Girl, the party is going to be off the hook. Let's go!"

"Okay, okay I'm coming!"

Before leaving Shanae told her momma, "See ya tomorrow morning, Momma, love ya."

Looking out the living room floor to ceiling window as her daughter and Keya walked down the driveway laughing and talking. Dena shook her head. *I can't believe they think I am stupid. Senior all night party.* Dena stood there with a soft smile on her face. She thought, *my baby has graduated, will be going to college and she has a good head on her shoulders.*

Dena was proud of herself for raising such a wonderful child. However, Dena gave God the glory. If it weren't for Him, none of this would have been possible. He laid the foundation and Dena followed His path. She wanted her children to be so much better than she. She wanted them to overachieve and have their own houses, cars, money, and anything else they wanted. What she learned over the years was that there was nothing was like having your own. Nothing was better than a loving, honest and well thought of family.

1

6 Years Later

Shanae stretched over and hit the snooze button on the alarm clock. *Why won't this thing stop?* Then she realized it was one of those old-fashioned clocks that had two little bells on the top. She called it "The Big Tick." It couldn't possibly be seven o'clock in the morning. It seemed as if she had just dozed off. Her two-year old daughter, Sherrice, kept her up all night with a fever. Shanae tried everything to break the fever, but nothing worked.

Shanae felt Hasaun's side of the bed. It was empty for the second consecutive morning. This instantly pissed her off. Shanae and Hasaun used to be madly in love with each other when they were in school. Ever since Shanae moved into the housing projects Hasaun became more and more doggish. It wasn't that he didn't love her he was just too comfortable and took their relationship for granted.

Shanae didn't have anyone as far as family in her corner so he used the situation to his advantage. Hasaun thought he could have his cake and eat it too because they weren't married.

To no one in particular Shanae said, "The bastard knew I had a doctor's appointment. It is really over this time. After I have this baby, I seriously have to get my shit together. I don't need a no good for nothing ass nigga freeloading off me. Shit, I don't even have shit. Why am I thinking like this? When did I lose who I was brought up to be?"

She thought of that old song by Jesse James, "I Can Do Bad By Myself" and sung it over and over while she wobbled around the housing project in a haphazard aimless way, gathering all of Hasaun's belongings. Shanae was throwing all of Hasaun's shit into old wrinkled bags that somehow had gotten crammed into the corner of a closet. When she tossed in his cologne, the top came open and drenched his clothes. Shanae didn't care. She bagged up shoes, socks, clothes, clippers and anything else that belonged to him. Shanae could not believe Hasaun had the nerve to not come home. Not just one night but two nights. He was really trippin'. She had never experienced this type of behavior from him and she refused to put up with it any longer.

After bagging up his belongings, she sat the three trash bags in the far-right-hand corner of the living room. It was a living room her mother would have had a coronary over. Dena hadn't raised Shanae to live like this. Overcrowding was common. The apartment over the sidewalk had several families living in it. Plumbing broke down, and human waste was thrown in the streets along with the garbage. Contagious diseases spread rapidly in such cramped, unsanitary housing. People were always on a mission to get their hands on the almighty dollar.

Once she completed her task at hand, she sat on the sofa to catch her breath. She rubbed her belly; she only had a couple more weeks before her due date. Shanae was twenty-four years old and knocked up with her second child by Hasaun. She couldn't believe it eight and a half months ago when her doctor told her she was expecting. She had been on the pill faithfully.

She had no intentions of having any more children. Sherrice was unexpected, and so was this one. Everything in Shanae's life was unexpected. Hasaun wasn't holding down a steady job. She was taking care of the house, bills and Sherrice. *What kind a man can't hold down a job?* She was beginning to doubt if he was a real man. She thought that to be a real man you had to know what you believe in. You had to understand that actions have consequences and that they are connected to everything that you are. Hasaun was doing this. She was fed up with his bull crap. She was tired. Tired of his lies, tired of his being disrespectful and tired of living in a hellhole. However, most of all she was tired of being tired. When a woman is tired there is nothing a man can do to change her mind. Hasaun was out of luck.

Things can't stay like this anymore! I was not raised like this and I will not continue to live like this. I have to change something!

Shanae stared into space with tears streaming down her face. She thought back to several years earlier when she was still living at home with her family. That's when the future was full of possibilities.

Then everything was the bomb; at least she thought it was. Until that dreadful day. Shanae didn't want to travel down that unpleasant path again so; she forced the horrible memory out of her head. She wanted to remember the jovial times they shared as a family. She was on her way to being a top-notch lawyer. Then with the blink of an eye everything changed.

Shanae snapped out of it and wiped the tears from her eyes. *Shit, that's when my life had meaning. Now my life is in total chaos.*

As Shanae sat there thinking about her once perfect life, she was unable to control the constant flow of tears. She couldn't believe how her future had vanished in a blink of an eye. She got pregnant and it seemed like everyone either walked or ran out of her life. It seemed as if no one could understand that she had made a mistake and was only human. Now she only had a handful of people in her pathetic life. She started to think about this and decided to do something about her own attitude. Shanae thought about all the things she was grateful for.

I have a roof over my head. I'm not homeless and starving. I have family and some close friends. Many people don't even have family or relatives to turn to. I have my health and people who really do care for me. I have food. I'm not hungry. I have my freedom. I can walk outside and do things.

2

Sherrice Nicole Ryder was the most valuable gift God has ever blessed Shanae with. Sherrice was a very beautiful little girl. Her skin was as smooth as jet-black silk. The majority of Shanae and Hasaun's friends told them they should have named her Ebony. Hasaun and Shanae didn't have the slightest idea to why her skin was so dark. The majority of the people in the housing projects call her dark and lovely.

Sherrice was the most adorable little girl you have ever laid eyes on. Her facial features stood out. Her eyes were the shape of almonds and she had perfect eyelashes any supermodel would love to have. The color of her eyes was amazing. They looked coal black but if one took a closer look, they were really dark brown. Her eyes were so mesmerizing they would put you in a trance if you looked too long. She had inherited her mother's long natural curly hair that dangled down her back.

Sherrice was Shanae's pride and joy. Sherrice had taught Shanae the true meaning of the two most important aspects of life. One being friendship and two being love. Shanae never had known the true meaning of love or friendship until Sherrice was born May 22, 2003.

When Shanae became pregnant, the majority of her family and so-called friends vanished; only a select few stayed around. Shanae was lost and lonely. With the birth of Sherrice, that feeling slowly faded. Loneliness was pure torture for Shanae. Everyone needs another human being even if it is just one to witness lives and prove that they were there. Only Sherrice gave that to her.

She couldn't understand how so called Christian folk could turn their backs on a person. When she first became pregnant, she thought her life was over. She had heard of all the statistics about young mothers. Close to twenty-five percent had another child within two years.

All her dreams went out the window. While pregnant, Shanae began to resent her unborn child. According to her momma what she was carrying was the end of her life. Shanae later realized that her child was a gift and a blessing from God because she would no longer be alone in this dreadful world. She finally had something that no one could ever take away from her and she knew Sherrice would never walk out of her life.

Besides being the apple of her eye, Sherrice was a very intelligent little girl. The apple didn't fall far from the tree. Shanae made sure she read, sang and played with her on a daily basis. She didn't want her daughter falling short like she had. Hearing her laugh, cry, yell and play was music to Shanae's ears those were the daily sounds that would push Shanae forward. Shanae knew for a fact that her daughter's love is sincere. Something that was non-existent in her life.

Shanae loves the special bond they share. Shanae finally knew what true love felt like. She was thankful for her child and she loved her with all her heart and soul. The bond between them was truly unique.

3

"No, I will not make an exception! You ordered the equipment and double-checked the purchase order and agreed to the invoice. Therefore, you are responsible for the entire payment!" Victor yelled as he hung the phone up.

He didn't understand why he was handling this matter. Being CEO of his company he felt his administrative assistant should be handling this matter. He made a mental note to remind Megan what time her shift started and make her aware of her job description.

Victor walked over to the bar in his simple yet luxurious office, deep toned and highly graphic wallpaper surrounds the desk. Sculptural console lamps and a mirror were a contrast against the walls that were covered in patterned paper; had they been solid black. He poured a class of Louis XIII Remy Martin. Victor took a deep breath and devoured the cognac. Victor Davis, Shanae's younger brother was the CEO of Sports

Unlimited, which was based in Chicago, Illinois. Victor was a very handsome six foot three, hazel nut skin tone, deep dark brown eyes, head full of deep waves and a muscular build bachelor, who is deeply into his business. He had time for nothing else. Victor was all work and no play.

Looking at the family portraits strategically placed on his solid wood and veneer in a walnut finish credenza, made him think about how much he missed and loved his family. His family was important to him and he just couldn't figure out what happen. One of the reasons he worked so hard was to forget about the problems of his family. Victor picked up the photograph of Shanae and smiled.

Shanae is so beautiful and intelligent. What went wrong with her?

He still had many unanswered questions as to why his older sister left the family. Victor loved Shanae completely and was very heartbroken to see her under the current circumstances. He could kill Hasaun for getting her pregnant before she graduated from college. Even though they didn't see each other often they tried to stay in touch with emails and texts. Victor made sure he always had a close relationship with his niece.

He also gave his momma pictures of her. These pictures kept momma posted on Shanae's whereabouts. He made sure Shanae knew nothing about this. For some reason, Shanae despised their momma and stepfather. Shanae really appreciated and loved Victor for everything that he had done for her and Sherrice.

Victor hadn't been able to see Shanae in a long time. He became despondent when he visited her the last time. He wasn't usually a judgmental person but he didn't want his sister living in the hood. Her apartment was immaculate but he just wanted to know she was safe every night. It just didn't look good; him being a multi-millionaire and his sister living in the projects. She didn't have to be there. He had enough money to build her the biggest house she ever wanted. He offered on numerous occasions to move her out of the projects. Shanae just kept turning him down. He wanted to visit his sister and niece but he just couldn't bring himself to doing it.

Shanae's biological father left her mother when she was seven and Victor five. Her father was a dedicated stalwart lawyer and hard worker. Being a hard worker and married to Dena just didn't mix.

Samuel Davis never had much time to spend with his family, which upset Dena tremendously. Dena complained for years but Samuel pacified her with expensive gifts, nice cars and an extravagant home.

That still wasn't enough to placate "Queen B," She wanted more. Dena felt that Samuel didn't understand her. He felt she was being unfair. Whenever he had free time he always spent it with his family. The marriage was becoming unbearable so Samuel hired extra help and cut back on his hours at the firm. He loved his wife and children and he didn't want to lose them so he did everything in his power to make them happy and keep them together.

However, it was too late. Dena had started spending time with Bernard Williams, a coal black six-foot neurosurgeon. When Samuel found out he divorced her. He refused to put up with an unfaithful wife. When he left he took Janae with him. Dena never fought to keep her daughter. No one understood how Dena gave her daughter up so easily. A mother and a child's bond should be unbreakable. No caring or compassionate mother would ever give her flesh and blood up willingly. This was one of Dena's mistakes she regretted for the remainder of her life. Samuel took Janae because Dena had always treated her differently from the other children. Still, to this day, Dena denied that she favored her other two children over Janae.

Janae and Shanae were twins but they were like night and day. They both loved each other and the split was very difficult for them. Even though they were twins, they looked nothing alike. Shanae was beautiful and Janae was just Janae. Victor and Shanae took after Dena. They both could turn heads. Samuel didn't want his daughter to be mistreated so he took her. The look on his other children's faces almost killed him when he walked out the door. Shanae always wondered what was wrong with her and why he left her and Victor behind. She still has a void in her heart because of this. Samuel and Janae moved away, and no one had heard from them since.

Dena didn't have a worry in the world she had whipped it on the doctor, and he was talking marriage. Dena, a high strung and high maintenance individual with a sense of entitlement who wouldn't settle for less, was up for another marriage. The ink wasn't even dry on her divorce papers from Samuel when she announced her upcoming marriage to Bernard.

Two months later she married him. He gave Dena a beautiful home built in Columbia, Missouri, and the family relocated. Dena's family thought she had lost her mind. Bernard took Victor and Shanae in as his own children.

He and Dena both made sure they had great childhoods. They went to all the tennis, volleyball, soccer, cheerleading tournaments and basketball games that both Victor and Shanae had. Victor and Shanae could always count on Bernard and Dena to cheer from the sidelines. Over time, they thought about their biological father and sister less and less. Shanae never forgot about them completely because she always wondered how things could have been.

Everything was amazingly incredible, and everyone got

along remarkably well. Shanae was happy because she thought she had the best family in the world. Bernard spoiled them rotten; they had everything. At the age of sixteen they bought Shanae a red Range Rover. Bernard always showered her with gifts. Dena warned him that they were creating another Dena. That's how things used to be. Shanae hadn't talked to or seen her mother or stepfather in years.

Victor always asked Shanae why she left because her mom and dad loved her so much. Shanae figured her momma never told Victor what really went down, same old Dena.

4

"Oh, oh Dee, please doesn't stop," Keya yelled as her new wham-bam-thank you-man handled his business.

Keya was getting her groove on while her best friend was across town having a mini mid-life crisis. Keya's phone rang as Dee was putting in work. She refused to answer it and whoever was on the other end refused to hang up.

"Damn, I really need to get voicemail!"

The ringing of the phone was really pissing Keya off. She reached over, picked the phone up and slammed it back down in its cradle hoping whoever was on the other end would catch her drift. Instantly the phone started ringing again. She was getting the best piece she had gotten in a long time, and her damn phone wouldn't stop ringing. Keya rolled over while Dee was still deep inside of her and rode his manhood like a champ while she answered her annoying phone.

"Hello!"

"Keya, why does your voice sound so muffled?"

"Bad timing, gurl. Bad timing!" moaned Keya.

Shanae replied, "Keya you are sick? Why even answer the phone?"

"Because ya ass wouldn't stop calling!"

The idea of Keya talking on the phone while she was riding him must have turned Dee on because he started working the middle. In the midst of it all, Keya dropped the phone and rode him like the black stallion he was. After Keya and Dee both reached their peak, Dee got up, grabbed his clothes, baggy jeans slung low around the waist, gold chains, boots and a large t-shirt. He went to the bathroom. Keya lay on the bed and thought that this might be the one. Nice car, educated, big dick, fine as frog hairs and no criminal record.

"Yes!" Keya thought to herself.

Keya heard water running in the bathroom and after about ten minutes Dee exited the bathroom fully dressed. Dee walked over to Keya's Goodwill nightstand picked his keys up, grabbed his leather coat and walked out of her room. Watching him the entire time she was in awe. She wanted to know why and what changed his demeanor.

"What's up Dee?" With a smile on her face she said, "I can't get a kiss good-bye?"

He looked at Keya with his nose slightly turned up and said,

"If you want one you can?"

Keya didn't understand where this attitude was coming from. "What's up with the attitude Dee?"

"Shit, I didn't know you wanted a kiss. It ain't like we really know each other and shit."

Keya was hot. *I can't believe this bastard.*

"You didn't say that last night or this morning!"

"Kaia."

"It's Key Ah!"

"Well, KEY Ah, I don't think I kissed you last night or this morning and you didn't complain."

Dee had no interest in Keya. He needed a freak last night and she happened to be the first one he ran into. Keya and Dee stood there wordless for a brief second.

He decided to break the silence. "Look Kaia don't get me wrong, but you just ain't my type."

"I told you that my damn name is KEY Ah!"

Frustrated and taking a deep breath Keya yelled, "I seemed like your type last night and a few seconds ago!"

"Kaia, I do not mean to be rude but I think you are looking for something more than what I am looking for. I am just not into you like that."

Keya felt as if she had been completely insulted. She stood there with her mouth wide open. She wanted to say something but for the first time in her life she was speechless.

Dee continued, "Besides you give it up too soon, and you don't hold back anything. You don't even know my name." Dee turned around and walked through the living room and out the door. Keya was standing there stark naked and in total disbelief. When she heard the thud of the door, she snapped out of her trance. Keya staggered into the bathroom, took a shower and drove to the office.

Shanae couldn't believe her ears as she hung up the phone. *Keya. Keya that trick isn't ever going to change. I love her though"* Shanae thought

Keya and Shanae were very tight meaning wherever you saw one you saw the other. No matter what they went through Keya always kept it real. Keya wasn't as attractive as Shanae and didn't carry herself as well as Shanae. However Shanae had coached her well and she was able to pull niggas. Keya used her tool between her legs to get what she wanted. That's why she didn't have a man.

Shanae has always told Keya, "You give it up too soon. What do they need to stick around for?"

Even though she wasn't material for Harvard, she had managed to succeed in her own eyes. After high school, she went to Degree Technical School in Kansas City, Missouri. She received her associate's degree in business and completed paralegal school. She worked full time at a law office as an administrative assistant. She ran his shit while he got the big bucks and she received the scraps. Shanae and Keya's plan was for Shanae to become a lawyer and hire her at her law firm. Shit doesn't always go as planned though.

Keya and Shanae had been through thick and thin. She had always been there for Shanae and vice versa. Shanae couldn't remember a time when she wasn't in her life. They had been friends since their first year of high school. They used to run shit when they were in school. Both fly, intelligent and having the top of the line gear. Most females didn't like them, and they preferred to keep it that way. The more bitches, the more problems you have. Both Keya and Shanae had the fellas at their feet. Shit, those were the days. Shanae and Keya consider themselves sisters. Shanae had Keya's back and Keya had Shanae's back. It had always been like that and it would remain like that. When Shanae thought she couldn't go on anymore it was Keya who gave her that extra nudge. She always told Shanae to keep her head above water and not to let anything in life bring her down. Keya had always been there to lend a helping hand or a shoulder to cry on. Shanae was truly grateful for her.

5

When Shanae moved to the housing projects, she had just had Sherrice. She was living with Ms. Ryder but things didn't go as planned as usual. Ms. Ryder always walked around with a chip on her shoulder. Shanae couldn't understand why she constantly had an attitude. She kept Ms. Ryder's house cleaned and she helped her whenever she needed it. That still wasn't enough for her. Shanae could feel the tension in the air. She heard about public housing that gave people apartments based on their income. One day she stopped by the office and completed an application.

A few months later and tired of walking around on pins and needles Shanae decided she would clear the air. She politely asked Ms. Ryder. "Why are you always so angry and upset?" She wished she had kept her big mouth shut. Ms. Ryder told her where the bear shits in the woods and that it was time for her to go.

Thankful that she had applied for public housing she went to the office and pleaded her case. Shanae couldn't believe that she was going to be living among the same people she had tutored and help during high school.

She was living in a world that was different now, and not simply because of the profane graffiti sprayed across its walls. It appeared to her that the kids perched on the steps and leaning out of windows and milling around the yellowed lawn were training not for college or jobs but for their destiny as loiterers, hustlers and single mothers. The bright side of the situation was that Shanae knew it was not permanent, and she didn't have to deal with Ms. Ryder's attitude.

Shanae's life had taken a turn for the worse. She had to settle for bullshit. Not accustom to not having money was a change for Shanae. Living in the housing projects was very drab and depressing. With the drab and depressing living situation Shanae began to isolate herself from society and people.

Shanae had been living in the housing complex since 2003 but had only planned to live there until she got on her feet. Only thing she didn't know how she was going to get back on her feet. She wasn't doing anything she planned to do. She spent her days getting sucked into the hood. Having a job wasn't at the top of her list. Most days she slept in. She was becoming another statistic.

Even though Shanae lived in the projects and was

pregnant with her second child, she still had dreams and goals she wanted to accomplish. She still had nice clothes and a little money in her savings. Shanae could not splurge how she used to but she had enough money for a rainy day. One day Shanae went to check her mailbox. She was dressed in such a way to look impressive. She knew she was looking good. She didn't have many friends in the neighborhood and she preferred to keep it that way. The more friends you have the more problems. Most of the females in the hood didn't like her because they thought she was stuck up. They confused her confidence with conceit, which was so far from the truth.

She exited her apartment and strutted to the mailbox. An elderly lady across the way watched her leave her apartment, walk past all the thugs receive her mean mugs from the hood rats, check her mailbox and walk back towards her apartment. Shanae saw the lady looking at her. She thought the lady would stop staring, but she didn't. The lady made Shanae anxious.

Before Shanae made it back to her apartment, the lady yelled, "Hey, you."

Shanae pointed her index finger to her chest and looked at the lady.

I do not need this crazy ghetto shit today. I just need a place to live. I do not want any friends. Damn! Shanae thought to herself. Shanae had convinced herself that she didn't need anyone in life. If she had friends, they would hurt her and turn their backs on her. So she continued to isolate herself from others.

"Yes, you who else you think I'm talking to," yelled the elderly lady.

Shanae approached her with a smile on her face, "Yes ma'am."

"You ain't from around here are you?" questioned the older lady.

"No ma'am. I am not,"

"My name is Ma Rose and I noticed that you carry yourself differently from the rest of these young ladies. What's your story?" Living in the projects all her life, Ma Rose had seen it all. She knew they all had stories. However, this one seemed different.

Shanae had a lump in her throat and had to force her words out, "I had some unexpected troubles and had to move here."

Shanae noticed that the woman wasn't bad looking but with age and living in the ghetto, she looked tired and worn out. She was a clean lady and was dressed nicely. Shanae looked at her and thought of her grandma. *My grandma is old. She has wrinkled skin and soft hands. When I feel her hands, it reminds me of the soft fluffy clouds in the sky. When she smiles, it always reminds me of the sun when it shines bright in the morning.* Her hair was curled and frosted. Shanae thought probably to hide the gray.

Shanae broke the silence and told Ma Rose, "I don't plan on being here forever. I have goals and dreams that I still want to fulfill."

Ma Rose whispered, "Like I told you, my name is Ma Rose. I don't miss anything that goes on in this here complex. I know you have potential. I can see it in ya. I've lived in these here housing projects all my life. I have seen it all. So don't get sucked into this system, young lady."

Shanae felt sorry for her. How did she manage to survive living in the projects all her life? Shanae was so confused. She didn't understand where all of this was coming from. Shanae had no idea what the crazy old lady was talking about.

Stuttering Shanae replied, "M-Ma Rose I don't understand where all of this is coming from."

Ma Rose yelled, "Child, listen to what I am saying; don't get caught up in this hood. Don't let these hoodlums and hood rats know your business. Don't let them in your apartment and don't let them walk over you. You have the right to be respected."

For a second Shanae thought the old lady just liked hearing herself talk because she was on a roll.

"Okay, Ma Rose I will take your advice to heart."

Ma Rose looked from left to right and then she focused on Shanae and said, "There is a lot of shady ass shit that goes down in these here projects, child, don't get involved in them."

Shanae's eyes were the size of golf balls. Shanae could not believe the words that were coming out this old ladies mouth. She had never heard such an elderly person use those kinda words. She had to laugh. She had never heard an old woman cuss like that before. This would be the first of many cuss words that would pour out of Ma Rose's mouth.

"Thanks for the information."

Shanae was convinced that Ma Rose was certifiable. Shanae turned around and breathed a sigh of relief as she began to walk away from the crazy old bitty.

Her sigh of relief was cut short when she heard Ma Rose say, "What's your name child?"

Irritated Shanae turned around, walked back over to Ma Rose. "My name is Shanae Davis."

"Where you from?"

"I am originally from Saint Louis. Well, I like to say Saint Louis but we really lived in Ladue, Missouri," boasted Shanae.

"Ladue! Well your family must have a little money. What you doing living here?" questioned Ma Rose.

Defeated Shanae replied, "Sh— I mean stuff happens."

"Well, I say," joked Ma Rose. Not happy with Ma Rose's comment, Shanae turned and tried to walk away.

Ma Rose grabbed her by her arm and looked her directly in her eyes and said, "Shanae Davis from Ladue. You just gave me too much information. You don't know me from Adam.

If you give the wrong person that information it could be misused. I see I will have to look out for you too. Baby, you have to be smart and tough in this war zone. You ain't in Ladue."

At that very moment, Shanae caught the old lady's drift.

"Ma Rose, I see where you are coming from."

Nodding her head towards Shanae's apartment Ma Rose said, "I just have one more thing to tell you then I will let you go. Seems like your better half is getting antsy."

Shanae looked over her shoulder, and Hasaun was standing in the door holding Sherrice with an impatient look on his face.

"He will be okay," she said smiling, "I like to think of myself as the better half."

"Well, baby that expensive truck and all that extravagant furniture you moved in, if you want it you better go put it in storage because you may come home one day and it all might be gone. I have a friend who sells nice used furniture, and I can take you down there to get something if you don't mind."

"Thanks again for the information,"

Shanae began to walk off cutting across Ma Rose's grass.

"Shanae!"

Smiling and turning around, Shanae replied, "Yes, Ma Rose?"

"Off that grass, baby, don't nobody walk on Ma Rose's grass."

Shanae jumped back onto the sidewalk and waved bye to

Ma Rose. Ma Rose looked at Shanae as she headed home and hoped she had her head on right. *Pretty little thing like that would't last a minute,* she thought. *That girl needs to realize ain't nobody out here got her back.*

The next day Shanae called a moving company and put all her valuable items in storage—her coin collection from all over the world. Her Barbie dolls still in their unopened boxes, her original Mickey Mouse ring, plus all the jewelry her dad had given her. She and Ma Rose went to Treasure Chest Flea Market where Shanae bought furniture to furnish her project. It wasn't the expensive Italian leather she was accustomed to, but it looked nice. Hasaun was pissed about her truck and Shanae told him to get a job and get his family out of this hellhole. This was the beginning of a great friendship between Ma Rose and Shanae.

Over the years, Shanae and Ma Rose became very close. She schooled Shanae on the hood and taught her well. Ma Rose was the next best thing Shanae had to a mother. She was the only person besides Dena who knew the real reason she was living in the projects.

Ma Rose did not care for Hasaun at all and from the jump she let Shanae know that she did not care for him. When Shanae became pregnant with her second child, Ma Rose felt like dying. Ma Rose knew she had to get her out of this trap and fast. She just hadn't had time to talk to Shanae lately.

Ma Rose was like a mom to Shanae. Shanae could always count on her. Ma Rose told it like it was. She didn't bite her tongue for anyone. Although Shanae wished sometimes she would. Shanae and Ma Rose were family.

6

Hasaun Nicholas Ryder the love of Shanae's life has been

missing in action for two days. It never used to be like this

between Hasaun and Shanae. Shanae used to have to duck and

dodge Hasaun for breathing space. After their lives changed

they began to grow apart. Hasaun used to be so charming and

romantic.

The only individual that Shanae thought about was Hasaun.

She used to call Hasaun "Sexy Chocolate" but now her sexy

chocolate was becoming bitter. The sight of Hasaun used to

make her toes curl. He is so fine and breathtaking. He gave her

anything that she ever wanted. Hasaun's physique was

mesmerizing. Six foot-two inches tall and one hundred a ninety

pounds, of pure muscle. The best way to describe him is cut.

You saw muscles on him that you never knew existed. His

physique reminded you of D'Angelo when he was singing in the

video half naked. Just a different complexion; Hasaun was a

deep mocha, had beautiful eyes, nice succulent lips and a head full of waves. The man had it going on. Besides being handsome, as ever, he also knew how to lay the pipe, another reason Shanae was knocked up again.

However, over time, his attitude and demeanor towards Shanae changed drastically. She couldn't believe some of his comments he would say to her. Shanae didn't have any eyewitness accounts that Hasaun was cheating on her, but her heart told her he was and the heart never lead her off course. Her assumptions were now confirmed because he had not been home in two days. Shanae loved Hasaun but she just refused to put up with his shit any longer. She made a promise that as soon as he knocked on the door she would toss him out on his sorry ass. *You really have to be a stupid fuck if you get kicked out of the projects.*

"Hasaun where are you going?" questioned Jalisa

With his back towards Jalisa, Hasaun replied, "Home, where the fuck you think I am going?"

Jalisa yelled, "You promised me you weren't going back!"

With a shitty grin on his face Hasaun replied, "I have an obligation to my family and besides I love Shanae and Sherrice."

Jalisa looked as if she were going to die and Hasaun kept talking.

"Why y'all think a nigga going to leave a good woman

for y'all? I fuck you and that is about all I do. You knew the situation from jump and you said you were down, so don't get it twisted. You know that Shanae and Sherrice are my life and I am not leaving them for no one. If you can't handle it then you can kick rocks."

"What do you mean y'all?"

Shaking his head and laughing he replied, "You really have no clue what y'all is?"

No, Hasaun I sure don't know what y'all refers to."

"Hoes, you hoes always think it's going to end differently."

Jalisa could not believe her ears; she wanted to cry. She still had this nigga's dick on her breath, and he was telling her he loved his baby momma. Lifting her face from her hands, she saw Hasaun walking towards the door. Her heart sank and instead of cussing him out and telling him where to go she found herself begging Hasaun.

"Hasaun, please make sure you come back to see me. I am sorry for questioning you. Please forgive me," pleaded Jalisa.

Never looking back Hasaun exited the apartment. Jalisa fell on the couch and cried. Jalisa was an appealing girl. She went to Hickman High with both Shanae and Hasaun. As of the present day, she thought she had it going on because she was dating Hasaun Ryder, Shanae Davis' man. The only thing she took for granted was how open Shanae had Hasaun's nose and that his love for Shanae was much stronger then sucking his dick and letting him hit it whenever he wanted to.

Hasaun walked to his car with a smirk on his face. I guess HR still got the magic touch. At that moment, the smirk left his face, and he thought of Shanae. He had never cheated on her before, and he prayed she never found out about this little fiasco. Driving home the only thing he could think about was his family. *"What will I tell her? I have been gone for two days. Shit, what will she do?"*

Hasaun turned on his radio and he instantly felt his gut sink. Alicia Keys was on the radio talking about a woman's worth. He knew he had fucked up big time. Hasaun was preceding home when he realized he had forgotten to pick Shanae up for her doctor's appointment. *Damn! Damn!*

Hasaun did not want to face Shanae so he went to his boy's instead. Hasaun had a feeling that he had not experienced since sophomore year in high school. He knew he messed up and he would have to face her sooner or later. He decided on later.

7

(The Past)

Sophomore year heads turned when the fellow
students of Shanae saw her pulling into a parking lot of David H.
Hickman High School. She was rollin' in her candy apple red
Range Rover bumping Pony by Ginuwine. Shanae was singing at
the top of her lungs. She didn't care that she couldn't carry a
note. She continued rocking to the upbeat tempo. Shanae loved
all types of music. She would listen to Eryka Badu, Bob Marley,
Red Hot Chili Peppers and any other genre of music that she
liked.

She maneuvered into the parking space with skill, exited
the SUV and activated the alarm. Shanae walked with poise and
skill towards the entrance of the school. Aware all eyes were on
her, she worked her hips extra hard and paid the gawkers no
attention.

She spoke when spoken to and never broke her neck to

be friendly to anyone. On the same token she wasn't a mean or disrespectful individual. She was intelligent, beautiful and a trendsetter. She didn't take shit from anybody. If you stepped to her wrong she handled her business. She had to put her demo down several times during her ninth-grade year when people stepped to her incorrectly. The word around the school was the cutie from the private school could go. Shanae knew how to throw her hands and everyone knew that and they didn't mess with her.

Shanae had a great relationship with her momma. Matter of fact she was a splitting image of her momma. She loved her stepfather very much and was very thankful for him. She believed any man who took responsibility and raised two children who were not his was an angel sent from heaven.

Later that morning when Shanae was walking to her second hour class, a group of senior boys gathered around staring and making passes. Shanae didn't even recognize them. She had the most attractive male specimen at Hickman.

Shanae knew they were jockin' her so she decided to give them something to look at. On this particular day, Shanae thought she was looking good. She had on a white Dolce & Gabana tee with D&G in black and red rhinestones in the middle of the shirt. The expensive and exquisite shirt hugged her torso and made her breasts look even more voluptuous. She wore a black Dolce & Gabana belt with a pair of Dolce & Gabana capris that hugged in all the right places. She had on a pair of black Gucci mules and a black and red Gucci backpack. Her hair was pulled up in a ponytail at the crown of her head, exposing her intriguing facial features. She was natural and didn't like a lot of makeup. She only wore a little lipstick with lip liner and eyeliner on special occasions. She tossed her head up high and walked down the hall as if she was on the runway. She made sure she switched extra hard.

In the distance she heard the guys yell, "Work it, gurl!"

Before she made it to the end of the hallway her man was standing there with a smirk on his face. She walked towards him. He pulled her close and kissed her on her forehead. The guys whom she had been putting on a show for looked as if they had been defeated.

With pure envy in his voice, one of the guys said, "I don't know why she thinks he's all that. He was with Jalisa last night."

After kissing Shanae on her forehead, Hasaun said, "Stop showing off, gurl."

Pointing back at the guys Shanae replied, "Shit, they were staring so I decided to give them a show."

"Save the shows for me."

"No doubt, baby." teased Shanae.

As Hasaun walked off he replied, "Get to class before you set off the fire sprinklers."

"See ya at lunch."

Shanae headed to her second-hour class. Before making it to her class she ran into Jalisa and her click that happened to be the biggest haters there were at Hickman. She didn't have a problem with them, but they didn't care for her.

Evidently, Jalisa was the baddest beezy before Shanae came along, and she hated competition. Well, there really wasn't any competition. Shanae was top of the line. Even the gear she wore the hoochies could not pronounce and the whip she drove said it all. Besides, in spite of all the materialistic shit she was a smart student and a nice person. Most of her problems came from people being jealous of her, why she had no idea. They never said anything to each other or for that matter have words but you could feel the tension between the two of them. Today when Jalisa saw Shanae she burst out laughing.

Shanae thought, *what is this heifer's problem? Keep trippin with me she'll get chin checked.* Shanae ignored the haters and continued walking to class.

Hasaun made it down the hall and was nervous as hell. When he saw Shanae he almost turned and ran in the opposite direction. He did something so stupid last night, and the entire school was talking about it. He was so relieved to find out Shanae still hadn't heard the bad news.

Shanae and Hasaun had a relationship that no one could touch. They both loved each other and planned to marry after college. Everyone knew that. A number of Hasaun's friends tried to get him to cheat on her, but he wasn't going for it. He didn't want to lose her.

Shanae thought she had Hasaun's nose opened wide but after second hour the rumors she heard about Hasaun were confirmed. Hasaun didn't think the information would get back to her or at least not so quickly. But what's that old saying, "What's done in the dark will come to light."

Thanks to Hasaun's best friend, who had been trying to get with Shanae, for a while, he threw salt in Hasaun's game the very next day. Jason was the main guy forcing Hasaun to get with Jalisa.

This was something she did not understand about bruthas. They would listen to their friends about cheating but never once consider why their boys want them to cheat. They wanted them to cheat so they could holla at their girl.

Quite naturally she was hurt and furious but she didn't let anyone know. She wasn't one to walk around showing her emotions. The talk around school was Hasaun cheating on Shanae.

When Shanae didn't meet Hasaun for lunch as usual; he knew something was up. Jalisa kept walking past him smiling and looking goofy as hell. He wanted to smack the shit out of her but he had vowed never to hit a lady. Keya walked past Hasaun and rolled her beady eyes.

He grabbed her by her arm. "Where the hell is Shanae?"

Turning up her nose and snatching her arm away from him Keya replied, "She went out for lunch. She figured you wanted to have lunch with Jalisa."

"Fuck you, Keya!"

"No, fuck ya self, Hasaun!" Keya was upset because she had never seen Shanae so rattled before.

She's handling it betta than me because I would be upside that skank's head thought Keya.

Hasaun ducked and dodged Shanae for the remainder of the day. He had never been that paranoid in his life. Shanae left her last class fifteen minutes early and was sitting on his Mustang when he came out of the school. The sun was shining on her face enhancing her caramel complexion making her look gorgeous. When he came outside, he saw her sitting on his car. He was going to turn back around but she spotted him before he had a chance to.

Damn, I thought I would miss her; I can't even face her. The look on Shanae's face told Hasaun he was in deep shit. He unlocked the car doors, walked over and opened her door for her and they got inside. She never spoke above a whisper, and he knew she meant everything she was about to say.

"Who do you think you are? I don't know what is going on, but I'm having mixed emotions and they don't feel so good. First off, I don't play second to anyone. Secondly, dick comes a dime a dozen and I have plenty of money."

Hasaun tried to get a word in edgewise, but it wasn't happening. Shanae was not bullshitting, and she was on a roll. She had not taken a breath. The words that were coming out of her mouth cut deep into Hasaun's heart. The feeling he felt at that moment made him sick to his stomach and it left him feeling empty inside.

Shanae took a deep breath and continued, "I'm sorry that you want your cake and eat it too but this diva ain't going for it. Hasaun what were you thinking about?"

Hasaun had asked himself that exact question all day. Again Hasaun tried to answer but was cut off.

"I refuse to put up with this shit! So I have come to the conclusion if you think we should explore other options and opportunities, I'm cool with that."

The thought of Shanae holding, kissing and spending time with another guy infuriated Hasaun. Hasaun wanted to say something but he was too afraid. He had never seen Shanae's eyes look so cold. He could only remember seeing her eyes filled with joy. *What have I done?* The void he was feeling was incomprehensible all because of a stupid kiss. He could kick himself. Hasaun would later learn that being unfaithful to someone you love could cost you dearly.

Shanae ended the conversation by saying.

"So when you are ready to kick it with me and only me,

holla at a playa."

Hasaun wanted to tell her he wanted to be with her and only her right now and didn't want her to leave him. He was scared to say anything. Hasaun didn't know what to do as he watched her get out of his car. He had always had control in relationships. No one had ever told him to get to stepping. This was a new feeling for him and he didn't like it one bit.

While Hasaun was trying to absorb everything that was taking place, he continued to watch Shanae. He watched her switch to her truck, unlock her doors, get in, put on her designer shades, let her hair down, roll down her windows and exit the parking lot.

Bobbing her head to Total's "What About Us" Shanae turned right on to Providence Road to go home. Hasaun was damn near in tears, but too many eyes were on him, so he held his cool. He pulled out of the parking lot, speeding right behind her. Before going home, Shanae stopped by the convenience store at the corner of Garth and Business Loop. She strutted in the store, bought a bottle of water and left.

Walking out of the store, the bruthas who noticed her walk in were standing there when she exited. They were yelling and telling her how good she looked. Shanae was use to this type of attention and ignored them. Until, she glanced and saw Hasaun sitting in the Payless Shoe Store parking lot across the street. One guy walked up to her and gave her a piece of paper with his number and a note that said, "Call if you ever get lonely."

She smiled and waved as she made her way towards her truck. Shanae tossed the paper on the floor and thought how lame it was.

Hasaun was in the parking lot across the street observing her every move. Seeing Shanae flaunt around other dudes enraged him. He took his fist and punched the steering wheel. He felt like hurting somebody. They were looking at his girl and she was smiling and switching her ass like there was no tomorrow. At that moment he knew he could not live without her. He came to the realization he would have to do everything in his power to get her back.

Over the next five and a half months Hasaun tried everything, but she was not having it.

He made the first mistake by trying to approach her in front of a crowd. It had been two weeks. Hasaun figured she had cooled down; wrong answer. He stepped to her trying to have casual conversation and apologize. She walked past him like he wasn't even standing there. He stood in the middle of the hallway looking dumbfounded. All of his so called boys just laughed at him. Hasaun's heart felt as if someone had jabbed a knife into it. He didn't know how to handle this kind of rejection. Usually, females sweated him twenty-four seven. The one and only female he was interested in wasn't giving him the time of day. This went on for several more weeks. Hasaun was let down after every attempt of reconciliation.

Two and a half months into the breakup, Hasaun left school and instead of driving home he went to Shanae's house. He knew she was at cheerleading practice and would not be home for about an hour. He sat on her porch contemplating what he was going to say to her. Hasaun had a feeling she would respond to him in a positive way because she was not around a crowd.

He had a smile on his face when he saw her pulling into her driveway. He prayed this would be it. His smile and hope vanished when he saw Shanae pulling back out of her driveway with a look of repulsion on her face after she noticed him sitting on her porch.

Slowly backing out of the driveway she thought, *what the hell is he doing here? Why can't he take a hint?*

Ms. Ryder and Mrs. Davis-Williams both became concerned about their children. They both lacked their usual happy inner being and they both appeared to be slowly dying inside. They recognized that their children stilled cared for each other. Ms. Ryder knew her son was doing everything in his power to get her back, but Shanae was not having it.

Being women, both Francis and Dena admired Shanae for not putting up with a dishonest man and standing her ground. This was just one strong characteristic of Shanae Davis. She still loved and cared for Hasaun with all her heart, but she refused to let anyone trample on it. Not even the love of her life.

Hasaun was hopeless. He was hopeless on the court, and his grades were on a downward spiral. He wasn't keeping his sexy and stunning appearance up anymore. He felt he had no one to impress so why spend all the extra time looking good for nothing. On the other hand, Shanae kept her appearance up and was looking better than ever.

He understood that he had messed up tremendously, but he could not believe she was tormenting him like this, over a stupid kiss from Jalisa. He didn't even care about Jalisa so why would Shanae be tripping so hard. It wasn't like they were married. They were still kids and were bound to make mistakes.

Five and a half months after the breakup it happened during an assembly Hasaun was recognized for outstanding sportsmanship. He was called to center stage where he was given a plaque, a thousand dollars scholarship and asked to give a brief comment about his accomplishments regarding basketball. Hasaun was so nervous about receiving this award. He knew he would be receiving an award but he had no idea what he was receiving an award for. His mom had let it slip that she had to go to the assembly because he was being honored. He made sure he had on some fly gear, clean fade and his face was trimmed and perfected. The crowd was rowdy when he walked towards the stage, especially the females. They thought he was so fine. Shanae didn't like the fact that so many heifers were on his nuts. Hasaun was a damn good ball player. He had broken all the records and was leading the Kewpies to victory almost every single game. He had to clear the lump out of his throat when the microphone was placed in his hand.

Shanae noticed that Hasaun was sharp as a tack. Hasaun had a fresh haircut; waves were bumping and his face was trimmed nice and neat. Shanae also observed that his goatee had finally connected and looked good against his smooth chocolate skin. *Damn he looks good!* She continued studying Hasaun. He had on a pair of Timberlands with a solid Ralph Lauren Polo Shirt that matched his boots and a pair of dark denim jeans. Hasaun was looking good and she could not take her eyes off him. For almost six months, she had a routine where she avoided him but today the school assembly ambushed her routine. He was on the stage and she was forced to look at him. Shanae closed her eyes so she would not have to look at him. When she opened her eyes he was staring in her direction. Shanae said to herself, *damn he looks good.* Shanae was becoming uncomfortable. The crowd had calmed down and silence swept over the entire gymnasium.

She leaned over and told Keya, "I don't like the look on Hasaun's face. He has something up his sleeve."

With a confused look on her face Keya said, "Shanae stop tripping. He would not do anything else to further humiliate himself in front of the entire school."

Keya was getting tired of Shanae. *She has the finest dude in school chasing behind her stuck up tail and she was trippin'. Sometimes Shanae did not realize how beautiful and sexy she is.* Keya was reminded everyday by all of the fellas asking her to hook them up with Shanae. *Stupid heifer,* thought Keya.

While Shanae was sitting in the bleachers made of wood, oak to be exact, and are painted gray, she was mesmerized by Hasaun's appearance. She thought she heard her name. She snapped out of her trance to find the whole school staring at her. Hasaun was on stage trying to get her back. She looked at Keya as if she had said, "I told you so." Shanae stood up to exit the school assembly but was pulled down by Keya.

"Shanae you know you want him, so stop fronting," whispered Keya.

Shanae rolled her eyes at Keya and said, "There is a time and place for everything and this is neither the time nor the place, Keya!"

Keya pulled her down again and told her, "Bitch, he has tried everything to get you back but you must have a wild hair up ya ass because you keep dissin' him. I am tired of hearing y'all sob stories. So you need to get with the program!"

Looking a little perturbed Shanae told Keya, "Really, I don't know what crawled up your rear end and died, but you can drop the attitude!"

Keya and Shanae went back and forth with Hasaun still

45

standing center stage. He cleared his throat, which caught their attention.

Before Hasaun said a word Keya snuck in one last comment, "Shut up and listen to ya guy."

After clearing his throat Hasaun said, "Shanae, I know I made an awful mistake and I am truly sorry. I promise you it will never happen again. Over the last five months I have realized that I cannot live without you. I love and care for you and only you. I want to be with you for the rest of my life." Hasaun took a deep breath and continued, "Jalisa didn't and she still doesn't mean anything to me. I haven't looked her since that terrible day."

The crowd turned toward Jalisa as she jumped up and ran out of the gymnasium. Hasaun was not trying to hurt anyone's feelings he just wanted his girl back.

The entire assembly clapped and the principal took the microphone from Hasaun and smiled at him. The principle said, "That was a great speech, and I hope you and Shanae can work things out. This concludes our assembly."

Shanae could not believe what had just occurred. She was so happy that school was over after this dreadful fiasco. Hasaun was waiting by the exit door after the assembly. Shanae marched passed him and out the doors without even looking at him.

Everybody in the school thought she was crazy. Here it

was, she had the finest dude in school and she played him every chance she got. Hasaun felt as if Shanae enjoyed hurting him, his feelings and his pride. After the way Shanae treated Hasaun today after the assembly, he vowed never to speak to her again. He would leave her alone forever. Hasaun skipped basketball practice and went straight home. He pulled into his driveway, got out of the car and went in his house. Hasaun slammed the front door, which in turn shook the entire house.

Ms. Ryder came out of the kitchen wiping her hands on her apron, "Boy, what is your problem?"

Hasaun looked at her, with hurt in his eyes. "It didn't work, your bright idea. The only thing I did was further humiliate myself. Fuck Shanae! I can't keep letting her hurt me!"

Ms. Ryder looked at him with a stern look on her face, "Boy, you better watch your mouth. You should have thought about that before you destroyed her trust in you. That is what's wrong with men; you think you can do anything you want, and women will take y'all back. Ha ha. You have a person who is difficult to deal with and if you really want her back, you have to keep at it. But if you don't, I definitely don't want to hear shit when she has another boyfriend."

Hasaun knew deep in his heart he could not handle that, and he knew his mother was telling the truth. Deep down Hasaun knew he should have been faithful to Shanae. He shrugged his shoulders and walked to his room. While in his room, he undressed and put on some basketball shorts and a tank top, which did wonders for his body. He fell back on his bed and cried. Cried because he made a silly mistake and because he had been careless with Shanae's feelings.

Downstairs his mother could hear him and a part of her was hurting for him. These were the times when he needed a man around. She knew Hasaun was hurting but he should have never kissed that other girl. This was going to be a life lesson for him.

Across town, Shanae pulled into her driveway and ran into the house. She had every intention of calling Hasaun, but she wanted him to suffer for a while longer. She ran down the stairs and took her shoes off in the living room. She walked into her bedroom, picked up the phone and fell back on her bed.

"What a day?" Shanae said to no one in particular.

Shanae hit the Number 1 on the phone followed by the pound sign calling Hasaun's house. His phone rang three times. When she was about to hang up on the fourth ring she heard Ms. Ryder's voice through the receiver.

"Hello," Hasaun's mother screeched.

"Hi, Ms. Ryder, may I please speak to Hasaun?" asked Shanae.

"Honey, do you know how glad I am to hear your voice? Hasaun has been a mess since y'all split he'll be so happy to hear your voice. Shanae please put some life back into my baby.

It is killing me to see him like this. I don't know what you have done to him but I sure wish I had what you got when I was in my prime. That boy is going insane without you."

Shanae wanted to tell Ms. Ryder the only thing she had was pride and if she allowed someone to take that, then she had nothing. She decided against it because she did not want to step on anyone's toes.

"Well, Ms. Ryder, I can't make any promises but I will do the best I can."

"Thank you, baby."

Shanae could hear Ms. Ryder telling Hasaun to pick up the phone. Hasaun had dozed off after he went to his room. He still could not believe Shanae was playing him. Shanae also heard Hasaun telling his mother to take a message because he did not want to talk. Shanae's feelings were a little hurt when she heard Hasaun say, "take a message." This is what she wanted now she would have to live with it.

Ms. Ryder, in her brashest voice, got back on the telephone and said, "Hasaun does not want to talk Shanae, please call back later!"

Hasaun heard Shanae's name and jumped all the steps except two, ran into the kitchen and grabbed the phone out of his mom's hands, nearly knocking her down. Hasaun accomplished all of that within a split second. His mother couldn't figure out why he didn't answer the phone in his room.

"Ms. Ryder, please tell Hasaun to call me when he has time."

"Shanae," Hasaun pleaded.

"Hasaun, I thought you didn't want to talk?"

"That was before I knew it was your stubborn ass." Ms. Ryder took the rolled-up dishrag, soaked with dishwater and dish detergent and swiped at him. She almost felt guilty about hitting anything with it but hit Hasaun across is back. He ignored her but he could not ignore the stinging from the wet rag.

"I just wanted to let you know that you didn't have to do that today."

"I know I didn't have to but I have to do something to get you back."

"Hasaun, what if you never get me back?"

That never crossed his mind. He always assumed she would eventually take him back. The thought of her never taking him back made him sick.

"Well, Shanae, I always assumed you would take a brutha back."

"Well, you know what they say when you assume. You're making an _ass_ out of _u_ and _me_," replied Shanae.

"Why did you call, Shanae? To further humiliate me?"

"Hasaun, I hope you really meant what you said."

"Shanae, what more can I do to let you know if I can't be with you there is no point in living. I love you damn it!"

"I love you too, Hasaun."

Hasaun could not believe his ears. He was stunned. His mom told him he had to do something off the wall to get her back, to do something that will surprise her and shock her at the same time. After school today he thought his mom didn't know a damn thing about relationships. However, like always she proved him wrong.

"Shanae, you do not know how long I have waited to hear that."

"Yes I do, five and a half months, twelve hours, twenty-two minutes and fifteen seconds. Hasaun, can you come over so we can talk? I think we need to get everything out in the open and start fresh. Hasaun. Hasaun."

The only sound Shanae heard was the phone hanging up. She figured he was on his way to her house. Hasaun's mom stood in the kitchen of her house and let out a sigh of relief. Her son finally had that special glow in his eyes that had been absent for months.

The usual twenty-five minute drive only took Hasaun ten minutes that day. Before Hasaun arrived, Shanae took a seven-minute shower and freshened up. She put on a pair of black Spandex shorts and a beater. Shanae's hair was pinned up, and she was laying on her bed reading, "I Know Why the Caged Bird Sings" by Maya Angelou, who happened to be her favorite author. The doorbell rang and Dena went to the door to answer it. She was so pleased when she saw Hasaun standing there. She gave him a hug, told him that Shanae was downstairs and to go on down. Dena and Bernard were on their way to the Hickory Hills Country Club to play tennis when Hasaun arrived. Bernard and Dena were both happy to see Hasaun. Despite Shanae's appearance, they knew she was also dying inside. Their credit card bill proved it. Shanae had charged over $2,000 in who knows what.

When Hasaun walked into her room and saw her lying on her bed in those tight shorts, he prayed he could keep his composure. Shanae stood up with her hands on her hips, which made her braless breast poke out even more. She was looking so good. Hasaun walked over and gave her a hug. She embraced him. Hasaun wanted to kiss her but he didn't know if it was the appropriate time. They sat on the California king and had a long talk.

Shanae let Hasaun know that while she loved him with all her heart, she was never going to let a man or anyone for that matter misuse or mistreat her. She made sure Hasaun knew where she was coming from. Hasaun assured her he understood. Hasaun also promised Shanae he would never deceive her or hurt her again in his life. They hugged again and Hasaun's nature began to rise when he felt her supple breast against his chest.

Shanae noticed his manhood bulging in his pants and said,

"Down, boy, down."

Hasaun and Shanae both laughed. It felt so good to share a laugh with the girl he loved. His life was finally getting back on track. Hasaun knew what type of party it was. Shanae had made it clear that she was only having sex with her husband. Therefore, they did a lot of kissing and clothes burning but never the real thing. He looked her over and knew it was no coincidence that she was dressed so provocatively.

He told her, "Nice get up."

She smiled and poked her bottom lip out. He took his warm mouth and sucked her bottom lip. They held each other while lying in her bed talking and smooching. From that day forward Hasaun promised himself he would never look or think about another female. Shanae Davis and Hasaun Ryder were inseparable. Those were the days.

Hasaun was brought back to reality when he realized he wasn't sitting in the Davis-Williams mansion and that he wasn't with Shanae in her old bedroom.

8

Shanae was reminiscing and forgot that she was sitting in the living room of her housing project because up and down and across the grid of residential city streets, everyone was outside. Plumes of dark smoke that smelled of seasoned meat rose above the houses from backyard cookouts. Elderly women opened their front windows wide and sat there all day behind fans that blew across bowls of ice cubes. Cards, dice, checkers, jacks, jump rope, hopscotch, craps, step dance–offs, stickball, handball, basketball—one could not turn a corner without encountering a game being played, often with the elderly cheering on the young, dispensing their peanut gallery wisdom gained from decades of playing the same games on the same blocks.

She was so disappointed with the outcome of her life. She always wanted more and expected more of herself. She made mistakes in her life, and now she was paying dearly for them.

She wanted to scream. She wanted to let everyone who was passing judgment on her know that she was going to turn her life around.

"I will change my life for the best!" Her voice bounced off every nook and cranny in the small apartment. She wanted to be heard. Her life was in an uproar.

When she lived at home, she didn't have to worry about anything. She just wished she could turn back the hands of time. She would have, without a doubt, done many things differently. Now the few thugs and dealers whose presence kept her inside on most other evenings like this characterized her neighborhood. When she was in school, she helped people with schoolwork and self-esteem problems that lived in the same projects she now lived in. She never thought she would be living among the same people she helped in school. Life is so unpredictable and ironic.

Shanae got up from the couch, walked over to the phone and called her doctor. She had to reschedule her appointment for tomorrow. After talking to her doctor, Shanae cleaned the few dishes that were in the sink, ran the sweeper and cleaned the bathroom. Shanae didn't know where she was getting all this extra energy.

She woke Sherrice up, fed her and gave her a bath. After taking care of Sherrice, she ran some bath water for herself. Shanae wobbled into the bathroom to take a bath. She took off all her clothes and put one foot in the tub, but the water was too hot. She turned on the cold water to cool down the bath water.

While waiting for the water to cool, she looked at her naked body in the mirror. She had gained about forty pounds with this pregnancy and was pushing one hundred eighty pounds. She still looked good even though she was nine months pregnant. She carried her weight in her hips and butt. Other than that, she looked great. Even while pregnant Shanae exercised to stay in shape. Her doctor told her it was okay to exercise, so she didn't miss a day. Shanae took a bath, dressed, brushed her hair into a ponytail and put on some makeup. She felt and looked hundred percent better.

Walking into the living room, she put a Barney tape in for Sherrice who was tired of coloring. While Sherrice watched, Barney, Shanae called the housing authority and told them she had lost her keys and needed her locks changed immediately. They told her the work order would be completed within the next hour. With the growing crime rate in the projects, they wasted no time changing locks when keys were lost. They didn't want to be held liable for any mishaps. Shanae went into her bedroom, lifted up her mattress and got fifty dollars to pay for the work order.

Shanae kept the majority of her money at home. If she put it in the bank, she would more than likely have to pay some type of rent. The housing projects looked into all your records. When she applied for public housing, she felt so low. They want to know every little detail about her life.

While in the bedroom, she walked to her closet and retrieved a shoebox. Inside the box was a college application she had picked up last week when she went to check on her college credits from the University of Saint Louis-Missouri.

After leaving the campus, she was happy because she only needed twenty-five more credits to have a bachelor's degree in political science. She went to the kitchen table and completed the college application. All her credits would transfer with no problem from The University of Saint Louis-Missouri to the University of Columbia-Missouri. Shanae put her application in an envelope, addressed it and placed a first-class stamp with the United States of America flag on it.

"Sherrice," Shanae yelled.

"Yes, Ma," replied Sherrice.

"Go get your coat so we can walk to the mailbox."

"Okay! Okay!"

Sherrice was always excited to walk to the mailbox. Before they left for the mailbox, there was a knock at the door. Shanae opened the door and it was Calvin from the housing authority.

"Hey Shanae, I've come by to change your locks," said Calvin. "But it looks like you are going somewhere."

"I was on my way out to check the mailbox, but I can wait

until your work is done."

"Oh, it will not take me long. I will have these locks changed in no time."

"Thanks so much. I thought I would have found the keys by now but I haven't been able to locate them for days."

Shanae lied to Calvin. Her keys were actually in her pocket. She didn't want anyone to know her business.

"Shanae, you should have called this order in days ago," scolded Calvin. The locks on your doors are your strongest line of defense against intruders. Without functioning or secure locks, your home will be vulnerable to burglaries and intrusion. Knowing the situations in which it is prudent to change your home's locks can help you secure your property and keep your family safe."

Shanae said, "I know it's just that I have been so busy lately." Shanae felt bad as each lie rolled off her tongue.

Calvin said, "This won't take any time."

Calvin had the locks changed within minutes. Shanae paid him, locked up the apartment and walked to the mailbox.

While walking to the mailbox she knew Ma Rose was watching; there was no sense in dodging her. She probably had already put two and two together. On the way back from the mailbox, Shanae and Sherrice stopped by Ma Rose's project.

Shanae was getting ready to knock on her front door when she heard Ma Rose say, "Come on in, Suga." Shanae knew she was in the window.

"Well, don't you two ladies look darling? What is the special occasion?" smiled Ma Rose.

"There's no occasion."

Ma Rose double-checked the sadness in Shanae's eyes. Her heart went out to her.

"Sherrice, honey, take your coat off and go play in your toy room while Ma Rose and your Momma have a talk."

They both smiled as the beautiful little girl walked into her toy room. Shanae knew what this meant. Ma Rose looked at Shanae with concern in her eyes.

"What's going on, Suga?"

Shanae inhaled, then slowly exhaled and said, "I don't know." Silence filled the room. Ma Rose sat there waiting for Shanae to continue her statement.

Shanae shook her head back and forth and then replied, "It has to change, and I am going to change it somehow and some way!" Tears were pouring down her cheeks and her nose was red.

Handing Shanae some Kleenex, Ma Rose looked confused, "And how do you plan to change it, Suga?"

She had heard this so many times before and just didn't believe Shanae. She knew Shanae had the potential, but she had been slacking.

In a whisper Shanae replied, "He has to go. My nerves

can't take this anymore. He is going to send me to an early grave if I don't change this situation."

There was no reason for Ma Rose to comment about Shanae's situation. Shanae knew exactly how she felt. Ma Rose had been telling Shanae to put him out for over a year. She decided to change the subject.

Ma Rose questioned, "Suga, why did you go to the mailbox so early today?"

"I mailed a college application. I plan to complete my degree. School starts in two months. I only need twenty-five more credits. I have to get myself together."

Ma Rose smiled and said, "Suga, I didn't expect to see you taking it so well. I mean Hasaun hasn't been home in two days. I just knew you were going to be sad and upset, and Lord knows that unborn child does not need all this stress."

Shanae asked, "Ma Rose how did you know Hasaun hasn't been home for two days?"

Smiling Ma Rose said, "Suga', I told you I don't miss nothing. I am the eyes and ears of this here neighborhood. But I'm not a person who meddles or pries into the affairs of others.

"Shanae said, "Well, thanks for being concerned."

"No problem, Suga," Ma Rose replied.

"One more question, baby. Why was Calvin at your apartment today?"

Damn, Ma Rose doesn't miss a beat. She knows what's

going to happen before it happens, thought Shanae.

Shanae replied, "I had my locks changed so Hasaun can't get in."

Ma Rose jumped up and gave Shanae a hug and a kiss. "Shanae, if you need anything, please let me know," said Ma Rose.

"I will," replied Shanae.

"Shanae, make sure you go sign up for child care to help you while you're in school, and you need to find a cheap car. I will help you get one," said Ma Rose.

Shanae hesitated and then said, "Ma Rose, I don't want to take your money. I have money in a savings account that I haven't touched in years. I never knew when I would need it, but I need it now. Besides, I still have my truck in storage. I might as well put it to use. I have been paying taxes on it for years."

Ma Rose looked puzzled, so Shanae decided to put all her questions to rest.

"I told you that my family had some money."

"Well, yes you did, but you got enough money to pay for college all by yourself and childcare for two children. How ya gonna do that, Suga?"

"I had money put away for school but I got a full ride, and all the money came to me. I am pretty much set for life if I finish school. There was even a trust fund set up by my biological dad for Victor and me. There are many stipulations. One is getting a bachelor's degree. So stop worrying about me."

Shaking her head Ma Rose replied, "Shanae, you mean to tell me all you had to do is take ya yellow ass back to school and you were set for life!"

Shanae replied, "Yes, ma'am. I did not know all the details until last week when I talked to Victor."

Ma Rose said, "Gurl, I ought to slap you right now, and I thought you were smart." They hugged each other and both laughed.

"Ma Rose, before I leave I need you to do me a favor. Hasaun might be coming home soon. If he is in my apartment, more than thirty minutes, please come over and check on Sherrice and me."

Ma Rose asked, "Baby, is there something wrong?"

Shanae replied, "No, but lately he has had a temper. The pressures of trying to find a job and the stress of family are part of life. Anger is as much a human trait as happiness. I don't know how he is going to react when I tell him it is over."

Ma Rose said, "You know I will be in my window."

In a hushed tone Shanae said, "That I do."

"Excuse me?"

Smiling Shanae replied, "Oh, never mind. I was just thinking out loud."

"Shanae, now don't think I won't slap you in that pretty

little face of yours," threatened Ma Rose.

9

After leaving Ma Rose's, Shanae felt as if all her burdens had been lifted off her shoulders. She felt lighter in spirit. Shanae was excited and determined again. Approaching her apartment, she used her new keys to let her in. Those keys represented a new beginning for Shanae and Sherrice.

Looking around the tiny cluttered apartment Shanae felt sad. She knew she would be moving in a couple of months. She had established a sense of belonging, and she had a few friends sprinkled around the housing complex. They were depressing clusters of close by and interconnected buildings. Even though it wasn't the greatest apartment or neighborhood, she had been in the projects for a few years. The place looked different now and she felt at home.

Sherrice appeared to be tired, so Shanae took her into the bedroom and put her down for a nap. Shanae strolled back into the living room, sat on the couch and started composing a to do list. There were so many things she needed to do. There just wasn't enough time during the day considering she was nine months pregnant. She was limited to what she could do. She needed to stop by the bank, buy school supplies, call Ms. Ryder and stop by her storage unit to pick up her truck. Shanae decided to knock one off her list today. She picked up the phone and called Hasaun's mother. After several rings, Ms. Ryder answered the phone.

"Hello," said Ms. Ryder.

Francis Ryder always sounded like you were disturbing her when you called.

"Hi, Ms. Ryder. How are you?"

A little surprised from the phone call, Ms. Ryder was a little reluctant to answer. "I'm great, how about yourself?"

"Oh, I'm maintaining under the circumstances."

Ms. Ryder and Shanae still got along even though she kicked her out on her butt two and a half years ago.

Ms. Ryder cut to the chase, "Shanae, what makes you call me?"

"I was wondering if you have two daycare openings for your grandchildren."

Hesitantly, Ms. Ryder replied, "Shanae, you know I don't mix family and business. Just too many problems."

"Ms. Ryder, I really need someone I can trust to take care of my kids. If it is the money you are worried about I will pay in advance for both kids."

Shanae couldn't believe she was trippin about keeping her own damn grandkids. She didn't want her to do it for free.

Ms. Ryder was puzzled. She knew Shanae didn't have that kind of money.

"And where exactly would you happen to get the money from?"

"What difference does it make if you get your money?" Shanae could not understand why some people had to be so meddlesome.

"It makes a difference because I do not want some thugs kicking my door down looking for you and their money," stated Ms. Ryder.

"Have you ever known me to be shady or do anything illegal?"

"Shanae, I do not have time for games."

"Why would I be playing? I need a sitter and one that will take good care of my kids. If I didn't need your expertise, I would not be calling you."

"I just want to know how you are going to get your hands on that type of loot," Ms. Ryder knew that her parents were loaded but they disinherited her a few years back.

"Ms. Ryder, I will have it if I go back to school," Shanae had decided to keep as much of her business as she could to herself. She was not planning on telling Ms. Ryder more than she needed to know.

"Shanae, what are you talking about?"

Annoyed Shanae said, " My biological father had money put away for my education since I was a child. I never used it, so I still have it. I plan on going back to school in January."

That was an ear full of information, but Ms. Ryder was able to absorb it, especially when it came to money.

Immediately after hearing Shanae's explanation, she replied, "Well, I do happen to have two spots available. I will bring the paperwork over tomorrow. I need to see my granddaughter anyway."

"Thanks Ms. Ryder. I will be gone the majority of the morning and early part of the afternoon running errands. If I am not at home, please leave the information with Ma Rose."

Ms. Ryder didn't particularly care for Ma Rose. *The lady thinks she is my granddaughter's grandmother,* thought Ms. Ryder.

Annoyed Ms. Ryder replied, "Sounds good to me. Shanae, I am so glad you are getting your life back on track." Excited Ms. Ryder replied, "What does my son think about this? Maybe he will go back to school."

Shanae really didn't want to tell Ms. Ryder anything in case she saw Hasaun first, but she knew the truth was important right now.

"Honestly, I don't know what he thinks. I haven't seen

Hasaun in two days, and when I do see him, I will be informing him that it is over."

Hasaun's mother could not believe her ears.

"Shanae, are you telling me he hasn't checked on you and Sherrice in two whole days!"

"Yes ma'am, two whole days. Forty-eight hours." Shanae replied.

"Do ya'll have everything ya'll need?"

"Yes ma'am, I had a doctor's appointment today but Hasaun didn't come home. So, I missed my appointment."

Ashamed Ms. Ryder said, "Shanae, I am so sorry."

"Ms. Ryder, you do not have to apologize for anything. Hasaun's a big boy who knows right from wrong."

Shanae, I will see you around five-thirty tomorrow."

Shanae ended the conversation by saying, "See ya' tomorrow."

Shanae was exhausted mentally and physically so she decided against making any other phone calls. Before taking a nap she went into Sherrice's room to check on her; she was still asleep. She wobbled into her room to rest and crashed within minutes.

Bang! Bang! Shanae sat straight up in the bed and wiped her eyes. *Who the hell is that beating on my door like the police?* She glanced at the clock on her nightstand. It was only two-thirty in the afternoon. She could not believe how slow time was moving. She walked slowly towards the door, looked out the peephole, opened the door and let Hasaun in. Sherrice was still asleep, which was a plus because she knew the shit was about to hit the fan.

Hasaun looked so dense right now. In a masculine voice Hasaun said, "Shanae, my keys don't work."

At this point, she wanted to say "Duh!" It took everything in her not to slap the dog shit out of him. He was tripping on his keys not working. He didn't care that he hadn't been home in two days. Or for that matter that she missed her doctor's appointment because of his immaturity.

Disgusted Shanae replied. "Duh! That's because you no longer live here."

Hasaun looked confused, "What the hell you mean?"

"I mean get ya mutha—get your trash bags and get the hell out. I don't need your sorry ass."

"I ain't going anywhere!"

"Hasaun, you don't have a police record, and if you don't want one, you need to leave now." She talked back to him, and that was one of the reasons he loved her. But she could shut him up with just a few words, Shanae's basic confidence in her own sense trumping all of Hasaun's verbal tricks and back doors. She never let him talk her in circles like she never let him be right when he was wrong.

Hasaun knew she was not budging, and he couldn't believe

she was so pissed off. Then again he could, because he had never stayed out all night. She didn't even ask him where he had been. So the outlandish story he had concocted on the way home wasn't even going to work. There was no way he could even bullshit his way out of this one.

"Shanae let me explain. I w—," uttered Hasaun.

Shanae cut him off and said, "...Hasaun, you have been gone for two days. There is nothing to explain. Leave!"

"Just where in the hell am I supposed to go?"

"I don't care. That's not my problem anymore! Oh, you can go where you have been for the last two days."

"When will I get to see my daughter?"

Shanae did everything she could not to laugh. Hasaun had been gone for forty-eight hours and didn't give a shit about his daughter. Now he was so concerned.

"As of January they will be at your mother's daycare from six in the morning until three-thirty in the afternoon. Make time during those hours.

"Shanae, why?"

Shanae was tired of trying to be nice to Hasaun and finally let him have it.

"You self-centered son of a bitch! Fuck you! You have been M.I.A. for two damn days. Two damn days, Hasaun. Now, for the last time get your shit and get out before I call the police!"

Shanae was crying and breathing so hard. She couldn't

believe he had the audacity to consider that she would stay with him. She was upset because she was emotional. She always vowed to never wear her emotions on her sleeve. She wanted to be strong when she kicked him out. He was so persistent in trying to tell her where he had been. Shanae didn't want to hear any of the bullshit, and she continued to ignore his pleading and deceitfulness. She felt light-headed and walked over to the sofa to catch her breath.

Concerned Hasaun asked, "Baby, are you okay?"

"I will be when you get the hell out of here!"

After yelling, Shanae felt a sharp pang in her stomach. She grabbed her stomach and scrunched her face up in agony.

"Shanae, are you okay?"

"Hasaun get your stuff and get out."

Shanae was fed up. She couldn't stand to hear his voice any longer. He had to go. She wanted him out, and she wanted him out now. Hasaun looked around the apartment, and nothing was his except the phone he had bought.

He walked over to the kitchen and snatched it out of the wall saying, "I will be taking this."

Shanae rolled her eyes and said, "I don't care just leave!"

Pissed because he could not keep an argument going he yelled, "Where's my shit!"

Shanae pointed her neatly manicured finger to the corner near the living room at the three trash bags.

Annoyed Hasaun said, "I'm going to take my shit to my car and come back and give my daughter a kiss!"

"Oh, no you won't. If you want a kiss, you'd better kiss her now!"

Hasaun wanted to smack the shit out of her stupid ass. He walked into his daughter's bedroom and gave Sherrice a kiss good-bye. Sherrice never moved.

Before leaving, Hasaun took it upon himself to further humiliate Shanae.

"So now what Miss Goody Two Shoes? Even after you hit rock bottom you still think ya shit don't stink. Ain't nobody gonna want you. Twenty-four with two kids, no job, no goals and no ambitions. You ain't shit anymore but a baby having project HO!"

Shanae was crushed. Hasaun had never called her names. She would never let him have the satisfaction of knowing how those words hurt her. His words cut to the core.

Nonchalantly, Shanae replied, "Hasaun, go fuck yourself!" Shanae got off the worn torn couch and walked into her spotless kitchen to get a glass of water.

Looking at Hasaun because he was truly confused, she laughed at him and said, "See ya!"

Hasaun could not believe this arrogant bitch. He lost it. He ran over to Shanae and shoved her in the middle of her back as hard as he could. Shanae's head jerked back, the cup of water fell out of her hand, and she landed on her stomach beside the cup. She hit her head on the flea market dining room chair on the way down. She was stunned because she hadn't expected it. Her stomach was hurting, and so was her head. She managed to roll over and sit up with her back supported by the dented used refrigerator. The look on Shanae's face told Hasaun she was obviously in pain.

He looked at her and said, "What can make you laugh can also make you cry!"

Because of the pain, Shanae was unable to yell. She told Hasaun. "Get the hell out! Like father like son."

Hasaun could not believe what she had just uttered. He became enraged. He ran over to her grabbed her by the collar of her shirt with his left hand and balled his right hand into a fist and yelled,

"I can show you like father like son. You conceited slut."

Spit was all over Shanae's face. Hasaun had officially snapped. He was furious and for the first time. Shanae was scared and speechless. She prayed to God he would let her go and not ram his fist down her throat, or worse. She just remained quiet. Finally, he released her shirt and furiously walked away from her. Shanae was terrified, and the pain in her stomach did not help the matter.

Hasaun gathered his bagged up belongings and left. He was lucky because Ma Rose was putting her house shoes on, and had her straight razor getting ready to clean house. It had been twenty-nine minutes. Before she walked out the door, she spotted Hasaun leaving with all his belongings. She was relieved, and happy because she had seen too many young women fall victim to the hood. Shanae could do it. Hasaun walked to his car and was taunted by the thugs standing outside.

"Looks like you fucked up royally this time. Maybe one of us can take your spot."

Hasaun looked at the hoodlum and said, "Fuck you!" All the bystanders snickered at Hasaun as he pulled off.

10

Shanae lay there immobilized in a fetal position, rocking back and forth. She knew she had to get up but the pain in her womb was excruciating. She had never felt pang like this before.

What the fuck has Hasaun done!

Shanae was crying and scared. Then she remembered that she was in the kitchen. She knew the telephone was near, so she felt a little relieved.

She told herself to reach on the counter, grab the phone, and call the ambulance.

Shanae didn't feel the phone.

Damn, Hasaun had taken the phone!

She sat there, and when the pain slowly began to ease up, she managed to get on all fours, and crawl towards the front door. Before she made it to the door, the pain hit her like a sharp knife, which caused her to fall over in the middle of the floor. She was screaming and yelling at the top of her lungs.

Please God, give me the strength to make it to the door.

The pain eased up, and she lay there trying to catch her breath. All the screaming and yelling woke Sherrice. Sherrice came toddling in the living room as happy as ever.

Sherrice jumped on Shanae's back and said, "Getty up horsey."

Shanae screamed. "No, Sherrice. Ma has a boo boo!"

Sherrice got off her mother and sat by her side rubbing her mother's head. Shanae hadn't noticed her head bleeding until Sherrice touched it. It started stinging. Then she saw the blood on her daughter's hand.

I have to get up!

Shanae was scared and desperately in the need of help. Seeing the blood on her daughter's hand sent chills down her spine causing her to shed tears.

Meanwhile, Ma Rose had tried to call Shanae twice. When Shanae didn't answer, Ma Rose assumed she wanted to be left alone. She had been through a lot over the last few days. Ma Rose decided to check on her around dinnertime. Keya had also tried to call several times. She wanted to let Shanae know she was sorry for not taking her call this morning.

Keya thought, *why ain't she answering her phone? I guess I will have to stop by after work.*

Sherrice swaggered to the refrigerator; and got some juice to drink.

"Ma, I am hungry," cried Sherrice.

"Just wait, baby." Shanae had never felt this helpless.

"Sherrice, I need you to open the front door."

Shanae knew it was a long shot because her fine motor skills were not sharp enough to manipulate the lock, and the doorknob. Watching Sherrice struggle for twenty minutes trying to open the door was literally pure torture. A couple of times she almost had it.

"Ma, get up. Get up," cried Sherrice.

"I can't, baby," cried Shanae. The pain wasn't letting up. It was getting worse by the minute. Shanae thought she was going into labor. However, she had never felt pain like this with Sherrice. She prayed nothing else was wrong with her and her unborn child. Dealing with the pain and her daughter's cries, Shanae became exhausted. She wished she had fed Sherrice before she took a nap. Maybe she would not have been so hungry. Who would have thought Hasaun would show his ass. Shanae had had enough. She scooted to the door, tried to get up enough strength to open it. She did not have enough strength.

After about an hour and a half of being in pain and agony, Shanae loss consciousness. Sherrice was lying on her mother's back crying at the top of her lungs.

Three hours later on his way walking to the store, a kid from the neighborhood heard Sherrice crying. He was gone for about forty-five minutes, and when he walked back past the apartment, and still heard the baby crying. The kid thought; *that's unusual. You never hear anything from Shanae's house.* He liked Shanae because she was so kind and always told him to stay in school. He knew Ma Rose and her were tight, so he walked to Ma Rose's and told her what he had observed.

"Ma Rose, Shanae's baby has been over there crying for about an hour. I think something's wrong over there."

"What makes you think that?"

"Because when I walked to the store I heard her crying, and when I came back an hour later she was still over there crying to the top of her lungs," stated the boy.

Alarmed Ma Rose said, "Thank you, baby."

Ma Rose ran over to Shanae's apartment and beat on the door. She could hear Sherrice crying before she knocked. She turned the handle, and the door was locked. She ran to her apartment and grabbed her spare key. Ma Rose ran back to Shanae's to let herself in, but the key would not fit. *Shit, Shanae had the locks changed today!"* Ma Rose walked over to the window and looked inside. She could not believe her eyes. Shanae was unconscious, and lying in a mixture of blood and mucous. It did not look good.

Ma Rose grabbed a brick from Shanae's flowerbed and broke the window. She stuck her hand inside and unlocked the front door. Ma Rose ran to the kitchen to call 911 but there was no phone. She ran outside and told the little boy to call an ambulance.

Ma Rose grabbed Sherrice and held her. "My God, how long has my angel been like this?"

Ma Rose went inside Shanae's bedroom and got a blanket to put around Shanae's motionless body. She stood outside waiting for the ambulance. A crowd of people had started to gather, and rumors were spreading like wildfire. Hasaun was the last person in the apartment, and people figured he had done something to her.

Keya pulled up to find an ambulance flashing red and blue lights in front of Shanae's project.

When Keya spotted Ma Rose, she asked, "What is going on?"

With tears in her eyes Ma Rose said, "I don't know, but I need a ride to the University Hospital."

Keya replied, "Let's go!"

They locked up both apartments and followed the ambulance. Shanae had been unconscious for a while and had lost a lot of blood. It was not looking good. They immediately gave her a blood transfusion and were about to perform an emergency caesarean, but it was too late. They could not find a heart beat for the baby. They induced labor, and Shanae gave birth to a stillborn, six pound, eight ounce beautiful baby girl.

Keya and Ma Rose were waiting in the lobby. Both were

scared. Ma Rose knew Shanae was strong, but this was really going to test her inner strength. No one had come out to tell them anything.

Keya was upset. "Where in the hell is Hasaun?"

"Baby, there is no need in your getting upset. I called his mother. She is on her way. She doesn't know where Hasaun is. Shanae threw him out this afternoon. He was the last person at her house."

Keya was at a loss for words. She felt so guilty because she had ignored Shanae this morning and hadn't stopped by to see her or her goddaughter in a very long time. She was so wrapped up in her drama she had not realized that Shanae was going through some hard times herself. Keya felt ashamed.

After a long pause Keya replied, "Oh, I wasn't aware of that."

Down the hall, they could see Ms. Ryder running towards them. She was so scared. The look of pain and concern was etched across her face. She had wrinkles in her forehead, and she was on the verge of crying.

She bombarded them with questions, "What's going on? How are Shanae and the baby? How is Sherrice? Where in the hell is Hasaun?"

Keya and Ma Rose both looked at Ms. Ryder and in unison they said, "Calm down."

Keya tried to answer some of her questions, "Shanae

was found unconscious in her apartment. We do not know how long she was unconscious. She has lost some blood and has been given a blood transfusion."

Keya caught her breath and continued, "No one knows where your son is. Sherrice is just fine. She's asleep, right over there. We don't know how the baby is doing either."

Ms. Ryder, apparently not getting the information that she wanted, marched to the nurses' station. She was upset when they told her the same exact information Keya had told her. Defeated, she walked over and picked her granddaughter up and rocked her.

She noticed that Sherrice was a little warm. After sitting with her granddaughter for a while, she walked over and sat with Keya and Ma Rose. Shortly, Shanae's doctor came out of the operating room to give them the long awaited status of their dear friend and her baby.

He cleared his throat and said, "I have some good news and some bad news." Keya, Ma Rose, and Ms. Ryder all sat with blank looks on their faces.

Ma Rose broke the silence by saying, "Tell us what you got to tell us. We are all big girls, Doc."

"The baby didn't make it. She was dead upon arrival. However, Shanae's body responded to the blood and she is doing great. All of her vital signs are normal and she is going to pull through. She didn't suffer any brain damage." All of the women were crying from the tear jerking news.

The doctor continued, "However, Shanae doesn't know that she has lost her child and will need someone to stay with her when we relay the terrible news."

Keya immediately said, "I will be here for her. I will stay."

Only if I would have talked to her this morning things might have been different, thought Keya.

Ma Rose asked, "Can we see her tonight?"

The doctor replied, "Only for a brief second. She is in room 615."

Entering the room, they all were in shock and just stood there. Shanae looked like an angel, so peaceful and content. Except for the bandage on her forehead, you would have never known she was hurt. Ma Rose knew that would change once she heard her child didn't make it.

After about twenty minutes Ms. Ryder, Ma Rose, and sleepy Sherrice left the hospital. Ms. Ryder dropped Ma Rose off at home and took Sherrice to her house. Keya stayed with Shanae at the hospital.

11

Pulling into her driveway, Ms. Ryder noticed Hasaun's car in her parking spot.

Just the person I want to see.

Ms. Ryder didn't remember taking Sherrice out of her car seat or walking to the guest bedroom to lay Sherrice down. The only thing she remembered was standing in her kitchen watching her grown ass son eating a bowl of cereal as if he didn't have a worry in the world.

She yelled, "Hasaun where have you been? Why haven't you been home in two days?" She was known for asking several questions right after another.

This chic done already told my mom.

Hasaun never heard his momma enter the house. He was heavy in thought. He had so much on his mind. When his momma yelled, he spilled milk all over the front of his shirt and pants.

Hasaun replied, "I see Shanae has already broken her neck to tell you. I have been at a friend's house. I needed a break."

Perturbed and crying Ms. Ryder said, "It's too late for a break. You're a grown ass man with a family. You need to start acting like it."

Hasaun didn't understand why his mother was crying and flipping out over his business. After all, he was a grown ass man who didn't live at home and whose mother was in his business. He wanted to tell her to mind her own fucking business. However, he knew if he did, he would most definitely be picking his teeth up off the floor. He, for damn sure didn't want to go that route.

Confused Hasaun asked, "Mom, why are you crying?"

"Why am I crying? Why am I crying? I'll tell you why I'm crying. You don't have the balls to be a man. You have a family, Hasaun. It is you're responsibility to take care of your family. Hasaun, you are so clueless. I never thought I see the day you would lie to me."

Hasaun was lost. He didn't know where all this was coming from, but he could only imagine what Shanae had told her. He made a mental note to pay "Miss It" another visit tomorrow. She didn't take heed to his actions earlier. He would just have to go back too get his point across. He wanted to let her know she didn't walk on water.

Hasaun tried to defend himself, "Mom I—"

She yelled, "Shut the hell up! You have been over to some bitch's house and walked out on your family. I never thought you would be like him."

Ms. Ryder hadn't cussed in a long time. However, what Hasaun was doing to his family brought back to many harsh memories and she was furious. She wanted to hurt her son and his good for nothing father.

"Mom, we talking about you or me?" He was tired of hearing her ranting for no damn reason.

Hasaun didn't even see it coming. The bowl went one way and the spoon went the other way. With every ounce of her power, she slapped him. Holding his cheek in disbelief Hasaun was hurt physically and emotionally. He couldn't believe his mother was carrying on like this. He wanted to know exactly what Shanae had told his mother.

This bitch got my mom mad at me I am going to whoop her ass.

"Hasaun, what difference does it make. You know better. You saw what your father put me through. What he put us through for that matter. Why would you put Shanae through this? If you didn't want her, you shouldn't have knocked her up. You need to start thinking with your head and not that little one between your legs either. You need to be a man about the situation, not a coward."

Hasaun felt like shit he had actually turned out to be like his old man.

"Well, at least you haven't resorted to putting your hands on women yet," she replied.

Hasaun's heart sank and he felt nauseous. He had put his hands on Shanae, and she was in so much pain when he left. He felt so bad for hurting her. He knew he was in the wrong but never in a million years did he think she would kick him out. He hoped that she was okay.

Disgusted with Hasaun and wanting to end the conversation she told him, "Hasaun, I don't know how to tell you this. Nevertheless, something happened to Shanae tonight. She lost consciousness and went into labor. There was no phone to call the ambulance. I gather you took it after she kicked you out. She was out for several hours and—"

Concerned, Hasaun asked, "And what? What is going on with Shanae? Where is she?"

Ms. Ryder knew there was no easy way to break the news to him, so she cut to the chase. "Hasaun, calm down and let me finish. She lost the baby. She had to have a blood transfusion. She is okay right now. Keya is sitting with her at the hospital. However, it is not her place it is your place. I don't know what was said or done, but Shanae was fine when I got off the phone with her earlier. You were the last person she talked to and to see her. Did she seem okay?"

Hasaun felt sick. He sat there in disbelief. He could feel the cereal working its way back up his digestive track. He ran to the bathroom and hurled.

I killed my fucking baby. What in the hell was I tripping on? Hasaun walked back into the kitchen. He looked pale and lost.

"Hasaun, was she okay when you left the apartment?"

Hasaun could not tell his mom the truth, so he lied. "Yeah, she was cool. We had a few words but other than that she was straight."

What the fuck have I done?

"Hasaun, I don't care what happen tonight. You need to get to the hospital and be there for Shanae. I don't care if she hates your guts but be a man and do what is right by your child's mother!"

"Speaking of children. Mom, where is Sherrice?"

"She is in the guest bedroom, Hasaun."

Hasaun walked over to his mom and gave her a hug. She felt so bad for him, but she also blamed him. Hasaun left his mother's and drove to the University Hospital to be with Shanae. On his way to the hospital, he felt horrified. All of this was his fault. He had deliberately tried to hurt Shanae and never took into consideration the outcome of his actions. Now, he had to live with the fact that he killed his unborn child. What kind of a man was he? Maybe the apple didn't fall too far from the tree. Maybe Shanae was right. Maybe he was just like his old man. In fact, he felt he was even worse because he killed something before it was even born. He didn't want to face Shanae. He knew she would be devastated. He had caused her so much unnecessary pain and heartache. He wished he could turn back the hands of time. But turning back the hands of time is not possible.

12

As Hasaun approached the hospital, he began to tremble.

What have I done?

Hasaun parked his car in the garage and walked into the hospital. The stench from the hospital smacked Hasaun in the face and made him nauseous. It was the smell of illness, death, antiseptic and cold. Hasaun hadn't been in a hospital since his first child's birth. It was ironic that he was there for his second child's bereavement. His baby was dead, and he was responsible for the baby's death. Hasaun felt so bad for what he had done to Shanae and his family. Not knowing how, he would apologize to Shanae.

He proceeded to the nurse's station to find out Shanae's room number. Hasaun was so scared and confused as he walked to the elevator and pressed the button that would take him to the sixth floor. Hasaun got out of the elevator and walked to Shanae's room.

I have to be strong. Even if Shanae never wants to see me, again. I have to be here for her.

All the way to Shanae's room, Hasaun continued to psych himself up. He entered the room to find Keya and Shanae. Keya was in a recliner with a thin hospital blanket over her. Shanae was asleep in the bed with a bandage on her head and an IV in her left arm. She didn't look as bad as he had expected her to be.

When Keya heard the door open, she sat straight up in her chair. She put her index finger to her lips telling Hasaun to be quiet. She stood up and motioned for him to come outside. Hasaun followed Keya into the waiting room. Hasaun knew Keya had her two cents to put in so he just followed her without any hesitation. Keya was pissed because he should have been there for her hours ago.

"Hasaun where have you been?"

He had heard that same damn question all day. In addition, he was sick and tired of every fucking body wanting to know where he had been.

"Keya, I have been riding around trying to clear my mind. Shanae kicked me out, and I was upset. After riding around I went to my mother's. While I was there, she came in and bit my head off. So I guess you are ready to do the same thing?"

"No, Hasaun. I am not going to bite your head off. I want you to know that you and Shanae both lost a child tonight, and I am deeply sorry for that."

Hasaun could not believe his ears. Was this Keya Lewis talking to him?

"Keya, my mom told me everything and I want to be here for Shanae when she wakes up. You don't have to leave, but I know I am not leaving."

Instantly Keya replied, "I know I don't have to leave so we will both be there when she wakes up. I have been here for hours, and I will stay."

Hasaun knew it wouldn't take long for the old Keya to surface.

"Whatever floats your boat Keya? I don't have time for you," Hasaun replied as he walked back into Shanae's room.

Keya was right behind him, and she was furious. For all she knew he was the cause of all this. Shanae would most certainly shed light on this entire situation in the morning. Hasaun walked into the room, pulled a chair to the side of Shanae's bed and rested his head on her legs. Gently rubbing her hand Hasaun lay there thinking about how happy they used to be and how if she took him back he'd promise to change. While sitting at the edge of the bed reminiscing, Hasaun fell asleep.

Keya sat in the recliner staring at both Hasaun and Shanae. She was upset because Hasaun had the last word and because Shanae had a man that cared about her. Keya loved Shanae with all her heart, but she had always been jealous of her. Keya finally dozed off after midnight.

The next morning the sunlight peeking through the blinds woke Shanae. She tried to open her eyes, but the sun was too bright. She quickly closed her eyes and tried to sit up. Shanae felt weight on her legs when she tried to move her legs. The movement woke Hasaun.

Hasaun jumped from the side of the bed. "Shanae, stop moving. You are in the hospital."

Shanae tried to open her eyes but the sunshine was blinding her. Hasaun noticed her trying to focus her eyes. He ran over and shut the blinds.

"My baby? Is m-my baby okay?" murmured Shanae.

"Shanae, try to remain calm. The doctor wants to see you as soon as you wake up. I will go get him."

Hasaun felt like shit. This was harder than he imagined it to be. He had to tell the woman he loved their baby was dead, and he was to blame. *Why did I put my hands on her?* Hasaun felt sick and ran to the bathroom. He was so thankful Keya had stepped out of the room. Hasaun tossed some cold water on his face and went back into the room with Shanae.

In a groggy voice, Shanae bombarded him with questions, "Hasaun, what is going on? Where is the baby? How long have I been here?

Hasaun was at a loss for words. Shanae was concerned, anxious and she wanted answers. Hasaun had no choice but to tell Shanae what was going on. He cleared his throat and before he could utter a word Shanae passed out as her monitoring machine was beeping. The doctors entered the room and ordered Hasaun to leave.

Shanae was suffering from an overload of stress that in turn caused her to blackout. Hasaun stayed by her bedside day and night. On the third day her eyes began to flutter and she was wiggling her fingers. Hasaun had been praying nonstop and was so thankful his prayers had been answered.

Shanae questioned, "Baby?"

Hasaun could not believe his ears. What would he tell her? How could he explain the situation? He had fucked up. She tried to open her eyes but it felt as if weights were holding her lids down. She remembered yelling with Hasaun. She remembered lying on the floor.

"How did I get on the floor?"

Hasaun sat quietly. What could he say? He prayed she didn't say anything else about being knocked on the floor he could be in serious trouble.

"Hasaun, how long?"

Hasaun cleared his throat and said, "How long what Shanae?"

"Have I been in this damn hospital?"

"Shanae, you have been in the hospital for three days. You are okay and the doctor would like to talk to you."

"No, Hasaun you knocked me down! How long was I at

home?"

Hasaun was looking around the room and praying no on heard Shanae. No matter how tough he thought he was he didn't want to be sitting in Boone County Jail.

"Shanae, it's bad," replied Hasaun with tears running down his face.

Tears were streaming down Shanae's face also and she yelled, "She didn't make it did she!"

Hasaun didn't say anything. He was crying and his face was covered with tears. Hasaun walked over, sat on the bed and hugged her. Shanae held on to him like there was no tomorrow. She buried her face in his chest and wept. She wept because of her loss and she knew she would never love Hasaun the same again. Shanae was crying so hard Hasaun couldn't control her. She was devastated and had never felt this way before. Hasaun held her tightly and rocked her ever so gently.

At that moment, Keya walked through the door with coffee and donuts. Like Hasaun, Keya refused to leave her friend's side and the little scare three days ago had Keya shaken up. When she noticed that Shanae was awake, she sat the coffee and donuts down on the metal rolling nightstand and stood against the wall with her hand over her mouth. Keya instantly started crying. She knew how Shanae felt about her children and she could empathize with her.

Shanae pulled away from Hasaun and asked him, "Did our

baby make it?"

"Shanae, why don't you calm down while I go get the doctor?"

"NO! I don't want to hear it from an outsider, please! Hasaun tell me the truth. Did my baby make it or not?"

Shanae used my baby because she felt that Hasaun hadn't been there for her during her pregnancy so why give him any recognition. Hasaun hesitated because he didn't know what to say and he knew this whole ordeal was his fault.

Hasaun looked Shanae in her eyes and said, "Shanae, I am so sorry. She didn't make it," Hasaun could barely get the words out of his mouth.

Keya could see how the information was killing them both. She walked over and rubbed Hasaun's back and told them, "In time it will all get better."

After Keya said that, she didn't know if she wanted it to get better for Shanae. She would enjoy having some one-on-one counseling with Hasaun. They sure as hell wouldn't be talking about the death of his child.

Shanae pulled away from both Hasaun and Keya. She looked like she had been on a drug binge for weeks. Her eyes were swollen and her hair was all over her head. Shanae took a look around the room and slowly said, "I don't understand what happened. Why did this happen to me? I have lost so many people in my life."

Keya and Hasaun were both speechless. They sat there while Shanae lost control of herself.

Hasaun ordered Keya, "Go get the doctor!"

Keya ran out of the room at top speed and brought back Shanae's doctor. The doctor came in took her vital signs. Everything was okay except her blood pressure. It was elevated, which was normal under the circumstances. However, it still was not safe.

Dr. Todd said, "Shanae we have some bad news. Your daughter didn't make it. We—"

Shanae interrupted him,

"Dr. Todd, I have already been informed that my child didn't survived," all the while staring holes in Hasaun.

Dr. Todd was relieved because he didn't want to be the bearer of bad news.

"Well, I am so sorry for your loss."

"Dr. Todd, what happened?" questioned Shanae.

Dr. Todd looked about the room as if to say, "Are you sure you want me to discuss it in front of everyone?"

"It's okay. He is the father of my children and she is a very dear friend. I don't mind if they hear." Hasaun didn't want to know how it happened. He already knew.

Dr. Todd cleared his throat and said, "You went into labor and evidently loss consciousness. While unconscious you lost a lot of blood, which in turn decreased the oxygen supply to the baby."

Hasaun cringed at the thought of his daughter gasping for air all because of him.

Dr. Todd continued, "The baby was dead on arrival. We had to give you a blood transfusion. Other than that, everything has been okay. Except for now your blood pressure is elevated and you have a nasty bump on your head. Shanae, if you don't calm down I will have to give you something to put you to sleep. I know it is hard to be calm considering all that you have been through but I can't let your blood pressure keep escalating. Okay?"

Shanae took a deep breath, laid flat on her back and replied, "I'm calm."

How the hell does he expect me to be calm? I just lost my child!

Walking out of the room Dr. Todd said, "Ms. Davis, if you need anything please call your nurse. If she can't help you, have them page me. We have to get your blood pressure down before you can be discharged."

With her eyes closed Shanae replied, "Okay." Shanae was a strong girl and she knew she could beat this. She just needed time. Right now she was hurt and confused. She fell asleep. She tried to fight it but it engulfed her body and she was a prisoner to sleep. While asleep, she had an awful dream. Both her daughters were dressed in white and they kept repeating the same thing over and over.

"Mommy, we have to leave you. We are in a better place." Shanae was confused because Sherrice was with her little sister and they appeared to be so happy.

She woke up to find Hasaun still sitting beside her and that the sun was no longer shining. Her breathing was loud and quick. The nightmare was weighing heavy on her heart. She was so confused by the nightmare. She was beginning to sweat.

Concerned Hasaun asked, "Shanae, are you okay?"

Shanae saw Hasaun's mouth moving but she didn't hear a single word he uttered. She was mad. Mad at Hasaun. Mad at the doctor for not saving her baby. Mad because her mother abandoned her. She was just mad at the world. She was distraught but she knew Hasaun had to be taking it really hard. After all, he killed their child.

Shanae laid in the bed with her eyes open and tears silently streaming down her face. Hasaun lifted his head from the bed. His eyes were swollen and his face tear drenched. Shanae actually felt sorry for him. Why, she had no idea. For about thirty seconds Hasaun and Shanae looked into each other's eyes without saying a word. The eyes never lie. They told so much about a person. Both Shanae and Hasaun's eyes showed hurt and pain. They were both going through hard times. They both wondered what had happened to their once perfect lives.

Hasaun broke the silence, "Shanae, I am so sorry."

"Hasaun, I know you are," she thought in more ways than one.

"Shanae, what will I do? I killed our baby!" Shanae wanted to tell Hasaun to go to hell but she held her composure.

"Hasaun, you will have to live with that for the remainder of your life. I guess you should begin by asking for forgiveness." Hasaun didn't understand how Shanae could be so strong. He felt so bad. He wanted to die. He wished he could switch places with his child.

"Shanae, I wish I hadn't put my hands on you. I knew better. I was just so mad. I know there is no excuse for my actions. I am so sorry. I am sorry for disrespecting you and I am sorry for being a sorry nigga."

Shanae agreed with Hasaun, but once again decided to spare his feelings.

"Hasaun I accept your apology and I hope it is sincere. I want you to know as of right now I have a lot of mixed feelings. I know that I love you but I also hate you right now. I am angry with you. But I was always taught that hatred and angriness would wither away at a person's soul. So, I know I will not feel this way towards you forever. You will always hold a special place in my heart but never in my life. I don't want to be with you anymore and I hope you can understand why."

It took everything in Shanae to utter those words. This was the man she wanted to spend her entire life with.

Hasaun heard this speech yesterday and if only he would have done the right thing and accepted it, their baby would be alive. He decided to do the right thing now.

"Shanae, I understand and I will respect your wishes. I just want you to know that I don't know where to go from here."

Hasaun was crying and he couldn't get his breath. Shanae pulled him close to her and hugged him. She hugged him because it hurt her to see him like this and because he needed it.

Silently crying inside Shanae said, "Hasaun, I can't tell you where to go from here but you have to learn from this mistake. I hope you will never put your hands on another female or for that matter, anyone. You also have to take into consideration that we have another child. We can't die with this child. We have to make sure Sherrice has a happy and meaningful life."

"I know Shanae. I know. It's just I haven't been there for you guys and I am sorry."

"Hasaun, I have accepted your apology. You need to focus on the present and future. Stop dwelling on the past. No, you haven't been there for us but you can't change that. Put the past behind you."

Hasaun knew he had to get his shit together. He realized he would have to do that without Shanae. Something he never imagined.

Hasaun gazed into Shanae's eyes and said, "I love you so

much. Shanae."

Hasaun bent forward and kissed Shanae on her forehead. Shanae pulled Hasaun's face down and kissed him on his succulent lips. They held each other and relished the sensuous kiss. Tears were streaming down both their faces. This would be their last kiss before they would go their separate ways.

As Hasaun stood to leave he held on to Shanae's hand and said, "What will we say happened?"

Hasaun didn't want Shanae to lie for him but he didn't want everyone to know he had killed his daughter. So in a sense he did want her to lie for him so people would not judge him.

"Hasaun, I don't think this is anyone's business but ours. I will never tell anyone what happened."

"Thank you, Shanae."

Again, Hasaun bent down and kissed Shanae on her forehead, turned around and walked out of the hospital room, leaving behind the most precious gift in his life.

13

Later that evening when Keya and Ma Rose arrived at the hospital, Shanae was asleep. They both walked in and took a seat. Shanae heard them and opened her eyes. Ma Rose was so happy to see her awake. She had been on pins and needles all night worrying about Shanae. That scare the other day had her on edge. Ma Rose knew that Shanae's life revolved around her children and she felt sorry for her.

Smiling Ma Rose said, "How are you feeling, Suga?"

Shanae replied, "I've been better. I feel okay though. I'm happy I'm not in any physical pain. The doctor will be discharging me whenever my blood pressure drops."

Shanae couldn't wait to see Sherrice. The dream she had was unnerving.

Looking around Keya interrupted, "So where's Hasaun?"

Shanae had been waiting for this question when Keya walked in and perused the room. Shanae replied, "He just left."

Keya questioned, "When will he be back and is he giving

you a ride home in two days?"

Shanae really didn't feel Keya's smart-ass today. *Keya ain't ever going to change always sticking her nose in other folks business.*

"Keya, who said I was leaving the hospital in two days?"

Shanae didn't give Keya enough time to answer her question. She continued talking, "And why are you so worried about Hasaun? He left because I asked him to leave. Hasaun and I aren't together and I don't want him here. We had a long talk and we both are on the same page!"

Ma Rose couldn't believe Keya had the audacity to be so mean considering Shanae's condition.

Keya rolled her eyes in her true ghetto fashion and said, "And what page is that?"

"Keya, it is none of your damn business! We are not a couple anymore. That's it!"

Ma Rose watched the two-sided conversation and saw it getting ugly so she jumped in.

"Shanae, Victor said he would be here first thing in the morning."

Shanae questioned, "How did you get his number?"

"I guess you gave him my number. He said he called your house several times and there was no answer. So he called me I told him you were in the hospital."

Shanae replied, "Thanks, Ma Rose."

Shanae glanced over at Keya who was looking out the window heavily in thought. Ma Rose had a couple of questions she wanted answered but decided this wasn't the time. They all sat there in silence avoiding eye contact with each other.

Shanae broke the silence, "I can't believe I am sitting here in the hospital and my baby died. I expected to be having her in a couple of days and holding her in my arms. Things never go as planned when it comes to me."

At that moment, Keya felt bad for badgering her. Keya spoke first, "Shanae, I am so sorry for acting like a bitch. It's just that I sort of hold myself responsible if I would have taken your phone call that morning maybe there would have been a different outcome."

"You were a little preoccupied that day, Keya," joked Shanae.

"Sorry, Shanae."

Shanae was crying and having trouble getting her words out. She managed a whisper and said, "Keya, by no means was my baby dying your fault. Don't think this was your fault. You are not responsible for a person living or dying. None of us in this room are. So for my sake and yours, please don't hold yourself responsible for this."

Crying, Keya said, "Thanks for the reassurance but I don't understand what happened."

Again, Ma Rose jumped in the conversation, "Honey, this

ain't for none of us to understand. God works in mysterious ways. I don't mean to sound calloused but he knows what is best for each and every one of us. There was no guarantee that Shanae would make it, but she did. God knew Sherrice couldn't live without her. So he does what is best." Ma Rose paused and wiped the tears from her eyes and continued talking, "Shanae, you are hurting right now and that is reasonably expected. I just want you both to remember God will NEVA—I mean NEVA put more on you than you can bear. It may seem unbearable now but time mends a broken heart. Just put your faith in God."

Both Keya and Shanae knew that she was speaking the truth. But the only thing Shanae knew right now was she was miserable. Shanae inhaled and said, "I know that everything you said is correct but it hurts, Ma Rose. It just hurts so badly and I am hurting and I can't do anything about it."

"Honey, it is going to hurt. Ten years from now, it will hurt but you will have to learn how to cope with this terrible loss. I am hurting. You are hurting. Keya is hurting. And Hasaun and his family are hurting. Death hurts, baby."

This was way too deep for Keya and she couldn't take this conversation. She jumped up and said, "I am going to the cafeteria and grab a bite to eat."

She didn't want to sit and listen to Shanae wallow in her sorrow, or her old bestie, spitting her scriptural knowledge. She wanted to know where Hasaun was and if he had something to do with the baby dying. Sitting here listening to these two talk about their God was not what was up.

As if reading Keya's mind Shanae said, "Wait, Keya, before you go I know both of y'all want to know how this happened."

Ma Rose and Keya both had their own assumptions and wanted to know if they were accurate.

Shanae wiped the tears from her eyes and said, "Hasaun came over and we had a heated argument. We screamed, yelled and cussed at each other. While we were arguing I felt a sharp pang in my stomach. I sat down on the sofa to catch my breath. Hasaun asked me if I was okay. I told him I would be when he'd get the hell out. Earlier that day I packed everything that belonged to him, including the phone he bought. After he left I wobbled into the kitchen to get a drink of water. A pain hit me and I fell to the floor. I tried to get up to call the ambulance but I had packed the phone. I crawled to the front door but couldn't go any further. I tried for hours to open the door but the pain wasn't letting up. I guess I lost consciousness because I just remember waking up in the hospital."

Keya and Ma Rose were both happy that Hasaun didn't do anything to her. They both were sad because she was helpless and no one was there for her.

Ma Rose said, "That's why you never answered the phone when I called. I thought you wanted some time alone so I didn't bother coming over." Ma Rose knew this couldn't have been prevented. The baby was going to die no matter what. If God sought after the baby, He was going to seize it.

Keya said, "I called also and you never answered the phone, so I decided to stop by after work." Keya walked back over to the recliner and took a seat. The conversation was finally going somewhere, so she decided to stay put.

Ma Rose looked at Keya suspiciously and stated, "I thought you were going to get something to eat."

"Naw. I changed my mind," Keya replied.

Ma Rose noticed something different about Keya for the first time. It seemed as if she was happy about Shanae's circumstances. She decided to keep a watchful eye on her.

The women sat around for a couple of hours and had small talk before they left. Ma Rose and Keya both gave Shanae a kiss before they left. They told her they would see her when she got home.

Shanae watched her friends leave her room and was actually happy to have some time alone. She buzzed the nurse and requested a notebook and pen. She knew she would have a healing process and decided to start today. She was grief-stricken. Her baby died and at the same time she was also happy. She asked God to forgive her for having those feelings. She was happy he took her at birth and not after she had grown attached to her. It was an ironic feeling but she was relieved her child was not one or two years old when he decided to take her.

She blocked those thoughts out because they seemed immoral. After about five minutes, the nurse brought her a notebook and a writing utensil. Shanae thanked her and the nurse left. Shanae opened the book and wrote:

Dear God,

I know the grieving process can be difficult and long. I don't want to diminish because I have lost a child. I want to live for the child and family I have. Dear God, please give me a helping hand to make it I also need strength.

Thanks,

Shanae

Shanae decided she would keep a journal and write all her feelings about her loss and life. She realized she had been through a lot in her life and maybe she would see a shrink to help her cope with all her misfortunes.

Shanae dozed off after dinner. She couldn't believe the food the hospital tried to have the patients consume. Shanae was jarred from her sleep when she heard a tap at the door. A middle-aged white woman with a clipboard and several papers walked through the door. Shanae sat up and greeted the stranger.

"Hi, my name is Mary Hines. I am the social worker for the hospital and I just wanted to know if you had any questions or concerns."

Shanae thought it was a little late for a social worker to be working. "I have a couple of questions. However, I don't know if you can help me."

"My job is to make sure you are stable mentally to go home."

She didn't have the credentials to make sure I was mentally stable. So why was she here.

"Oh, I have to be. I have another child I have to care after. I guess my first question is do you know of a credible shrink that I can see?"

Mary was pleased with the question. This was going to be easier than she thought. She was used to being attacked after suggesting a patient see a psychiatrist.

Smiling Mary said, "Yes, as matters of fact I know quite a few. I have a list right here," Mary gave Shanae the list of psychiatrists and a schedule for grief classes.

"Thank you so much, Ms. Hines, for this information. I am under a lot of strain right now and I know I can't deal with it all by myself. I know what I have to do to get over this. I actually started a journal today. I can't let this incident break my mold."

Amazed at what she was hearing Mary said, "Shanae, you appear to be handling the situation great. After all, you made the first initiatives to better yourself. I think your recovery will be great." Shanae was pleased that Mary was on her side and smiled.

"Shanae, did you have any other questions?"

"Oh, yes. I was wondering if I gave you the information of the father of my children if you could help him out with this. I do not think he will be able to handle this ordeal at all."

"Well, yes, if you can just write all his information on this piece of paper." Dr. Hines handed Shanae the standard issued clipboard and jotted down all of Hasaun's information.

"Shanae, it has been a pleasure meeting you and I am so sorry for your loss. I have to go make the rest of my rounds. Here is my card. If you ever need any additional information please give me a call."

"Thanks, Ms. Hines," replied Shanae.

Shanae got out of bed and went inside the bathroom to tinkle. She exited the bathroom and walked to the sink to wash her hands. She caught a glimpse of herself in the mirror. Her eyes were red and swollen, lips chapped and cracked, hair was tangled and all over her head. She had dried up tear stains on her face and sleep in the corner of her eyes. She cupped her hand around her mouth and blew in her hand. Her breath was hot and she looked a mess. Shanae looked at the reflection in the mirror and began to laugh. She was laughing because she could not believe that Ma Rose and Keya left the hospital without telling her that her face was dirty and her breath was hot.

Shanae didn't have a shower in her room so she buzzed the nurse and told her she wanted to take one. Within minutes, the nurse came and escorted Shanae to the shower room. The nurse pointed to the cabinet and said,

"Everything you need is in the cabinet."

"Thanks a lot," replied Shanae

"You're welcome. If you need anything just buzz." The nurse said as she left the shower room.

Shanae went to the cabinet and retrieved a towel, washcloth, soap, toothbrush, toothpaste, shampoo, comb, brush, robe, gown and lotion.

Shit the hospital has the works.

Shanae walked into the shower turned it on and exhaled. After her shower, Shanae looked one hundred percent better. She walked to her room. When she went inside Ms. Ryder was sitting in the recliner.

She stood up hugged Shanae and said, "Hello, Shanae. How are you?" Shanae had been asked this question all day.

She shrugged her shoulders and said, "Under the circumstances, I am doing okay."

"You look great, as usual."

Shanae laughed and said, "You wouldn't have said that about thirty minutes ago. I looked like hot trash."

"I can hardly imagine your looking like hot trash." Shanae was glad Ms. Ryder stopped by to see her but she was hoping she brought Sherrice.

"Where is Sherrice?"

"She is still under the weather. I can't get her fever under control and it keeps coming back. I didn't want to bring her to the hospital. I think I may need to make her an appointment. Oh, that reminds me." Ms. Ryder grabbed her purse and pulled out a blue piece of paper. She handed it to Shanae. "Sherrice drew you this picture and wanted me to bring it to you."

Shanae looked at the picture her daughter drew. It was a picture of a rainbow and the sun. At least that is what she thought it was. She hoped the sun would shine in her life soon. She had too many rainy days to even count. Shanae looked at the picture and started crying.

Ms. Ryder walked over and hugged her. Ms. Ryder thought to herself that Shanae was handling this a lot better than she would.

"Shanae, everything will fall into place. Put it in God's hands and He will see to it that you will be alright."

Ms. Ryder was so hurt. Deep down inside she knew this was all Hasaun's fault. Ms. Ryder loosened her grip and said, "Stay strong." She knew her son played a major role in this child's death. Only Shanae and Hasaun would not confirm it. She went with their bogus story even though she didn't believe it.

"Shanae, I am so sorry but I know it will get better."

"I know. It's just I can't believe the terrible hand in life I have been dealt."

"Days ago you told me you had plans just stick to your plans. God will work it all out baby."

"That's what everyone keeps telling me," replied Shanae.

"Then Shanae, take heed and believe what we are telling you," consoled Ms. Ryder.

"I want to but it is so hard," cried Shanae.

Looking at Shanae crying hurt Ms. Ryder more than anything.

"Shanae, this is only the beginning. Do not expect so much from yourself. I know this is hard but take your time and make it through this at your own pace and never give up on the Lord."

Shanae looked defeated. She had something else she wanted to say. She just wanted her baby and the happy life with Hasaun that she had envisioned for so many years.

Ms. Ryder stood, walked over to Shanae and wiped her tears. Then she gave her a hug and told her, "Well, I have to get back home because I know Hasaun is lost. Sherrice is not feeling good at all. I can't break her fever."

Shanae knew exactly what she was talking about. "I know she kept me up the other night. I tried everything."

"She had a fever the other day?"

"Yes. The day before I came to the hospital."

"Oh, I didn't know that. That is about four or five days. If she doesn't get any better I am going to bring her in."

"Sounds good to me. Please look after my darling."

"You know I will. I will see you when you get out of the hospital."

"Ms. Ryder thanks for everything!"

"No problem, baby," replied Ms. Ryder as she walked out of the room.

14

Victor called the University Hospital and asked for

Bernard Williams.

"Hello, Dr. Williams speaking."

"Hey Dad. This is Vic. I heard Shanae was in the hospital. What's up?"

Hesitant Bernard replied, "Well, Victor, you know Shanae doesn't talk to your mom and me. So, I haven't been up to see her. However, from the information I gathered she went into premature labor and lost her baby. I heard she is handling the situation great and has had plenty of visitors, so she is not alone."

Victor was upset his parent's hadn't been to see her. Annoyed Victor asked, "Why haven't you and mom been to see her? This is the perfect time to put aside your differences and make amends."

Bernard knew the reason he would never go to her room. He stammered and said, "Victor, what do we say to her after all this time? You know how hotheaded Shanae can be," replied Bernard.

"What difference does it make she lost her child! You guys are in the same town and haven't been by to see her. I will be there in the morning."

Victor didn't wait for Bernard's reply. He slammed the phone down. After hanging the phone up, Victor called his administrative assistant into his office and gave her the last minute errands and jobs to take care of while he would be gone. He hadn't had a vacation in a lengthy time so he decided to take two weeks off to be there for his sister. Victor left his office around five. He called his personal assistant and requested some vacation clothing and evening attire for his trip to Columbia, Missouri.

After a long day at work, he arrived home. Once he was at home Victor pitched his keys on the dining room table. He was so angry that he didn't even notice the table that he had searched for over two years to find just the perfect one. He loved this round base table with glass on the top and a handpicked and polished wood root as the pedestal. He walked over to his bar and poured a glass of Remy Martin. He loved the taste of cognac. He consumed the cognac and savored the taste. He couldn't wait to go home.

He hadn't been to Columbia in a couple of years. He had some friends he couldn't wait to see. Victor called it a night around seven that evening. He never left his office until around nine, so to be at home packing was something new to him. He took pleasure in the additional down time.

His alarm went off at four the next morning. Victor woke up, took a hot shower, dressed and waited for the car service to arrive. His flight left at five thirty. His secretary, who knew everything he needed before he has to ask for it, had taken care of everything for him. The car service arrived, loaded his luggage and headed to the airport. Victor loved early fights because the airport wasn't as congested as the later flights. He boarded his plane and took off without any problems. While in the air, Victor had several questions he wanted answers to and he had plans for his sister. He was going to get his sister out of the hood first and foremost. He was going to find out the real reason his parents weren't communicating with his sister.

Shit, we already have another sister out there somewhere. Momma knows better. I don't really remember my biological dad or Shanae's twin sister. I will get everything in order and we will be a happy family again.

Victor didn't realize he had his work cut out for him. While thinking about all the things he was going to change, Victor dozed off. Victor woke up when the flight attendant tapped him on the shoulder and told him he was in St. Louis. Victor looked around the plane and noticed he was the only one remaining. Victor jumped up grabbed his Gucci carryon and left the plane.

I don't remember falling asleep.

Victor still had another hour and a half to drive to Columbia. To be a college town it had no decent airport. There was the Columbia Regional Airport, but a man of Victor's caliber would not be caught dead flying on one of those little planes. He had been contemplating about buying a jet but never really gave it much thought. He reminded himself he needed to check into purchasing a private jet.

15

The car service was waiting on Victor as soon as he stepped out of Lambert Airport. It was a bright clear day for a November morning in Missouri. Missouri's weather was so unpredictable. It could be raining one minute and bright and sunny the next. Victor took a deep breath and relished the smog free day. The air wasn't the greatest in St. Louis but it had Chicago beat by a long shot. Victor was in high spirits because he hadn't been home in years and he was only an hour and a half away from being there.

He walked towards the black Lincoln Town Car and got in. As soon as he sat in the supple leather seats he relaxed. His relaxation was halted when the chauffer asked, "Where to?"

Victor wanted to stay at a hotel but he knew his parents would be offended. Victor gave the chauffer the address and dozed off again. The chauffer exited the airport and headed west on I-70. Victor could not wait to see his parents and his sister. He prayed she would be strong.

The chauffer unloaded Victor's luggage and took it to the door. Victor gave him a tip and told him he enjoyed the ride. Victor didn't worry about renting a car because he knew his momma had an extra one and didn't mind his using it. He would be rolling in his mother's sleek black E500 Mercedes His mother was known for her exquisite taste and her cars were always a year ahead of the present year. If it was 1999 she drove a 2000. Everything she possessed was top notch. Dena was a stunning lady and loved life.

Victor walked into the huge estate and was amazed by the decorations and renovations. Dena had transformed the entire place. Victor walked to his room and was glad to see not much had really changed. There was a new bedroom set and bathroom decorations but other than that everything was still intact. He positioned his luggage neatly in the closet, walked to the bed and sat down. Victor kicked off his expensive loafers and fell back on the king size bed. Victor wanted to take a nap but he had entirely too many errands to run.

The first thing he did was change out of his tailored suit that fit his physique proportionately well. Victor maneuvered into a Ralph Lauren golf sweater and a pair of Ralph Lauren khakis. Victor left the room with his briefcase and the car keys his momma left on the nightstand for him. Before leaving the house, he took a tour. Everything was well organized and arranged. Out of spite, he moved one of his mother's figurines to a different location to see if she would notice.

After leaving the realtor Victor was ecstatic. He had just purchased an executive home for Shanae and his niece. He could not wait to see their faces. He was aware of her taste and he knew she would fall head over heels for the home.

Before he went to the hospital he made a detour. Victor walked the steps to Ashlee's by Design. His mother had been using this interior decorating company for decades. He sat down with a very attractive African-American young lady named Jade and gave her all the details that he needed accomplished within twenty-four hours. Jade was in total shock.

"Excuse me," looking at the papers. "Um, Mr. Davis, this is a lot of work. I don't know if we can have everything completed within the twenty-four hour time frame."

Victor was a little annoyed by the comment. He took a deep breath and in a deep sexy baritone voice said, "I don't care what it takes. It really should have been completed yesterday. I don't care what the expense is. I really need this done."

Smugly, Jade replied, "This lady must mean a lot to you."

Victor knew exactly what Jade was insinuating. "As a matter of fact, she does mean a lot to me. I would move heaven and earth to ensure she has everything she needs and wants.

Impressed Jade smiled and said, "We will have to go with one of the more costly decorators because they have more staff and people to work around the clock."

Victor smiled and said, "Actually, I would like to use the exact decorator my momma uses. She has been a customer of this establishment for a while." Looking around the quaint establishment he hoped it lived up to what his momma said it did.

Jade eyed Victor curiously, "And who might that be?"

Victor was looking Jade over. She was very striking and he had examined her body earlier, which happened to be out of sight.

Again Jade asked, "And who might that be?" She had a smirk on her face because she knew he was sizing her up.

Victor, totally embarrassed, said, "Dena Davis-Williams."

Jade's eyes lit up when she heard Dena's name. Dena had spent so much money with her there was no way in hell she was going to let her son down.

Smiling Jade replied, "I have worked with her on several assignments. She is an interesting woman."

"Thanks," replied Victor.

"She never mentioned she had a son."

"She is secretive woman."

"Well, I would say. I think we can get this decorated within twenty-four hours. It will be a long shot but I will see to it personally that it is completed in a timely manner."

"Only because I mentioned my momma's name," joked Victor.

Laughing Jade replied, "Sometimes it helps to know people."

"I don't care what the cost; just make sure each and every room in the home is decorated and childproof," demanded Victor.

She thought, *this man has the nerve to have a child and a wife and has been devouring me with his eyes.* Then she remembered why she was still single because men aren't any good.

Victor was confused by Jade's change in demeanor. He cleared his throat to get her attention. Jade snapped back into reality when she heard Playa Playa clear his throat. She had to keep telling herself. *This is business. No matter how much he has my stomach doing flips, no more married men.*

Jade and Victor completed all the necessary paperwork for the strenuous assignment. Victor and Jade said their goodbyes and set a meeting for the next day.

Victor walked to the Mercedes and drove to the University Hospital. He stopped by the gift shop, purchased a teddy bear and a dozen of beautiful red roses. He impatiently waited for the elevator and rode it to the sixth floor. As he approached Shanae's room, he felt hopeless. She had fallen short and now he had to help her out. He enjoyed helping her and he wished she would move to Chicago with him. He tapped on the door and let himself in. To his surprise, Shanae was sitting in the bed writing in a notebook. When she heard the door open she turned towards the door. It was her baby bro. He had really grown up. He looked as handsome and dapper as ever.

"Victor, how are you doing? You look so handsome."

Victor ran over to Shanae and gave her a big squeeze.

"I am doing great! I just had to come and check on my big sis. How are you doing, Shanae?"

Shanae could feel the tears welling up in her eyes, "I am doing okay. Even though I don't really understand what I have done to have such a terrible life."

Victor was fighting back tears also. However, he was not strong enough. This was the big sister who told him to make good grades, never settle for less and ensured him he could be anything he put his mind to.

"Shanae, your life is far from terrible. You are a strong person and I know you can overcome all this heartache. Remember you were always telling me that God would never put more on you than you can bear."

"Vic, I'm not saying I can't overcome the heartache. I just don't comprehend it. Why me?"

124

"Shanae, God is trying to tell you something. Remember what Grandma used to say. "Quit saying why me and say why not me." You have to stay strong and get your life back on track. I believe God has more in store for you than heartache."

Shanae knew what Victor was implying so she enlightened him.

"Vic, I know you don't understand why I left the family or quit school. I will never be able to explain the circumstances to you but I had to do what I had to do in order to survive."

Perturbed Victor said, "And what is that, Shanae?"

"I can't tell you but one day you will understand."

Victor decided to flip the script. "I have a great surprise for you when we leave the hospital."

"Sorry to burst your bubble but my doctor will not be releasing me until my vital signs are in order. My blood pressure has been elevated so he wants to monitor me closely."

Let down Victor stated, "Well, doctor knows best." Victor wasn't pleased that his sister had to stay in the hospital longer. He made sure she got a private duty nurse. But this would give the interior decorators another day or two to decorate the home. He made a mental note to call them and let them know they had extra time.

"I can't wait to get out of the hospital. I haven't seen Sherrice in days. I miss her so much."

"I talked to Hasaun's mom and she said my niece has been under the weather."

"Yeah, I know. I really hope she gets better soon. We have a lot of catching up to do. I do so want to hold her."

"Shanae, don't worry about anything. I will be here as long as it takes to get you back on your feet."

"Victor, I really want you to know that I deeply appreciate all you have done for us."

"Don't even mention it, Sis." He couldn't contain the smile.

"No, Vic, you don't understand. I am so thankful for you. If it wasn't for your love and Sherrice's I most likely would have given up a long time ago."

Tears were running down Shanae's face. Shanae took her forearm and wiped the mixture of tears and snot off her face.

"Now. Sis, I know you are upset but Momma taught you better than to wipe snot on your arm," joked Victor.

Shanae laughed and proceeded to the sink to wash her hands.

"Imagine if she would have seen me do that."

They both shared a laugh.

"You uncouth fool. You know better than that," mimicked Victor.

"Oh boy, you sound just like her," laughed Shanae.

The both shared a chuckle, however, Shanae laughed a little longer. Victor knew deep down that she missed their momma.

"So what is going on?"

Shaking her head and trying to get her composure Shanae took a deep breath and replied, "Vic, I do not know. It seems as if I am losing a never-ending battle. I have lost so much I do not know if I can keep it together."

"What's up, Shanae? What can I do? How can I make it better? What do you need?" stammered Victor.

"I need you to quit asking so many questions at once." Shanae said seriously but lovingly.

"Sorry."

"Please, you are far from sorry." Dropping her head, Shanae continued, "Unlike me, I am a sorry case."

"Shanae, do not talk about yourself like this. You are smart, beautiful and have a sense of humor. I know you will be okay."

Balling Shanae replied, "Vic, it hurts so badly. Why me? Why is this happening to me?"

Victor held Shanae and tried to console her but she was so distraught it broke his heart to see a once strong individual go to pieces. Victor held her and continued to let her know he was not going anywhere until she was one hundred percent better.

Victor and Shanae talked for hours. They caught up on lost time. Shanae wanted to know when she would have a sister- in-law. Victor avoided that topic all together. He promised Shanae he would be at the hospital first thing in the morning. They hugged, kissed and Victor left the hospital.

Before heading to his mother's, Victor decided to stop by his sister's new home. He pulled into the circle driveway, which was well lit. Victor put his key into the lock and walked inside the spacious home. He looked around and was shocked that work had actually been completed. Victor also noticed that lights were still on. He made a mental note to talk to the decorating company about the lights. As Victor approached the master suite he heard music playing. The soft jazz playing behind the door was relaxing. He snatched the door open and there she stood, Jade in a black spandex body suit, deeply in thought. She hadn't noticed or heard Victor enter. She was busy perusing blueprints and layouts of the task at hand. He noticed that the company had purchased some beautiful art work. However, the one thing that stood out the most to Victor was Jade. Victor took in her amazing body. She was beautiful. After gawking he cleared his throat, which in turn startled Jade.

"Ahh," screamed Jade.

"It's me. Mr. Davis," replied Victor.

It was too late. Jade ran over and punched him in the chest, "You scared the shit out of me!"

Laughing, Victor said, "Sorry."

Jade's facial expression let Victor know she didn't think it was the least bit funny. "What are you doing here anyway?" demanded Jade.

Still laughing, Victor said, "I just wanted to see what your company accomplished today. I didn't mean to scare you honestly." Rubbing his chest Victor continued, "Remind me never to sneak up on you again."

"Sorry, you really scared me. I never even heard you come in the house. I really didn't mean to hurt you."

"I'll get over it. Why are you still here?"

"Well, there is a lot stuff to complete and I relieved one of our decorators so he could get some rest."

Victor said, "Oh well, since you're here I can tell you in person. Something came up and you have an extra day or two to finish decorating the house."

Jade smiled, "That is great news. We were going to be so busy trying to find exactly the right accessories." Still smiling Jade said, "I have a questionnaire about favorite colors and furniture. If you could have your special lady complete the questionnaire that would be great. We try to personalize the living quarters as much as possible."

Victor frowned and said, "That's going to be a big problem because she doesn't even know I purchased this home for her. It is going to be her surprise when she is released from the hospital."

"That is so sweet of you," replied Jade.

Smiling Victor said, "I just want to surprise her and move her out of her current living conditions."

"No problem. Maybe you can help by completing the form for her. I know the paperwork you completed at the office asked a lot of questions but this one will really add some great finishing touches to the home."

Without thinking Victor said, "Maybe we can grab a bite to eat and discuss this over dinner." Victor wanted to grab each and every word he just uttered and throw back in his mouth. His flushed face showed his embarrassment.

This man had a lot of heart and nerve. He was purchasing a home, having it decorated for his family and was asking her out. She kept telling herself that he was married or in a serious relationship. Tell him no. However, when she looked at his bulging biceps and his handsome face, she couldn't turn down the invite.

Jade smiled and said, "Sure as long as you give me time to run home and freshen up."

She didn't feel that bad because he did not have a wedding band on.

Shocked by her answer Victor replied, "Sounds like a plan. We can meet at seven-thirty at Teller's."

Jade and Victor both left the home to go get dressed for the evening.

Jade couldn't believe this beautiful man could be married. He opened doors, pulled out chairs, asked her opinion and was just an extremely courteous person. She was beginning to feel bad about having dinner and drinks with him.

"Jade are you okay?"

"Yes, why do you ask?"

Victor had noticed her apprehensiveness and was concerned for her. "Well, you look unhappy."

"I should not be here with you!" Jade said as she stood to leave.

Grabbing her hand and stopping her Victor said, "Whoa! Whoa! What is the problem? Did I say something to offend you?"

Jade just looked at him with a disdained look and never said a word.

"Take a seat and tell me what is bothering you so badly that you want to leave before we even have dinner," pleaded Victor.

Reluctantly, Jade sat down. She tried to smile but she felt disconcerted. She knew she had to leave even though her heart told her he was special in some way.

"What's up? Why are you angry all of a sudden?" Victor wanted to know what was up.

"I should not be here with you."

"Why not? Are you in a relationship?"

Jade shook her head and laughed at Victor. "You have some nerve. Here I am, decorating your lady's and child's home and you ask me if I am in a relationship. How hypocritical!"

Victor had no idea what Jade was referring to. He was glad she showed her real personality on the first date. He refused to put up with psychopaths. Hell, she seemed to have it going on.

Perturbed Victor replied, "What are you talking about?"

"You are married or apparently in a relationship. I mean for Pete's sake, you have bought her a home and having it decorated. You said you would move heaven and earth for her. If that's the case, why am I here and why do you keep staring at my breast?"

Jade was furious.

He sat across from her smirking and shaking, his head.

"Stop shaking your head at me!"

Looking around Victor replied, "Lower your voice. This is our first date and you..."

"We are not on a date," scolded Jade.

"Oh yes we are. Ms. Jumping to Conclusions."

"What do you mean by that?"

"If you really cared about my marriage why are you here?"

Jade felt like shit. She asked herself that the entire time she was getting dressed.

"I have no idea. That's why I have decided to leave."

Teasing, Victor said, "You ain't going nowhere. You said you would have dinner with me and that's what I expect. Besides we need to handle this decorating business."

Jade could not believe his arrogant ass.

"I am not going to have dinner because I don't want your wife and child to ride down on me."

"If I was married, do I look like I would have a wife that would ride down on you? Now give me some credit," replied Victor.

Jade's face frowned and she said, "What do you mean if you were married?"

Shaking his head Victor replied, "Does it look like I would have a ghetto wife?"

He really wanted to know.

"What difference does it make? We shouldn't be here together. It doesn't look good."

"Oh, so you worry about what others think about you?"

Victor was pushing her buttons. He planned to tell her she was decorating for his sister but he enjoyed watching her squirm.

"Not exactly, but this isn't right." She was rolling her eyes and shaking her head.

"Well, we came here to discuss the decorating of my sister and niece's home so I do not know what else to tell you, Jade," laughed Victor.

Jade felt so stupid. Her face was flushed and her nostrils were flared. She was so humiliated. Why didn't he just tell her he was not married?

Jade was at a loss for words so she said what needed to be said, "Sorry, Victor."

"You should be. You had me all worried that I was doing something wrong." Victor burst out laughing.

"You are so wrong for that. Why would you make me think you were married?"

"Why would you assume I was married?"

"Well, you said she was very important to you and you are so passionate about her home being perfect. I just thought."

Jade stopped talking in midsentence and stood to leave.

"I just need to go. I have made a big enough fool out of myself. Sorry for wasting your time."

Victor decided to lighten the mood, "Woman, you better sit down and eat dinner with a brutha."

He smiled and that was all she needed she sat right back down.

"Once again, sorry," replied Jade.

"Jade, when I say "I do" it is forever. I would never jeopardize my marriage. I do not care how good-looking a woman is. When I find my wife, it is forever. Just remember that."

16

When Victor woke the next morning he was still

exhausted. He and Jade didn't get in until after midnight. He

found out they had a lot in common and she was actually fun to

be around. He wanted to kiss her good night but he didn't want

to move too fast. They spent the first five or so minutes

discussing Shanae's likes, dislikes and favorite colors. After that

they were lost in conversation that had nothing to do with

decorating. They both hadn't dated in years and were busy with

their careers, so they didn't have time for a significant other.

They had plans to meet at the house in a couple of days. He

hoped Shanae wouldn't be released until late afternoon. Victor

got out of bed, took a shower, was dressed and headed

downstairs for some breakfast.   Victor walked into the kitchen

and gave his mother a much-needed embrace and a kiss. He

pushed his mother away from him and smiled at her. She was

still beautiful and didn't look a day over twenty-five.

"Still looking good, Momma," replied Victor.

"You don't look too bad yourself and you better stop moving my things around," commanded Dena.

"What sh— stuff are you talking about?"

Victor caught himself. He did not care how grown he was. If he cussed in front of his mother she would slap the living daylights out of him. The look she gave him with slanted eyes confirmed it.

His momma looked at him and rolled her eyes, "You know you moved my African statue."

They both shared a laugh looking at each other for a few seconds.

Dena broke the silence and asked, "What would you like for breakfast Victor."

"What ever you feel like making."

Victor loved his mother's cooking. It was the best. He could stay at the dinner table for hours feeding his face. Until he couldn't walk.

"How about fried eggs, bacon and French toast?"

Victor rubbed his hands together in anticipation for the meal. "That sounds like a winner. Warm the syrup and put powder sugar on the French toast."

"I see you still are demanding."

"Will you please do that for me?"

"Yeah, I guess. Where were you last night? You make sure

you make it in my house at a decent hour?"

"I had a date,"

"How? You just got here yesterday."

"Well, you know what can I say," laughed Victor as he rubbed his goatee.

"Poor girl," Dena said shaking her head.

"Momma, give me a break. It was just a date. Besides you know her."

With wrinkles on her forehead Dena replied, "How do I know her?"

"Her name is Jade. She said you used her company for decorating."

Dena turned around and pointed her finger at Victor and said, "You stay as far away from her as you can. She is a good girl. I don't need your hurting her feelings."

"Damn, I mean, dang Momma. What makes me such a bad person?"

"You just like to have your cake and eat it too. Poor girl." Dena said while she beat the eggs.

Dena whipped up breakfast within minutes. She and Victor sat at the table having small talk. They caught up on lost time and chatted for what seemed like hours. Victor helped his momma clear the table and wash the breakfast dishes. It felt like old times. The only thing that was missing was Shanae.

Then Victor asked the dreaded question that Dena had

been hoping would never come. "Momma, you want to go to the hospital with me to see Shanae today?"

Dena sat there speechless. She searched her heart and soul for words but nothing came out. She sat there looking into space and ignoring Victor.

Again, this time a little louder Victor said, "Momma, do you want to go see Shanae today or not?"

Dena whispered, "I can't. I just can't Victor."

Victor was furious. He wanted to cuss, scream and yell. This was the perfect time to put aside their differences and Dena couldn't even sacrifice her pride for her child.

With confusion and contempt in his eyes Victor said, "When will you want to see her? When it is too late? There is no way in hell parents should turn their backs on their children especially a mother. Momma, I love you but I despise you for turning your back on Shanae. I also hate the fact you let Shanae's twin leave. I swear I will not be coming back here tonight. I refuse to lay my head in this house. There is no love here! Until you make amends with Shanae, I will never set foot in this house again."

Victor stood to leave the kitchen and Dena yelled, "Victor, I am so sorry, but you will never understand. It's not as easy as you think. I have let her down and I can't fix the situation. You actually think that I am that calloused that I don't care about my children. I have lost two of them. Please don't turn your back on me. I have no one!"

Tears were running down Dena's face. Her body was shaking and she was gasping for air. Victor didn't know what to do so he ran over to her and sat her down on a custom-made dining room chair. He gave her a cup of water, told her to take deep breaths and pleaded with her to calm down.

"Momma, I really didn't mean to upset you but I don't understand what is going on. You didn't lose them. You turned your back on them. A true mother would have fought for her daughters."

Victor didn't want to keep upsetting his mother but he refused to sugarcoat the situation.

Dena whimpered, "Victor, I don't think you can ever understand this mess. It is so bad. I am ashamed of it."

"Momma, I am a grown man now. I believe I can handle it. What I can't handle is our family being divided. It's bad enough that we have a biological father and sister who knows where. We need to keep all the family we have together."

Yelling, Victor continued, "Either you swallow your pride or you'll lose all of your children!"

"Victor what will I say to her after all these years?"

"Tell her you're sorry, you love her and you want to put aside your differences!"

"Victor, I don't think it will be that easy. You just don't know what she has been through. I always told her I would have her back and I let her down tremendously."

"What actually happened to yours and Shanae's relationship?"

Crying Dena said, "Victor, I will never be able to tell you."

Upset, Victor replied, "Whatever the hell it is, it is causing this family too much unnecessary stress and it needs to be settled once and for all! Are you going to the hospital or not?"

Victor was distressed. He had never deliberately tried to hurt his momma's feelings but today he just didn't give a damn.

Dena answered, "Yes, Victor, I will go to the hospital. Victor, I know you are upset but you need to stop using profanity in front of me."

Ignoring his mother Victor replied, "Hell and damn are in the Bible."

"I do not care. I am your momma and I do not want to hear it. I told you I am going to the hospital so why are you still upset?"

Dena looked at Victor as if she wanted praises for making the right decision. Victor felt she should have closed this gap with Shanae years ago.

Victor ignored his momma's statement and advanced towards the door. Dena grabbed her designer bag and coat and ran towards the door after him.

The entire ride to the hospital Dena's stomach did flips. She hadn't seen her daughter in years. She was angry because once again she had allowed the same man to come between her and her daughter's relationship. Only if she had accepted what Shanae told her and done right by her daughter, their family would be a lot stronger. While Dena was reliving the mistakes she had made over and over in her mind she heard Victor's cell phone ringing.

"Hello."

"Hi, may I speak with Mr. Victor Davis?'

"Speaking."

The unfamiliar voice on the other end said, "My name is Marcus with M&M moving company. I was asked to call you to get the last minute requests, details and arrangements."

Excited, Victor replied, "I have been waiting for your call. I need all the furniture to be packed and put in storage. I need all the personal items to be packed and delivered to the house. Such as baby toys, books, papers and photos."

Victor took a deep breath and continued, "Ma Rose, her neighbor will let you in. She knows that you are coming and she lives across the way from her. Her number is 444-3333

Marcus replied, "Thanks for all the details. My crew and I will have this assignment completed within the next couple of hours."

Before Victor hung up the phone he said, "Thanks, I really appreciate it."

Victor immediately hung up the phone and called Ma Rose.

Dena was sitting in the passenger seat trying to figure out what her son was up to. Dena was about to ask her son what was going on when he started talking on his cell phone again.

"Hi, Ma Rose. This is Victor, Shanae's brother."

"Hey, baby. How are you doing?"

"I am doing okay. How about yourself?"

"Oh, I am okay. Just a little sad that my girl will be moving, but I guess a new beginning would be great for her."

"I think Shanae most definitely needs a new beginning."

With tears in her eyes Ma Rose said, "Well, let's get down to business, what is it that I need to do."

Silently laughing Victor replied, "The moving company will be stopping by Shanae's place today. I was wondering if you could let them in. The only thing that needs to go to the new house is personal items and Sherrice's toys and books. All the furniture, dishes, television and stuff like that."

Ma Rose wrote down everything Victor said. Then she confirmed it, "Let the moving company in, call storage and that's it?"

Smiling Victor said, "Yes, that is it. I don't know what Shanae would do without you. Thanks. I will talk to you later."

Before Victor had a chance to hang up Ma Rose said, "Victor, how is Sherrice holding up?

"I guess she is fine but I haven't heard from Francis."

"I was a little concerned because they had to take her to

the emergency room last night. I have been worried sick."

"What are you talking about? No one has called me."

"All's I know is Hasaun came over here last night looking for the medical card. He said the ambulance took her to Central Medical Clinic last night. He wanted her medical card so they could transfer her to University. He couldn't find it. I guess she is still at Central Medical Clinic."

"He did not need her insurance card for the ambulance to take her to the University. What is he talking about?"

"Baby, I do not know. I am only telling ya what he told me," confirmed Ma Rose.

"Ma Rose, let me get this straight. My niece is in the hospital and has been since last night and no one has contacted me?"

Quietly Ma Rose answered, "Yes, Victor."

Upset Victor replied, "Thanks for the information. I will keep you posted as soon as I figure out what is going on. Bye, Ma Rose."

"Bye, baby," replied Ma Rose.

Victor was irate. He wanted to know why in the hell hadn't the Ryder's called him about his niece. He made a U-turn in the middle of the street and headed towards Central Medical Clinic."

"What's going on, Victor?" questioned Dena.

Yelling, Victor replied, "Sherrice is in the hospital.

Somehow Hasaun and his mother neglected to inform me about the entire situation. Not only is she in the hospital but she is at Central Medical Clinic."

Victor took a deep breath and continued, "Momma, Shanae can't handle anymore drama. She will die if something happens to Sherrice."

So many emotions filled Dena's head. It hurt her deeply to see her children suffering. At that moment she realized it was time for her to step up to be a true momma. She had let all of her children down and she was not proud of it. However, she hoped she had another chance and knew what had to be done. She used to be the best mother in the world and she was going to reclaim that title.

"Victor, first thing you need to do is slow down. Your being in the hospital isn't going to do us any good. Secondly, calm down and drive to the clinic."

The ride to the clinic was a silent one. No one knew exactly what to say or do. When Dena and Victor entered the dark and gloomy clinic they both became sick to their stomachs. The clinic was in need of serious renovations. The paint on the walls was stained and peeling. Looking at the peeling paint, it was apparent that the employees had to be suffering from lead poisoning. They also needed to invest in a new housekeeping staff. The floors needed sweeping and mopping. The trashcans were over flowing with garbage and needed to be emptied.

When Dena and Victor approached the nurses' station Dena's maternal instinct went in overdrive.

"Hello, my granddaughter was admitted in this clinic last night and—"

Before Dena could finish her sentence the unit clerk, not even looking up from her crossword puzzle rambled, "Please take a number and we will see you when your number is called."

"Excuse me, Miss. I just need to know her room number," replied Dena.

Again the unit clerk rambled, "Take a number!" This time she put force in her voice.

This further upset Dena. She wondered how people in the medical profession could be so heartless. When Dena noticed that the lady wasn't willing to give her the time of day, she reached over the counter, grabbed the crossword puzzle and tossed it on the dirty floor with the rest of the debris.

Furious Dena replied, "Apparently you didn't hear me. I said my granddaughter is ill and I needed her room number, yesterday!"

Looking at the irate woman, the unit clerk noticed that she did not see her kind in this clinic too often. Judging by her Gucci coat and hand bag the unit clerk thought the lady thought she was better than her.

Upset the unit clerk replied, "Ma'am, if you don't calm

down I am going to have to call security." *See what her prissy behind thinks when she is sitting in Boone County Jail.*

The people in the shabby lobby were starting to stare. They all prayed the lady slapped the unprofessional clerk. She was rude to everyone for no reason.

At that moment Dena was beyond frustrated, "That's what it is going to take to get me off of your dumb ass if you don't give me the information I requested!"

Silence crept over the entire lobby. The gawking bystanders were hoping to see some action. The unit clerk stood and replied,

"Like I said, take a number. I don't know whom you think you are waltzing in here like you own the place. What you better do is get the hell out of my fa—!"

Smack! The unit clerk grabbed her jaw in disbelief.

"Who do you think you are? You don't know me."

Victor grabbed his momma's arm and walked her away from the lady.

"Have you lost your mind? Do you want to go to jail?"

Dena hadn't thought about jail. She was just thinking about knocking the taste out of the woman's mouth. When Dena turned around she saw a security guard and a tall slender Caucasian Doctor *great,* she thought.

The doctor asked Dena, "Ma'am, is everything okay?"

"No as a matter of fact it isn't. I need my granddaughter's

room number and the young lady behind the counter refuses to give it to me."

Dena wanted to call her an uncouth bitch but she held her tongue.

Dena continued, "I just can't believe that as much as we do for this establishment that the employees are so unprofessional."

Still holding her cheek the unit clerk yelled, "Bitch, you don't do shit for this place and I swear I am going to fuck you up if I ever see you on the streets!"

With a concerned look on his face the doctor said. "I didn't catch your name."

"I never threw it," replied Dena.

"Momma, calm down," pleaded Victor.

Taking in the lady's appearance the doctor knew she was well off.

"I am sorry that you have experienced an unprofessional staff member but I assure you not everyone on our team is rude. However, if you let me know what is going on I am sure I can assist you. Now what did you say your name was?"

"My name is Dena Williams. My husband is Dr. Bernard Williams."

Victor was oblivious to the entire conversation. He was in his own world. He was too worried about his niece and the effect it would have on his sister's well being. He knew that mentally and emotionally she could not handle any more drama.

After apologizing the doctor said, "Mrs. Williams, what is your granddaughter's name?"

Right on cue Dena replied, "Sherrice Nicole Ryder. She is two years old."

With a red face he calmly walked over to the unit clerk who was looking at the red welt that had formed on her face from the impact of Dena's smack, mumbled something and returned with Sherrice's room number.

"Thank you so much."

Then turning to the unit clerk, Dena replied, "It is nice to know that some people around here have sense and aren't ill-mannered."

The unit clerk had had enough of this high class heifer, "Fuck you and the boat you rode in on."

Dena was hot. Those were fighting words and she had insulted Dena's mother in the midst of it all.

"The boat I rode in on?"

Dena wasn't making a statement she was asking a question because she had worked hard to put these low lives behind her.

"The unit clerk replied, "Yeah, that's what I said!"

Walking back to the unit clerk Dena thought, *what kind of establishment hires some person who is undignified like this thing?*

Dena pranced over to the counter and looked the unit clerk in the eyes and whispered.

"I guess me smacking ya damn face didn't teach you anything?" Dena was ready to fight.

Victor grabbed Dena and walked her out of the lobby. Dena cussed the entire way to Sherrice's room. Victor had never, in his twenty-two years of life, heard his momma use such foul language. *I guess you can move out of the hood but you cannot take the hood out of some people.* He got a kick out of it. Silently laughing, Victor thought, *Ma was ready to throw down. What would her debutantes think about her behavior?* That's the momma he knew. She would move heaven and earth for her children.

17

When they entered the room they both were in a state of shock. Hasaun and his mother were the only two people in the room with Sherrice. Sherrice was hooked up to so many machines. It looked like a scene from the Twilight Zone. They were speechless. They both forgot about the events that had taken place prior to entering the room. All that was trivial. Here in this clinic there was a little girl fighting for her life and she seemed helpless. Hasaun stood up, walked towards the door and motioned for them to follow. Hasaun appeared to be drained. The bags under his eyes were evident that he hadn't had sleep in several days. His eyes were puffy and his face was stained with tears. He had just lost his second born child and now his first-born was fighting for her life.

"Hasaun, what happened?" questioned Victor.

Hasaun began to cry. The pain and agony he was feeling was surreal. Dena comforted Hasaun and said, "It's okay, baby, just take your time."

Hasaun hadn't heard her voice in years. He couldn't believe that everything about her was still the same. Her presence made the entire ordeal a little easier. She always could make a gloomy day bright. She had an essence about her that lifted everyone's spirits.

After regaining his composure, Hasaun began to explain, "I don't know what happened. Sherrice has been having a fever for several days. We have tried everything to break it. It just would not go away." Taking a deep breath he continued, "Last night when mom went upstairs to check on her Sherrice was jerking in the bed. The doctor said it was convulsions. Her temperature was excessively high. She had a fever-induced seizure. They don't know anything right now. They are still running tests. We have been here all night, worried sick. I do not know her medical insurance information and they are refusing to transfer her to the University Hospital. They also said it may be too risky to move her. I know for a fact Shanae can't handle this right now. I will not be the one to break this horrible news to her."

Crying, Hasaun continued, "I just can't do it."

Confused, Victor asked, "What are all those damn I mean darn machines?"

Hasaun replied, "They got her on so much shit I can't remember."

Shaking her head Dena replied, "Hasaun, I know that you are upset but you can stop cussing in front of me anytime now."

"I am sorry."

Victor could not believe his momma. She had just cussed and smacked a lady in the lobby.

"Hasaun, so what are the machines?" questioned Victor.

"Oh, I know she is hooked to an I.V., feeding tube and a couple of other things."

Victor thought that if it were his daughter he would know everything that was invading her fragile little body.

Dena asked, "Hasaun, how long did her convulsions last?"

"That's the problem. We don't know. Mom laid her down at six that evening. She went to check on her around seven-thirty. She could have been having them at the most for an hour and a half. We just don't know. Considering Mom was in her room reading until seven and didn't hear anything, we think maybe ten to twenty minutes."

Shaking her head and in a daze Dena walked to a corner and cried. She cried because she had let Shanae down. She cried because she was sorry and also because her child and grandchild were in so much pain. Dena realized that Shanae and Hasaun could be facing another loss and she would do everything in her power to prevent it. Dena never had a chance to meet Sherrice in person. Victor had given her pictures since the day she was born but she had never held, kissed or even touched her grandchild. When Sherrice pulled through this mess Dena promised to make up for lost time.

Dena dried her tears, walked back over to Victor and Hasaun and said, "We have to be strong for Shanae. We can't turn our backs on her. We have to make sure everyone is still standing after this, no matter what the outcome."

With that said she walked down the corridor and out of sight. Victor and Hasaun went back in the room with Sherrice and Ms. Ryder.

Dena returned about ten minutes later. She had the entire pediatric staff with her. They requested that everyone leave the room. They prepared Sherrice's little body for departure. Sherrice was transported to the University Hospital and the best doctors were going to see to it that she survived this ordeal. Dena explained everything to Hasaun and the rest of them. Hasaun rode with Sherrice in the ambulance while Ms. Ryder drove herself. Dena and Victor rode together.

When they arrived at the hospital, the doctors immediately began running tests. Sherrice's condition remained the same. There were no signs of improvement. Victor and Dena decided to go see Shanae and drop the bombshell. Before Victor left he asked Hasaun to call Ma Rose and Keya to let them know about Sherrice. He figured Shanae and Hasaun could use the extra support.

For some odd reason Victor had a feeling he couldn't shake. It was an eerie feeling. Something told him that everything wasn't going to be okay.

"Momma, let's stop by the chapel before we go see Shanae."

Dena replied, "Sounds good to me."

They made one last detour before they headed to Shanae's room. Dena didn't mind the detour because she had butterflies. She was nervous about seeing Shanae.

Meanwhile, Shanae was upstairs anxiously waiting on Victor. She was fully dressed and waiting to leave the hospital. Her vital signs had improved and she was given the okay for discharge. She could not wait to see Sherrice. It had been several days since she had seen her daughter. She was so eager to see her.

After praying for their family, Dena and Victor went to Shanae's room. When Victor opened the door he was surprised to see his big sis packed and looking good. Dena made one last stop by the receptionist desk and informed them about the current situation with Shanae's older daughter. After filling the team in, she ventured towards Shanae's room. Dena was scared and a little nervous. She was scared because she had turned her back on her daughter and nervous because she didn't know how her daughter would react to seeing her. Approaching the door, Dena heard Shanae and Victor deep in conversation.

"Victor, what took you so long?"

Stammering, Victor said, "Something came up and I had to take care of it. Why are you dressed and packed?"

"Well. Mr. CEO, if you would have come this morning you would know. They are discharging me TODAY!" Shanae was clapping her hands and smiling.

How could this be happening? Shanae will be right back in here as soon as we break the news to her about Sherrice, if not back in the hospital then in a mental institution.

"You don't look to happy."

"No, I am very happy, just a little tired," Victor tried to sound optimistic but he was literally about to pass out.

"Baby bro, what's my surprise?"

Dena heard the silence. It was taking Victor too long to answer. She knew she had to help him out. She had come too far to chicken out now. She took a deep breath, slowly turned the doorknob and entered the room.

18

Like an infection attacking a weak immune system silence spread rapidly throughout the room. Victor stumbled to the chair and sat. Shanae couldn't believe her eyes. She walked backward until she couldn't move anymore. Her back was against the vertical blinds. She shook her head in total disbelief. Dena walked towards her with tears flowing down her face.

Shanae had practiced this occasion over and over in her head for years. She had everything planned out. She knew exactly what she was going to say. She planned to hurt her momma like she hurt her years ago. Dena continued to walk towards Shanae. When she was within arm's length she reached and grabbed Shanae's arm. Shanae instantly jerked her arm away. Before Dena could respond Shanae slapped her face. The pain from the initial contact was nothing, compared to how Dena had been feeling over the years.

Dena grabbed her cheek and replied, "Is that all you've got? After all the years, that's all you've got for me. I want you to give me everything you've got!" Walking closer towards Shanae, Dena replied, "Because when it's all said and done, I am still going to be your Momma!"

Shanae balled her fist together and glared at her momma. She wanted to pounce on her. But something stopped her. Shanae assumed slapping Dena would make her feel better, but it didn't. She felt so bad for hitting her momma.

Hesitantly, Dena hugged Shanae. Shanae stood speechless with her arms hanging at her sides. Dena held her daughter as if her life depended on it. However, Shanae did not respond to the embrace. She pushed her momma away.

Wiping the tears from her face Shanae said, "Vic! I hope this is not your surprise."

Victor sat there speechless and in a trance.

Dena bridged the gap and hugged her daughter again.

"Shanae, I am sorry. I want to make this right. I know I have let you down. Just please give me another chance to make it right."

Dena continued to hold Shanae. Shanae continued to cry. Her arms slowly encircled her mother. All at once, Shanae wrapped her arms around her momma like she was a four-year-old child again.

For several minutes Victor watched them embrace and cry. He had no clue as to why they were crying and he for damn sure didn't know why Shanae had slapped their momma and why their momma didn't beat her down for doing it. He wanted to be filled in, but just not right now.

He was drained and more concerned about how Shanae would handle Sherrice's situation. Shanae and Dena had finally accomplished the hardest part of getting back on track, which was seeing each other for the first time. They both realized that they had a long way to go. However, this was a great stepping-stone. Shanae and Dena cried tears of joy and happiness.

"Shanae, I am so sorry," cried Dena

Shanae didn't respond so Dena continued to apologize, "I know there is nothing I can say or do to take away the pain and feelings of abandonment. I want you to know from this day forward I promise to be the best mother and grandmother."

Dena paused and waited for a response. There was none. Both Shanae and Dena continued to cry and hold on to each other. Dena took her hands and placed them under Shanae's chin. Dena slowly lifted her face. Shanae and Dena were looking each other directly in the eyes.

"Shanae, please say something," begged Dena.

"What do you want me to say? You turned your back on me," cried Shanae and then continued, "and what about him?"

Victor was at a loss. He didn't know what was going on. He wanted to know who the hell "him" was. He continued to listen to the complexities of the conversation. He finally decided to wait until later to figure it out.

Softly Dena replied, "I can do without him. I need my children,"

Crying Dena continued, "I let you down. I was too concerned about my status instead of your well-being. I vowed to always have your back. I let you down. I promise from this day forward if you give me another chance, I will always have your back."

For the first time in her life Dena was begging. She never had to beg. Everything and everyone always catered to Dena's every need.

"Shanae, please answer me. I am so sorry. My life hasn't been the same since I forced you away," pleaded Dena.

Shanae broke the embrace, wiped her tears away and said, "You hurt me bad, Momma. I had no understanding how you could do that to me. Once I had Sherrice I really could not understand your choice. Because never in a million years would I ever turn my back on my child. She is everything. My one true love and I will always be there for her. I would give my life for her. So how could you do it to me so effortlessly?"

Dena was at a loss for words. She did not know what to say. "I am sorry. I want to make it right, Shanae. Please let me make it right. I have missed you so much," pleaded Dena.

Crying, Shanae replied, "I have missed you, too. The only way we can have a relationship is if you believe in me one hundred and ten percent. You have to believe what I told you. If he is still in your life, Sherrice and I can't be in your life."

Quickly, Dena replied, "Shanae, I believed you the day you told me. I was just too scared to face reality. I haven't touched him since that day. We have different bedrooms. I will file for divorce ASAP."

Still a little reluctant Shanae replied, "Momma, we will have to seek some kind of family counseling."

"Anything you want baby. I will do this because from this day forward ya Momma has your back."

Shanae was reluctant but she smiled anyway. "Apology accepted."

Dena and Shanae sat on the hospital bed talking for a brief period. They seemed to be happy but they both knew they had a long way to go. Victor was still silently sitting in the chair. He had heard bits and pieces of his family's saga. He actually picked up on a couple of things. One thing for sure, his momma and sister were on better terms. He was hoping his ears were deceiving him when he heard his momma say she would divorce his step-dad.

Victor really needed a drink. He had entirely too much on his plate.

Shanae stopped talking to Dena and asked Victor, "Baby bro, what's wrong."

Victor replied, "Shanae, I don't know what is going on."

Pointing his finger from side to side at both Dena and

Shanae, "I'm just waiting for the two of you to enlighten me."

Dena and Shanae both looked at each other nodding agreement that he needed to know. Shanae took a deep breath and proceeded to tell Victor why she left the family.

Nevertheless, before she could utter a word Hasaun burst through the door yelling, "It's not looking good! We need you all downstairs now!"

Shanae thought, oh my, Hasaun has truly lost his mind. Hasaun looked around the room for some kind of a sign that Shanae knew about Sherrice. There was none. Dena and Victor wore a look of terror on their faces while Shanae wore a look of concern for Hasaun.

Hasaun looked at Shanae and realized she was too calm. At that moment he realized the news hadn't yet been broken to her. He closed his eyes and wished he could wake up from this dreadful nightmare. He hoped he wouldn't be around when Shanae found out, but he realized he would. He couldn't stand to see Shanae hurting anymore than she already was. He prayed she survived all this heartache and despair.

19

"**H**asaun, what in God's name is wrong with you?" questioned Shanae.

In shock, Hasaun replied, "Shanae, I am so sorry, but someone needs to break the news to you."

"Hasaun let me handle this. We have to take it slowly." interrupted Victor.

Hasaun yelled, "Vic, man I think I can handle this and besides we don't have a lot of time!"

Victor took a seat and let Hasaun have the floor. Dena motioned for Shanae to have a seat. Shanae was confused. She didn't know what Victor and Hasaun were talking about but she was becoming worried. For a brief second everyone sat in silence. No one knew exactly how to break the news to Shanae, but it had to be done.

"Would someone please tell me what's going on?"

Hasaun closed his eyes and said, "Shanae, I really need you to be strong. I don't know how to say this. Shanae, Sherrice is really sick."

Shanae could feel her stomach tightening and her palms become sweaty. She didn't comprehend what was going on. She knew that if something happened to Sherrice she would die. She couldn't handle any more stress. This would be the last unpredictable thing she could live with. If something happened to her baby she would die. No if, ands or buts about it, she would die.

"Hasaun, please calm down and tell me exactly what is wrong with my baby."

Shanae tried to remain cool, calm and collected but her gestures let everyone in the room know she was worried. Her legs were shaking, tears silently streaming down her cheeks. Her breathing was escalating.

"Shanae, I don't know what is going on but she is terminally ill. I need everyone to get to her floor and donate blood. She needs blood. The doctors are saying she has a rare blood disease they haven't seen in years."

Again Victor interrupted, "Hasaun, man, you don't even know the name of the damn disease. You don't know how long Sherrice was in the room and you weren't there when Shanae went into labor. What the hell do you know?"

Dena jumped in before the argument could go any further, "Not right now. You two drop the antagonisms right now and I mean it!"

Hasaun replied, "I'm sorry. I am just so worried right now. Victor, they are my fucking children, too."

Victor wanted to jump up and beat Hasaun's soft ass but the look his mother gave him he knew she wasn't going for any nonsense. Hasaun was literally talking so fast it was hard to understand him. He was so scared. After he had delivered the bad news Victor and Dena both prayed that Shanae and Sherrice recuperated from this ordeal.

Dena and Victor hadn't realized Sherrice's illness was so bad. They didn't think her life was in jeopardy.

Shanae was in a daze. She felt like dying. Not only had she lost a child a few days ago but also the one true love she had remaining in her life was fighting for her life. Shanae wanted to be strong and be there for her daughter. She kept telling herself not to let Sherrice down. *Stay strong. Stay strong.* Her body wasn't taking her advice. She tried to stand but she had no strength in her legs. Her entire body was shaking and she had no control over it. She couldn't talk and everyone's voice in the room sounded as if they were miles away. She heard Hasaun say terminal. *Terminal! Terminal!* Shanae passed out and slid off the bed. Terminal, as in fatal, deadly, life threatening and incurable.

Dena pressed the nurse's button and yelled, "We have a code blue! Something is wrong in here!"

Meanwhile, Victor and Hasaun were helping Shanae. They

knew this would be the end. She loved and adored her daughters. She had lost one and might lose her first-born. She couldn't take it.

The doctor ordered everyone to leave the room. While in the hallway they were bombarded by Sherrice's doctor and nurse. They wanted blood. They were informed that it was prudent that everyone donate blood because Sherrice needed it immediately. They also informed them that she was in critical condition. They escorted the three of them to the lab and drew blood. When they finished, they walked into Shanae's room and took blood from her. Shanae had had an anxiety attack but was going to be just fine. She needed her rest.

20

As Victor, Hasaun and Dena approached Sherrice's room they noticed a sign posted on her door, which informed them no one could enter the room. Seeing the note really caught them off guard. They all had questions and wanted to know exactly what was wrong with Sherrice. Hasaun suggested they go into the lobby. When they walked into the lobby there sat Keya, Ma Rose, Ms. Ryder and Rev. Thomas. They all had concerned looks on their faces. It was evident that some had been crying. Everyone said their hellos and sat in silence.

Victor broke the silence and directed his question to Ms. Ryder, "So what's going on right now?"

"Sherrice is not doing well."

Victor thought, *tell me something I don't already know."*

Ms. Ryder continued talking, "She has a disease called Blue Rubber Bleb Nevus Syndrome. It's a rare condition that is characterized by numerous malformations of the venous system that significantly involve the skin and visceral organs. The doctors are referring to it as BRBNS. Wiping the tears from her eyes, Ms. Ryder took a deep breath and said,

"According to the doctor, it is a rare disorder that consists mainly of groups of abnormal blood vessels. It affects the skin and gastrointestinal tract. There is treatment for it but Sherrice's is progressing faster than usual. They have never seen anything like it before. At least not in a child."

Victor was still confused so he asked Ms. Ryder another question, "Francis, why is it considered terminal?"

"I don't remember hearing them say that. However, this disorder forms malformations on the skin and visceral organs. Sherrice has many malformations in her throat, which are affecting her breathing. They had to give her a tracheotomy."

Ms. Ryder was crying and trying to explain the situation. She wiped her tears and said, "Guys, I want all of you to be prepared for the worst. It does not look good. The malformations are spreading rapidly. They also found out that the oxygen to her brain had been cut off for a while before we brought her in. I am just so sorry."

Ms. Ryder blamed herself. She thought this could have been prevented if she checked on Sherrice earlier.

"Also this disease is curable but for some unknown reason it is progressing rapidly and causing Sherrice's organs to function improperly. No one has ever seen anything like this before."

Keya handed Ms. Ryder some Kleenex and told her, "This is no one's fault. We all have to remember to be strong for Sherrice."

Hasaun added, "We need to pray for Sherrice and Shanae. She didn't take the news well. She passed out. They gave her a mild sedative to calm her down so she would sleep for a while. The doctors said she would be okay but I am worried about her mentally."

No one uttered a word. Victor was still upset. He wanted to whoop Hasaun's ass. He told Shanae it was a terminal disease; that's why she flipped out.

Instead of being rude and mean Victor replied, "I think we need to pray for Sherrice, Shanae and Hasaun. They all have been through a lot this last week,"

Everyone agreed.

After a prayer led by Rev. Thomas they sat in the lobby waiting to hear from the doctor about Sherrice and Shanae's conditions. Keya and Ma Rose were sitting together having small talk. Hasaun had dozed off. His head was lying on his mother's lap. Ms. Ryder watched her only son sleep. She wished his life could be peaceful but it was in an uproar. Victor was deep in thought. He was looking out of the window and he still couldn't shake his bad feeling.

Dena went to find Bernard. She located him in his office.

"Nard, Shanae's daughter is really sick and they need

everyone to donate blood. Will you please donate for me?"

Bernard walked over to Dena hugged her replying, "Baby, I will do anything you ask of me."

Bernard picked up the phone and called the phlebotomist to come and take his blood for the Ryder patient. Within seconds, a perky little white girl was taking Bernard's blood.

Prior to leaving, Dena broke the news to Bernard. "Bernard, I really appreciate your doing that for me but I have some more bad news. I have talked to Shanae and she is willing to work on our relationship and get it back on track."

"Dena, that isn't bad news. That is great news," Bernard tried to sound optimistic but he really didn't care one way or the other.

Dena paused before she continued, "Nard, the only way I can get our relationship back on track is if I divorce you. We haven't been happy for years and I am tired of sleeping in the guest bedroom. So come morning I will be filing for a divorce."

Bernard wasn't pleased with the information but he had been tired of Dena for years. Bernard replied, "Dena, if that is what you want, have your things you brought into this marriage packed and leave my house."

Dena couldn't believe this arrogant bastard. She told him, "Nard, it will be a cold day in hell when I leave that easily. You can either split everything with me fifty-fifty or I will take you to the cleaners. The choice is yours."

Bernard was in total disbelief. *Dena wanting a divorce?* He knew that they hadn't been happy in years but never in his wildest dreams did he think Dena would have enough nerve to divorce him. Bernard stood there speechless as he watched her exit his office. Dena walked out of the room, called her lawyer, informed him about the current situation and immediately started the divorce proceedings. On the elevator ride back to Sherrice's floor Dena said a quiet prayer for her family. She would find out if what she expected for years were the truth today. If it was, the family was going to need more than prayer.

Everyone was in the lobby on Sherrice's floor when the doctor came in to give them an update about Sherrice. He looked around the waiting area and said, "Let's all go into the conference room."

Upon entering the room he replied, "I have some news. First off, I would like to let you know that my heart goes out to Shanae and her family and I am sorry that you all are going through this."

He cleared his throat and continued, "We have just found out Sherrice doesn't only have BRBNS, she has also contracted the influenza virus. Her immune system is very weak right now and she is having trouble fighting the disease."

There were "no's" and "this can't be" circulating around the room. They could not believe what was happening.

The doctor continued, "We have tried everything in our

power to save her but it isn't looking good. I really don't know how to say this but I want to be honest with you all. Off the record, I don't see Sherrice surviving anymore than two or three days. The progression of the disease is baffling. The malformations are spreading rapidly and we don't understand it."

He paused to let the family absorb all the information.

Finally, he said, "Does anyone have any questions?"

No one uttered a word. Everyone in the room was either crying or in shock. His assistant was walking around the room giving everyone Kleenex. They were stunned.

The silence in the room bothered the doctor, so he decided to ask his last question, "Once again I am sorry and if there is anything the family needs please let me know. One last thing, do any of you know when the father will be here to donate blood. We are thinking maybe his blood would be a match."

Looks of confusion spread across everyone's faces. They all knew Hasaun donated blood.

With a little edge in his voice Hasaun replied, "Excuse me, doc, but I have already donated blood. I am Sherrice's father."

The doctor grabbed his clipboard, positioned his glasses on his face and perused his clipboard. He walked over to the computer on the desk and typed for a while. Then he walked back over to Hasaun and said, "Would you like to come to my office so I can talk to you?"

"No. Anything you have to say to me you can say it now." Hasaun was fighting to keep his composure.

Looking at Hasaun the doctor replied, "I don't have a match for her father. I will read the names I have received blood from: Francis Ryder, Keya Smith, Rose Hayes, Rev. Thomas, Victor Davis, Dena Davis-Williams and Hasaun Ryder. None of those were conclusive matches for paternity."

Hasaun stood there with a look of stun and loathing. He waited for the doctor to say he made a mistake. However, he never addressed his mistake.

He said nothing except, "You folks can remain in the conference room and once again if you need anything please call me."

With that said, the doctor and his assistant left the family alone.

Hasaun felt like shit. He wanted to die. There was no way in hell he could not be Sherrice's father. No one wanted to touch this situation. It had to be the truth. The doctor checked his paperwork several times. Hasaun was not her biological father. Hasaun watched as the doctor left him with the baffling news and felt sick. He knew he was Sherrice's father and he was going to talk to the doctor. Hasaun stormed out of the conference room to confront the doctor. Hasaun returned to the room minutes later and still had a look of skepticism on his face. He felt like strangling Shanae. *How could she do this to me?*

When her son walked back into the conference room with the same distraught look. Ms. Ryder had a tingling sensation. What she had just heard meant she wasn't Sherrice's nana. She felt nauseous, ran to the trashcan and deposited her lunch she had eaten earlier.

Dena stood and said, "I am so sorry, Francis and Hasaun. I am so sure Shanae can shed some light on this situation when she wakes up. Personally, I don't think the information the doctor gave you will change the love you have for that little girl in there. She is still your daughter, Hasaun and Francis she is still your granddaughter. Don't give up now you both have come too far to give up."

Crying, Dena continued, "She might not have the same blood as you guys running through her veins. What does that mean? She has my blood in her veins and I don't know her from Adam. Y'all, she knows so don't stop loving her. She has nothing to do with this mess."

As Dena sat down Rev. Thomas stood, "I think we need to stand and have prayer."

Victor yelled, "For what? This shit gets more complicated by the minute. I don't think prayer is going to help. My niece isn't going to survive, my sister is on the verge of a nervous breakdown and Hasaun isn't Sherrice's father. Forget praying!"

Victor stormed out of the room, down the elevator and outside for some fresh air. Dena wanted to stop him but she knew he needed to be alone. She, however, made a mental note to have Victor apologize. Then she thought differently. Everyone has a right to express how he or she felt however he or she wanted.

After Rev. Thomas concluded his prayer he left the hospital. Dena, Ma Rose, Keya, Hasaun and Ms. Ryder were still waiting in the conference room. They were all dealing with the fact that Sherrice's life was coming to an abrupt end. Her little body had decided to give up. She was too weak to fight. No one knew how to break the news to Shanae about her daughter. No one knew how to console Hasaun. They never commented on what the doctor had told them about Hasaun not being her father. They all sat in silence. No one uttered a word. The stillness in the room was unnerving.

Hasaun broke the silence. "Did anyone know that I wasn't Sherrice's father before today?"

Everyone except Dena said no. Hasaun turned towards Dena and asked, "Did you know before today?"

Dena didn't want to answer the question. She had always had doubts he was the biological father, especially after she had seen pictures of Sherrice. Sherrice had his eyes, lips, nose and skin color. Dena knew she would not be the one to let Hasaun know who Sherrice's father was.

Softly, Dena replied, "Hasaun, I didn't know for sure until today. I am sorry and I will not discuss this with you any further until Shanae is here to make light of the situation. Let's all try to stay focused and not forget about Sherrice. Hasaun, I know you love her. Please don't forget about the love you guys share."

Hasaun was speechless. Never in a million years did he ever think his life would turn out like this. Keya couldn't believe what she was hearing. How did Dena know something about Shanae that she didn't even know? Ma Rose had an idea of who the father could be since Shanae had only slept with two people. She admired Dena for being so strong. Ms. Ryder was tired, confused and mentally exhausted. She didn't feel like hearing anything else so she walked over to the couch and sat down. Within minutes she was sound asleep. Keya and Ma Rose decided to check on Shanae. Dena told them she would be there as soon as she located Victor. They were only allowing Sherrice's parents in to see her. Hasaun went to sit with his daughter. It was apparent from the wrinkles on his forehead that he was frustrated. He would have to get over it. Life was not fair and it often dealt people bad hands. Unfortunately, Shanae and Hasaun had been dealt several bad hands this week.

21

Victor was on the phone with Jade. He was explaining to her why he missed his appointment and rescheduled it. He made a few decorating changes for the home. He didn't want it to be child proof and he wanted the child's bedroom to be turned into a guest bedroom. He also wanted the playroom to be turned into a study. He gave Jade all the needed information regarding the decorating adjustments. After finishing his conversation with Jade, he called the moving company. He was so happy they had just arrived at the apartment. He told them to leave all the baby toys and clothing for Ma Rose to decide what to do with it. Victor also asked Marcus to pack a brown teddy bear if he saw it. Marcus assured him he would take care of everything. Victor took his cell and crammed it in the pocket of his Kenneth Cole slacks.

He couldn't believe the events that had taken place over the brief period of time he had been home. He was about to explode when he felt a soft gentle hand on his shoulder. He turned around and noticed it was his momma. He had so many unanswered questions and he knew that Dena and Shanae held the answers.

"Vic, everyone is going to check on Shanae. Would you like to go upstairs with us?"

Dena knew her son could be confrontational when he was confused or mad so she approached him cautiously.

Nonchalantly, Victor replied, "Sure. Why not?"

He knew this was the only way to find out what was going on. Pleased with the answer Dena grabbed his hand as they walked back inside the hospital and proceeded to Shanae's room.

When they entered the lobby everyone was there. Everyone was eager and waiting for an explanation. Victor hoped his sister could survive. Dena could see the eagerness in all of their eyes. They wanted clarification and they wanted it now. Dena assumed Keya just wanted to be nosey. She still had a bad feeling about her. In her heart, she figured Shanae had already told Ma Rose about the circumstances. Dena wanted everyone to know that Shanae was fragile and stressed. She wanted to make sure that no one said anything to hurt her when they went into the room.

Dena motioned for the group to come over. Like children obeying their mother they all came over.

"Guys, we've been through a lot and we are sad but no

one is more hurt and sad than Shanae and Hasaun. They have suffered tremendous losses. We are all grief-stricken and we need to be here for them. I also know that everyone is wondering who Sherrice's father is. I think we all know that Shanae is the only one to supply us with the answer. If any of you feel you can't be compassionate then I am requesting that you remain in the lobby and we will fill you in on the news. One last thing, this may all be news to Shanae. She may not have known who Sherrice's father was and if she did, I know for a fact she would have never had her. If anyone, I mean anyone, gets careless with my daughter's feelings there will be hell to pay. They all agreed to Dena's request and like soldiers marched in unison and entered Shanae's room.

Shanae was lying with her back towards the door. When she heard the door open she turned around. She was happy to see familiar faces. She knew exactly what was on their minds.

Sherrice's doctor and her doctor had already been down and informed her about Sherrice's illness and her paternity. She was literally unable to think. Her mind was like one big blur. She didn't have anything to live for anymore. The pain and anguish she felt was horrible. She was hurting and her eyes illustrated her pain. Shanae usually had joyful eyes that sparkled. Not today, today her eyes were cold and distant. She longed for her children and couldn't have them. She would have to come to terms that she would be alone again.

The doctor practically told her Sherrice would not recover from her illness. Her body and immune system weren't strong enough to undergo surgery. She would just have to wait it out. With everything else that was going on, Shanae had just been informed that Hasaun wasn't Sherrice's father. This was all news to her. Besides being heartbroken, she was puzzled.

Shanae sat in silence. She looked at everyone in the room. Her eyes stopped on Ms. Ryder. She was broken but she gave Shanae a sincere smile. The smile spoke many things. She wanted answers. When Shanae locked in on everyone in the room they were all sincere except for two people. One she could understand why he was so upset and not being cordial to her. The other one she could not figure out why she was so upset.

She knew it was a complicated situation but it had to be addressed. She took a brief moment of silence. She had been praying on a regular basis since she lost her unborn baby and she felt her prayers were falling on deaf ears. She hoped that they would understand and stick by her side. Shanae wanted to explain the circumstances to everyone.

When Victor noticed his sister's eyes he wanted to die. He had never seen her so worried before. He walked over to her, hugged her and kissed her cheek.

"Shanae, no matter what, I will always be here for you and I love you. You don't have to worry about anything," Victor walked over to the windowsill and sat with his arms crossed.

Ma Rose gave Shanae the thumbs up. This let Shanae know she was in her corner.

Keya walked over, gave Shanae a hug and went and sat next to Victor on the windowsill. Shanae felt that the hug was not sincere just like the look she received from her moments earlier.

Hasaun never budged. He was livid and he wanted answers. Shanae looked at Hasaun and he dropped his head. Immediately tears started running down her face. Dena walked over to Shanae and hugged her. At that moment, Shanae felt a sense of security from her momma's embrace. It was not enough from stopping Shanae's feelings of wanting to lie down and die.

Dena let go, looked into her eyes and said, "We have some very bad news. Shanae, I don't know where to start but—"

Before Dena could utter another word Shanae held up her hand and whimpered, "I know everything. The doctors have been here with me. They explained it all to me."

Shanae could feel her face getting hot. She knew that the tears would fall shortly. "I know that my baby isn't going to make it and I found out today that Hasaun isn't Sherrice's biological father."

Yeah, go ahead and cry you low life heifer. Hasaun thought to himself. Victor was biting his lip. He couldn't believe Hasaun he never once tried to console his sister. Shanae was supposedly, the love of his life.

Keya impatiently waited for the information. She wished Shanae would speed it up. She had a hot date tonight.

Ma Rose knew who the culprit was she hoped that Dena and the rest of the crew could handle the truth. Shanae couldn't believe how Hasaun was treating her. She had just lied and forgave him just days ago. She wanted this ordeal over with so she wouldn't have to look at him any longer. Shanae needed strength and again she asked God for help.

She closed her eyes and whimpered, "I never knew! I never knew until today that Hasaun wasn't Sherrice's father. I am so sorry for hurting and letting all of you down. What I am about to tell you will only make things worse. I have never wanted to relive this pain again. But in order for you to know the identity of Sherrice's father I will have to walk down that terrible path."

Shanae and Dena both looked at each other knowing what was about to be revealed would change many people's lives.

"Sherrice's father is Bernard!"

Dena grabbed Shanae's hand and held it tightly. Shanae never opened her eyes. She kept talking. She couldn't see the perplexed and dumbfounded looks plastered on everyone's faces. She couldn't see the tears running down Victor and Ma Rose's faces. She couldn't see the veins in Hasaun's neck tighten. She didn't want to see the hurt in her loved one's eyes. She wasn't accustomed to being hurtful or deceitful.

Victor began to say something but Shanae cut him off. "Please don't judge me. Let me explain everything before you judge me!"

Crying, Shanae continued, "I never asked for this to happen. I tried to stop him. I cried, screamed, begged and pleaded. I even fought back, but he overpowered me. No one was home. Hasaun was in Atlanta. Victor was doing a summer internship in Chicago and Momma was in Las Vegas. I was all alone. I tried to stop him but I couldn't! So please don't judge me!"

Victor walked over to Shanae and said, "Big sis, no one is judging you. I love you and will never stop, so don't worry." Shanae always knew she could count on Victor.

Ma Rose interjected, "Suga, none of us in this here room can judge you. Only The Man upstairs has that power."

Then looking at Hasaun she said, "We all fall short at some point and we all are ashamed of certain aspects in our lives but no one can judge us but God."

In her heart Ma Rose knew Hasaun was the cause of Shanae's miscarriage and by the way he started getting nervous he confirmed her assumptions.

"Baby, God knows where your heart is, so go on and get this mess over with. You've been holding on to this pain for too long. I can't stand it anymore. Tell them what happened."

Ma Rose was glad that the burden was finally being lifted off her baby's shoulders. The transgression had been holding her spirit down for years.

Keya couldn't believe her ears. She knew when they were younger he was just too nice to Shanae. Dena knew she would have questions to answer as soon as Shanae was done explaining the situation. Hasaun never once said a word. He was upset because Shanae had been holding out on him for years and now he was forced to face the truth.

Shanae sat up in the bed, looked around the room and said, "I want you all to know that Bernard never touched me when I was a child. He raped me. That was the first and the last time he ever touched me!"

With the last statement, Dena fell to her knees and began to weep. For so many restless nights she asked God to give her peace because she thought Bernard had been molesting Shanae all those years. He had finally given her peace and it felt good.

Dena was relieved. She worried for years that she had overlooked something.

Shanae continued her conversation, "I was waiting for Momma to pick me up from school. Instead Bernard showed up. I didn't think anything about it. He told me momma was in Las Vegas shopping for an evening gown."

Shanae thought back to the events that took place. She was in a trance depicting the chain of events that transpired that day. She remembered every meticulous detail. Everyone in the room sat and listened to her.

22

"I remember putting my last piece of clothing into my luggage and falling back on the twin size bed in my dorm. I couldn't wait until Mamma picked me up the next day. I was anxious and ready to relax in my king size bed. I had successfully completed my junior year of college. Normally, I would have driven myself home but my truck had been giving me problems. Bernard and Mom had picked it up a month prior. That was another reason I was excited about getting home. I had a brand new truck waiting on me. I couldn't wait to cruise the blocks."

She hadn't taken a single breath. She was afraid if she stopped she wouldn't be able to continue. She continued to ramble.

"The truck I was getting wasn't even on the market yet. They had it special ordered just for me. It was black with peanut butter interior and all the added luxuries. That morning I was sitting in the lobby waiting on Momma. I was reading a magazine when I saw my truck come into the circle drive of the dorm. Excited, I ran outside to see my truck, and of course, Momma. I was a little disappointed when I only saw him. I was confused because Momma had told me she would be the one to pick me up. I didn't think anything about it. This was the man who raised me since I was eight or nine. I remember asking him where my Momma was and he told me she was in Las Vegas shopping. I asked him if that was my truck. I remember walking around the truck touching every inch of the spectacular vehicle. I thanked him with a hug and we began to load my luggage into the trunk. After about ten minutes, I jumped into the driver's seat and Bernard got into the passenger seat. We headed west down I-70.

Bernard was happy Shanae decided to drive because he was exhausted. He performed an emergency operation the night before. Then he convinced Dena she needed a vacation. He was glad he had the next couple of days off.

Shanae was nervous and scared. She didn't know how her friends and family were going to act towards her.

She wiped her tears from her face and continued talking, "The ride home was long and quiet with the exception of Bernard snoring. I turned up the stereo to drown out his snoring. I made it to Columbia in record time. Before we made it home I made a detour at Sutton's. This was my first stop whenever I touched down at home."

"After about twenty minutes, I pulled into our driveway. The halt of the engine woke him. I remember his stretching and saying he couldn't believe we were home already. Briefly we joked about his calling the hogs. It was a running joke in our family when you snored extremely hard you were said to be calling the hogs. He apologized and I told him not to worry. I wasn't the one who had to sleep with him. Something I later regretted saying.

I told him to make sure he apologized to my momma when she got home. We both laughed and started unloading my luggage. After my luggage was in the house we went our separate ways. I was so happy to be home. I didn't have to put up with all those fake ass college females and I also had the luxury of being in my own bedroom, which happened to be ten times bigger than the dorm room. I wasn't willing to give my summer up. I promised Victor I would come and see him in Chicago I never did. Sorry, baby bro."

Victor could remember being furious when Shanae never showed up that summer.

Shanae didn't miss a beat and continued talking, "I decided not to unpack my clothes until later. I took off my linen dress, walked over to my dresser and pulled out some workout clothes. I jumped into my spandex outfit, grabbed a towel and Bob Marley's Greatest Hits and went to the gym on the lower level. I had wolfed down the entire chicken, rice and gravy meal so I decided to go work it off. I did a heavy cardio regiment and a mild weight lifting regiment. After about two and a half hours I was worn out. So I called it quits. I walked to the kitchen and got a bottle of chilled water."

Shanae's body was dripping with sweat and her hair was wet. She opened the bottle and gulped half of the bottle of water down in one swig. I was sitting at the kitchen table reading the Columbia Daily Tribune. Shanae didn't notice my glaring over the top of the paper. I was turned on at the sight of her. I stared at her physique in amazement. She was built like a brick house. Shanae was perfectly sculpted and flawless. I couldn't believe how fast she'd grown. She was breathtaking. She didn't know I was looking at her. When she walked over to the table and asked me when her momma was going to be home I acted like I didn't even know she had entered the kitchen.

"After I got my water I walked over to the kitchen table where he was reading the paper. I asked him when my momma was coming home. He never moved the paper from in front of his face. He told me she would be home in the morning. He seemed as if I was disturbing him so I went to my bedroom."

I refused to move the paper from in front of my face. I could not control my eyes from roaming all over her fascinating body. I wanted her. I wanted her bad.

Shanae's tears had halted and she was in deep thought

explaining every intricate detail of that dreadful day. She didn't want to leave anything out. She wanted everyone to know it was not her fault. She wanted her family to be by her side. Her family all sat quietly listening to her ramble on about everything that happened to her that day. They never once interrupted her. They kept passing the box of Kleenex around the room. They were all drawn to tears, except Hasaun and Keya. Each one never once shed a tear.

"Walking back to my room I decided to take a bubble bath and relax for the remainder of the day. I knew I would be busy tomorrow making my rounds to see my friends so I needed the rest. I walked into the bathroom, ran my bath water and squirted some cucumber melon bubble bath into the tub. While the water was running, I walked back into my room. I grabbed a Mizzou t-shirt; a pair of cut off shorts, a red DKNY bra and panty set and placed them on my bed. I walked back into the bathroom, took off my workout clothes and slid into the oversized tub. I turned the water off with my feet, laid back and closed my eyes."

Crying, Shanae continued, "It felt so good to able to relax in the luxury of my home. I can remember thinking about running my law firm as I lay in the tub with my eyes closed. I thought about all the cases I would win. After daydreaming the water became cold. Again, I used my feet and maneuvered the knobs to turn the water on. I took my washcloth and held it under the hot water. I rested my back and put the hot washcloth over my eyes. The warmth of the washcloth must have relaxed me because I dozed off. I was startled when I heard something fall in my room. Scared, I removed the washcloth from my eyes. I noticed that the tub was getting ready to overflow. I turned the water off."

Shanae stopped talking. She was just sitting there shaking her head from side to side. She could feel all the pain over again. She was taking deep breaths trying to remain calm.

Dena walked over and massaged her shoulders, "Take your time, baby. Get it together. I know you can do this. We are all here for you."

Shanae leaned back in the hospital bed, closed her eyes and began to talk again.

"H-he w-was standing in my bathroom naked. When I saw him I couldn't catch my breath. I wanted to tell him to get out but the words wouldn't come out. I was speechless. I slid further under the bubbles to hide my body from him. I was in total shock. I finally found my voice and I yelled get out of here!"

Shanae was scared. I couldn't believe she didn't want me. She was yelling telling me to get out. Ha! I wasn't leaving until I got what I came for.

"His demeanor told me he wasn't leaving. At that moment my heart sank and my stomach did flops. I sat there thinking of an escape route. I searched the bathroom nervously with my eyes trying to locate my bathrobe. When I saw that it was on the other side of the room I yelled DAMN! I was so confused because he had never acted like that before. I considered him my dad and we always got along. I knew I was in better shape than him so I decided to make a run for it. My plan was to run out of the bathroom, grab my clothes off the bed and run outside."

They all listened to Shanae. Everyone was stunned with the exception of Ma Rose. They all knew Bernard and they couldn't believe their ears. Never would they have ever thought he would lose his mind and rape his stepdaughter. After all he was a profound neurosurgeon and a pillar in the community.

Victor was furious. He knew as soon as Shanae finished telling them all the gory details he was going to find Bernard and beat the shit out of him. The man he called dad had betrayed the entire family. Bernard most definitely had to be handled.

"I jumped out of the bathtub at top speed. I was slipping and sliding everywhere. I ran out of the bathroom through the bedroom, grabbed my clothes off the bed and ran to the door. My heart was beating a mile a minute. I was almost free. My heart plummeted when I saw my dresser in front of my bedroom door. I couldn't believe he had planned this entire ordeal. Everything was going through my mind. I wanted to know if he had persuaded momma to go to Las Vegas."

Dena thought back and remembered how determined he was to get her out of town. He kept telling her she needed to get a nice gown for the hospital gala. He suggested she go to Las Vegas for the weekend to shop for her and Shanae. She hadn't thought twice about going.

Shanae was crying uncontrollably and her tone had elevated. Keya walked over and made sure the door was closed. She was ready to leave but not before she had all the juicy details of this sick story. Ma Rose watched Keya intently. There was just something about her that told her she was happy Shanae was experiencing heartache.

"With all my might I tried to push the dresser out of the way but he was on my heels and I couldn't move the damn dresser! I turned around and yelled "Why?"

Bernard didn't look like himself. He looked spooky. He had this sick sinister look on his face and from out of nowhere he laughed this atrocious laugh that sent chills down my spine. After I heard that laugh I knew I was in trouble. I held my clothes in front of me trying to shield my body from him. At the same time I was trying to get my underwear on. He ran over and grabbed my clothes from my hand and slung them across the room. At that point, my adrenalin kicked in. I started fighting for my life. I scratched him, kicked him and bit him, but he was determined. After about twenty minutes my stamina gave way.

My strength was gone and I knew within minutes so would my virginity."

Everyone's eyes in the room were glued on Shanae. They all felt sorry for her. She had been carrying this burden around for years and it was an awful burden to be carrying around.

Victor knew for sure he would kill Bernard. Dena was crying and Keya was shocked but happy that Shanae had been hurt. She had always envied Shanae. Keya couldn't have been happier.

Hasaun never cried but he was beginning to empathize with her. He never knew she had been raped. That's why she was so reluctant to have sex with him that summer. He kept pressuring her and she finally gave in. It wasn't until recently she acted like she enjoyed sex.

"He turned my drained body onto my back and straddled me. He took his hands and held both of my arms over my head. I tried to yell but it was no use. No one could hear me. I knew there wasn't a neighbor for miles.

Then in a voice I never heard before he yelled, *"Shut your damn mouth before I ram my fist down your throat."*

My entire body began to tremble and I could feel the Sutton's slowly coming up my esophagus. My heart and mind was working overtime. I knew there was no way out of this horrible mess. No one was home to help me so I closed my eyes and wished I were in a faraway place.

She took a breath. "Then he yelled in a deep baritone voice and ordered me to open my eyes. He told me if I closed them again he would break my neck. At that moment I wanted to die so I kept my eyes closed. I wanted him to put me out of my misery. He was getting more aggressive and pissed off. I wasn't complying with his sick ass. I yelled, 'Break my neck, you son of a bitch! Go ahead and kill me!' "

"I was brought back to reality when he hauled off and punched me in my face. I couldn't believe it. My face was burning and I felt lightheaded. I opened my eyes but I never looked at him. I started counting the bubbles on the ceiling. I could hear him talking but very faintly. I heard him say, 'I have waited so long for this."

He was sweating and moaning as he ran his thick gross tongue down my neck and over my breast. He sucked each breast one at a time. He continued moving down my torso leaving his sticky stale saliva all over my body. He stuck his tongue in my navel. His thick hot tongue going down my body made me numb and nauseous. I felt like hurling but it would not come up. He moved further down to lick between my legs but before he had a chance to go all the way I kneed him in the stomach. That must have pissed him off because he closed his fist and punched me in the mouth. Then h-he—"

Shanae paused and Victor ran over and gave her a hug.

He said, "Shanae, you can stop now. We all get the

picture."

"Victor, I have to tell everything. I want this to be over after today. I don't ever want to have to answer any more questions. I have to continue."

Shaking his head Victor replied, "If you insist. But we all get the picture,"

Bernard decided to handle his business and get it over with. He never expected this to take so long. Bernard tried to stick the head of his penis in but it would not go in. He never imagined Shanae still being a virgin.

"He tried to push it in but it was tough to get it in. He looked at me, smiled and said, 'Daddy's going to take your virginity, baby.'

Again he laughed that dreadful laugh. He forced his manhood in me with all his might. I screamed a long excruciating scream at the top of my lungs. I was in so much pain. I wanted to die. Bernard finished within minutes. It took him at least thirty minutes to rip away my pride and dignity! I hate that man!"

Everyone in the room was speechless. No one knew what to say. Dena held her daughter and rocked her. They both had tears streaming down their faces. Along with almost everybody else however, Keya and Hasaun were not crying.

Shanae regained her composure and said, "Hasaun, I never knew about Sherrice being his until today. I am so sorry that this is happening to you but you have to understand I never wanted anyone to know about this mess."

If looks could kill she would be dead. Hasaun was shooting daggers at her with his eyes.

He stood and said, "Shanae, you make me sick!" With that said he left the room.

Shanae cried. She could not believe him.

"Shanae, he does not mean that. He is under a lot of stress," explained Mrs. Ryder.

After the episode with Hasaun, Dena made everyone leave Shanae's room.

23

Shanae, Dena and Victor, sat in her room having small talk. They did not know what to talk about. There was so much tension, so much awkwardness. So much had transpired in the last few days that it was overwhelming to even comprehend. Shanae was silently asking God to give her strength to go see her little girl. She knew she had to go see her but she knew it would break her down. She was scared. Scared she would never bounce back from this mess.

Victor refused to go see his niece. He had no understanding of any of this; so much was going on the only thing he could think about was a drink. He knew his momma and sister were going to go see his niece but he could not muster up the courage to go see her.

"I have to go see her," said Shanae.

"When do you want to go? We will go with you," replied Dena.

Victor looked at his momma with raised eyebrows and replied, "I can't handle it, Momma. I can't see Sherrice like that. I'll pass."

"We are family. If one goes we all go," Dena insisted.

Victor could not believe his momma. He refused to argue with her. He shook his head yes and the discussion ended.

"Thanks guys. I really need the support. I love you guys so much," replied Shanae.

"That's what family is for," stated Dena.

Shanae was trying to get it together. She needed to go see Sherrice. She had to figure out what was next in her life. She had no clue as to what she would do.

The three of them walked to Sherrice's room. It was like an eighteen-wheeler hit Shanae when she walked inside. This was the main reason why Victor didn't want to come down here with them.

Dena escorted Shanae to the bed with one hand on the small of her back and the other on her shoulder. Shanae took both her hands and covered her mouth. *How could so much have happened so soon? One minute my life was okay. Then with a blink of an eye it was turned upside down.* She felt as if there was nothing she could do about it. Her life seemed to be getting worse by the minute.

She walked to her daughter who seemed to be hooked up to as many machines as she possibly could be. Shanae had no understanding. Her daughter did not look the same. It seemed as if her little body was retaining fluids. She was double her size. She had a tracheotomy. She was on a breathing machine, heart monitor and feeding tube. There were several other machines that she had no idea as to what they were.

Shanae walked over to the bed and placed her hand on Sherrice's forehead. It was damp. Shanae leaned forward and placed kisses all over her daughter's face. She could not believe what was happening to her baby. She held her hand and shed tears.

The room was quiet, with the exception of the machines and Shanae's whimpers. Shanae felt empty inside. There was something so strange about a mother having to say goodbye to her child. She was devastated. She just kept asking why. Why?

After about forty-five minutes of asking why, Victor gave his momma a look pleading for help. He wanted this scene over with.

Dena walked over and patted Shanae on the back. Shanae turned around and held her momma.

"Why? Momma, why? Oh, Momma why? Please tell me why? Why my babies? Momma!" Shanae felt as if her life was caving in.

Dena was at a loss for words. She just held her baby and let her release her emotions.

Victor could not handle it anymore. He walked out of the room. He needed to let off some steam and he knew exactly how. Once he found him he would beat the brakes off Bernard.

"Let it out baby. Let it out," cried Dena.

"How could this have happened? Momma, please! Please! Please tell me how," begged Shanae.

Dena was overwhelmed. She had no idea how she was going to get her daughter together. "Shanae you have to calm down. This is a time where you have to call on the man upstairs. He has all the answers," replied Dena.

"That's all you and Ma Rose know!"

Pointing her finger at Sherrice, Shanae whimpered, "I want her out of that bed and those machines off of her. That's what I want!"

Dena held her and whispered in her ear, "You need to calm down. What if she hears you and you are scaring her? Calm down. I know it is hard but we are here for you baby."

Dena ran her hands over Shanae's head and continued to try to calm her down. Shanae walked away from her momma and pulled a chair alongside her daughter's bed.

She looked at her momma and said, "I am not leaving her."

Dena shook her head up and down letting her daughter know she understood.

"I need to be alone with her. I want to be left alone," cried Shanae.

Dena walked over to her daughter, kissed her on the cheek and replied, "If you need anything I will be right outside this door."

Shanae shook her head up and down and continued to watch Sherrice. Dena turned around and left the room. She grabbed a chair and sat outside Sherrice's door.

Shanae had so much on her plate. She didn't know which to sample from first. Her second born was dead. Her first-born was on her deathbed. Hasaun was an asshole. She knew she would have to make some big decisions. She could not continue to watch her little beautiful baby girl suffer like this. Her breathing was labored. It was evident she was in pain. She pushed those thoughts out of her mind.

She held her baby's hand and talked to her.

"Hey, little angel. You're a strong girl. I know you can pull out of this. You need to hurry up and get better so we can go have some ice cream," Shanae's voice was cracking and her vision was blurred from tears.

Shanae wiped the tears and continued to talk. "Sherrice, I love you. I love you so much. Remember you are a big girl now. Get better for Momma."

Shanae sat looking at her daughter. She wanted her to be her normal size and all the machines gone. She needed that. She needed her baby at one hundred percent so they could walk out the hospital together. Shanae sat there in silence.

Sherrice was just lying in the bed motionless. Tears began to pour down Shanae's cheeks.

Shanae looked up to the ceiling and said, "Please do not put the burden on me to decide my daughter's fate. I pray you bring her through this. For some reason it is her time, please don't make me be the one to decide.

Shanae could not stand seeing her baby like this but by no means did she want to be the one deciding to take her off the ventilator.

Shanae only left her side to use the restroom. For three days Shanae read books, listened to music, sang and talked to her daughter. There was no response. Shanae did not waiver. She continued her routine and was happy to have the opportunity to spend time with her baby.

Dena and Victor stopped by everyday. Sometimes they stayed most of the day with her. Shanae was upset because Hasaun had not been back to the hospital to see Sherrice. She just wished he could love her no matter the situation. She figured it was his loss.

Shanae sat there talking to Sherrice and telling her she was a special girl. In the middle of the sentence her stomach growled. Shanae could not believe her stomach. Shanae realized she had not had anything to eat.

"Sherrice, I been sitting here with you running my mouth all day. I have not had a bite to eat," Shanae wished she would say something to her but she never did.

"Baby, I am going to run grab something from the cafeteria. I will be right back."

Shanae walked over to the bed, kissed her forehead and held her little hand and replied, "Be right back! Love you."

She turned the doorknob but before she left she took a glance at her baby and smiled. Shanae left the room. She stopped by the nurses' station to tell them she was going to the cafeteria. Once she hit the lobby there sat Victor, her Momma, Ma Rose, and Francis. Shanae smiled and walk towards them.

"What are ya'll doing here?" questioned Shanae.

Ma Rose broke the silence. "We have been sitting out here wondering if you would ever come out and have a bite to eat."

24

Shanae fumbled with the keys to her new home. She
finally opened the door and entered the foyer. Kicking off her
Prada boots, dropping her keys and Prada handbag on the
credenza in the crystal bowl, she wandered into the living area.
She sat on the Italian leather sofa and cried. She had just
returned from her child's funeral and she was in a state of
disbelief.

Her cries echoed throughout the massive home. She
wanted her children and no one could bring them back. She was
willing to make a pack with the devil himself if she could have
them back. She never even had a chance to say goodbye to
either of her daughters. She was hurting so bad. On a daily basis
she continued to wish the pain away but with each passing
minute it seemed to get worst. Sobs controlled Shanae's body
and she began to tremble. Her trembling led to uncontrollable
crying. She had never felt pain like this before. Nothing could
compare to what she was feeling. No mother was ever

supposed to bury her children. She could not believe she had
lost both of them. At that very moment Shanae wished she
were dead.

She left early because she could not take it anymore.
She hoped her friends and family understood. They had been
her saviors for the past two weeks. She never knew she could
be so vulnerable and emotional. One minute she could be
talking and laughing and the next minute she would be breaking
down crying. The sight of little girls instantly brought tears to
her eyes. There wasn't a night that she didn't wake up in a cold
sweat thinking about her children.

Shanae wiped her tear-drenched eyes and stood. She
proceeded to walk on to the terrace but stopped. Shanae
looked towards the ceiling and began to shake her head
vigorously.

"God, why? Why? Why do you keep doing this to me? I am
living in hell on earth. What have I done?

Shanae continued to question God.

"What have I done in my life to continue to suffer? What
kind of caring God are you who would place so many burdens
on one person's shoulders?"

Shanae was beginning to doubt the All Mighty.

"I am so tired. I hate this cruel world! What did I ever do to
deserve so much pain? Please just take me! I cannot go on
without them! PLEASE GOD!"

Shanae had fallen to the floor and was on her knees. She was rocking back and forth. She could not fathom how her life had spiraled out of control and she had hit rock bottom again. She wanted to know just what the man upstairs had in store for her and she wanted to know at that moment.

"Why are you doing this to me? What have I ever done? You cannot be a caring God! A caring God would never place so many burdens on me! I did everything right all my life and I even went to church every Sunday. To think this is how you repay me. You are a joke. Damn it. Why don't you answer me? The only feeling I have felt is heartache.

Shanae had lost all her common sense because she was hurting. She was unaware of the things she was yelling and saying. Most importantly, she forgot that she was talking to the Most Highest. Shanae had never questioned God as she did that day. She was livid. Her religious faith had been shaken and she wanted answers. She was upset with Him and continued to yell and question God.

"Why do you let children die? Why are there so many starving children? Why should I keep praising you and trusting you? You just keep letting me down! Tell me! Tell me! Nobody knows what I am going through. You hurt me!"

Pointing at the ceiling, Shanae continued to yell. "You! You! Now take it away!"

Shanae's voice was getting hoarse and she was tried. She

was tired emotionally, physically and mentally. She just lay on the floor wallowing in her own anguish. Shanae tried to get up off the floor but she could not move. Something was holding her down. Then she felt this tingly sensation running all through her body. She tried to get up off the floor again but she could not move. All of a sudden she felt as if her flesh was on fire. Her breathing was labored and she was sweating profusely. She was hot from the top of her head to the bottom of her perfectly manicured feet. Having trouble moving and being able to breathe, Shanae calmed down and focused on catching her breath.

Please God, don't let me die, thought Shanae.

Shanae thought it was ironic that she was calling on the same God who she had just questioned earlier.

"Please help me!"

Shanae wanted the feelings to stop. She was so scared and prayed that God would help her out. She felt as if she was going to black out. She tried to stay calm but was having trouble controlling her breathing.

After about five minutes of pure agony and labored breathing, everything subsided. She was able to move and breathe. The burning she felt had also left. Shanae realized that God had stopped by to pay her a visit. Her momma always told her to be careful what you ask for because you might not be ready for it. Shanae believed in her heart that God stopped by to show her what hell really would feel like. Shanae knew the death of her children would be hard to overcome but she also realized that she just might need God on her side.

Victor wasn't shocked that Shanae wanted to go home early and by herself. She hadn't had any time by herself to grieve. There was always someone at her side. When he walked into his sister's home, he picked her boots up off the floor and proceeded in to the living area. Once he entered the living area he noticed Shanae lying on the floor crying. Shanae was clutching one of Sherrice's stuff animals. She never saw or heard Victor enter her house. She laid there, swallowed up in despair. The sound of her whimpers made Victor's heart pour out to her. He knew she had been crying for a long time. She sounded so tired. He noticed that the tears were still pouring out of her eyes. Instantly, Victor dropped her boots and walked towards his sister.

Shanae jumped when she felt a firm hand on her shoulder. She knew whom it was before she even turned around. He had been so helpful and she was happy she could count on him. He was her brother. Victor could not believe the way that Shanae looked. Her eyes were puffy and barely opened. She was a total wreck. They both were at a loss for words. They did not want to speak because they both knew if the other said something they would both break down. Instead of saying anything, Victor just rocked his big sister to sleep.

After putting his sister to bed, Victor knew he would not be leaving anytime soon. His main focus was his sister.

25

Shanae was eager to go see the shrink in the beginning but now that it was time for her to walk inside the building she was nervous. She had so much on her mind that she did not know the first thing to discuss. She had walked back to her car three times because she was embarrassed to be seen walking inside the building. However she wanted to stop grieving. She knew Victor was tired of being her counselor. Besides he had found a woman.

Shanae finally gave in and went inside. She walked over to the receptionist's desk and was greeted with a smile. She gave the lady her name; she gave Shanae a packet to complete and notified the doctor. Shanae looked over the information and completed the packet. It was basic information. She finished it quickly. However, she became choked up when she got to the question that asked,

"What is it that you want to deal with while in these

sessions?"

Shanae did not know what to expect. She took a deep breath and closed her eyes and prayed everything would fall in place.

Dr. Trad called Shanae into her office and offered her a seat and sat a glass of water on the table in front of her. Dr. Trad perused her file and got down to business.

"What brings you here today, Ms. Davis?" questioned Dr. Trad.

Shanae looked at her with a concerned look on her face. She saw the doctor look over her packet so she had to know why Shanae was here.

"Well, I am having trouble dealing with some issues in my life right now, and I just need some help dealing with it," stated Shanae.

After Shanae answered her question, Dr. Trad wrote something down and asked, "What is it that you need help dealing with?" Dr. Trad was trying to get Shanae to say that she was dealing with the loss of her children but Shanae would not do it.

Shanae could not figure out while the doctor kept asking her the same question over and over. It was starting to work on her nerves. Shit, she had all her information on the packet but was not looking at it.

Shanae replied, "I am stressed and have a lot of stuff on my mind," Shanae was becoming pissed.

Dr. Trad walked over to her desk and sat down. She was not giving Shanae eye contact and the doctor was all over the place. "Shanae, what type of stuff is causing you stress? Can you give me specifics?"

What does she want from me? I was stressed. Stressed for so many reasons.

"It's just so much! Okay. Since you insist, I am stressed that my daughters are dead, my stepdad raped me and my baby's daddy killed our unborn child."

Shanae took a deep breath and continued. "Let me see what else I can think of—my dad and twin sister not being in our lives. I think that might be about it."

Shanae took her hand and wiped away the tears that were coming down her face. She was angry.

"Oh, I forgot one. Mad at God for turning his back on me. Yeah, that will be the last one."

Without any compassion in her voice Dr. Trad replied, "Which one would you like to deal with first?"

Shanae could not believe this expensive bitch. With attitude in her voice Shanae replied, "It doesn't matter to me."

"How about you go home and think about it? The only way I can help you is if you let me in. You go home and let me know which is holding you back. When you figure that out call back and make another appointment."

Shanae was at a loss for words. She had no idea what the doctor's problem was. Shanae grabbed her belongings and stormed out the door. She made a mental note to find another shrink.

Dr. Trad sat at her desk studying Shanae's file. She took several notes and concluded that Shanae was going to be a hard case because she did not want to face her problems.

Shanae sat in her car outside the doctor's office and was livid. She had no idea what had just transpired in the office with her head doctor. Nothing had been accomplished and she was told to leave. She sat in her car and thought about her life. What was it that ailed her the most? She thought about all her disasters in her life and she weighed them. Shanae cried and she knew what it was that pained her the most.

She jumped out her car ran back into the doctor's office and walked back into Dr. Trad's office without being told it was okay. When she barged in, Dr. Trad looked up from her file. She was looking over her glasses. Shanae and the doctor stared at each other.

Shanae finally broke the silence and said, "My girls. My girls. That's what hurts the most. My girls."

Shanae fell to her knees and wept

26

Once Shanae stepped out of her vehicle she immediately smelled rain in the air. She slowly approached the cemetery. Once she located their graves she knelt down beside them. It seemed like yesterday when she lost her children. She was feeling down and she had the desire to visit her children. Shanae was sitting in front of the graves with her pajamas and house shoes on. Kneeling, she meticulously cleaned the leaves and debris from around the tombstones. In her hand, she held the most beautiful pink and white roses. Tears were uncontrollably streaming down her face. Without her children she felt so lonely and empty inside. There wasn't a day that went by that she didn't think about her girls. If she could, she would change one thing. She would have never allowed Hasaun to enter her apartment that day.

Shanae closed her eyes, inhaled the air and imagined her life with her children. She saw two beautiful little girls running around laughing playing and bringing joy into her life. It seemed so real. Shanae had a euphoric feeling. She imagined herself pushing them on swings, eating ice cream, going to the zoo, playing with dolls and having the time of their lives. Shanae's tears had ceased and she had a smile plastered on her face. She could actually reach out and hold her daughters. They were so gorgeous. Shanae's beautiful dream turned into a dreadful reality when cold drops of rain began hitting her.

Shanae opened her eyes and looked around for the park, the sun and most importantly her daughters. Within seconds she realized she had been dreaming again. These were the worst because she knew that she would never have the chance to raise her little girls. God had taken that opportunity away from her.

For months she begged God to take her heartache away. It never happened. Now here she was on her knees once again pleading with the man upstairs. She wanted the pain to leave her heart, eyes and soul. She wanted to be her normal happy self again. All she kept hearing was how much it would get better. God will never put more on you than you can bear and numerous of other things. She had heard them all but she still felt the same.

After cleaning off the tombstones, Shanae placed the roses on her daughters' graves. Shanae couldn't believe she still had tears. She had been crying for months and she still felt like crap.

Shanae looked into the sky and let the raindrops hit her face. She wished they would wash away her pain. She closed her eyes and prayed she would get it together, sooner than later. Once she opened her eyes she kissed both of the graves and left the cemetery.

Shanae was drenched. Her pajamas were clinging to her perfect body. When she finally made it home she stripped out of her soaked pajamas, took a hot shower and found refuge in her bed. She wanted the pain out of her life. She stumbled out of bed and once again was on her knees.

"God, please help me. Lift this awful burden. I do not know if I can take much more. Please help me. I know I do not call on You often but I need Your hand. Pleases give it to me." Shanae cried herself to sleep that night.

Shanae jumped when she felt a firm hand on her shoulder. She opened her eyes to see her younger brother looking at her. Victor couldn't believe the way that Shanae looked. Her eyes were puffy and barely opened. She looked terrible. They knew as soon as they started a conversation they would both be drawn to tears. Victor told Shanae when she dressed to come down stairs so they could talk.

Sitting on the Italian leather sofa Victor said, "Shanae, I don't know where to begin or what to say. I just want you to know that I am sorry that you have to go through this. It hurts me to see your having to deal with this. What hurts me more is that I cannot do anything about it. Shanae, I know this is probably the wrong thing for me to say right now, but you have to be strong. I know you are a fighter and you can do this."

Crying, Victor continued, "I have always looked up to you. You always told me I could do anything I want as long as I put my mind to it. I just want you to use your own advice. Please don't give up. Please be strong."

Unable to find her voice Shanae just stared at Victor. She wanted to say she would be strong and that Davis' didn't give up. She was rendered speechless. Instead of saying what her brother wanted to hear she lost all composure and broke down in tears. Victor squeezed his sister and rocked her. Shanae dozed off and he carried her into her room. He placed her in her bed. Victor watched his sister as she slept. This was the only time she was at peace. He wished her life were peaceful. He turned out her light and walked back to the living quarters.

Victor refused to leave his sister there by herself. Hasaun was still upset and wasn't speaking to Shanae. Once Ms. Ryder heard the news she had forgiven Shanae and was by her side. Keya was on the go too much to realize her friend needed a shoulder to cry on. Shanae and her momma were on speaking terms but she was going through an ugly divorce. Most of her time and energy was spent on divorce proceedings. Ma Rose was a constant person in Shanae's life who had been helping her since day one. Victor decided he would stay for a couple more weeks. He wanted to make sure his sister was stable before he left. He would be lying if he said that was the only reason he wanted to stay.

Victor called his company and informed them that he would be extending his vacation. He put everything in motion. He decided to use Shanae's study as a satellite office. He had computers and phones installed that connected straight to his company. It would be like he was still in the office. His business was running smoothly and he had excelled where other sports companies hadn't. After taking care of the necessary business procedures, Victor decided to call it a night.

The next morning Victor was awakened by the smell of bacon and cinnamon rolls. He walked into the bathroom, washed his face and brushed his teeth. He figured his momma had come over to cook breakfast. He tapped on Shanae's door to see how she was holding up. There was no answer. He pushed the door open to find a neatly made bed without Shanae in it. He walked briskly into the kitchen to see what was going on and there stood Shanae cooking breakfast and listening to Kirk Franklin's, "Stomp," Victor was speechless.

Shanae saw the look on his face and said, "I never had a chance to thank you for the house and everything that you have done for me. So I am cooking you a thank you breakfast. You have time to take a shower and get dressed before I am finished."

Shanae shooed him away and Victor followed his sister's orders.

Breakfast was very quiet. Shanae looked better on the outside but she was feeling lost and lonely on the inside. Victor told Shanae he was staying for a couple more weeks and that was music to her ears. She was happy she was going to have her brother's company for a while longer.

"Vic, I know you love me and are staying here to help me but I think something else has you hanging around." Shanae loved to see her brother squirm.

"Shanae, I think you are meddling now. Mind your own business, sis."

They both laughed and finished breakfast.

27

Shanae could not believe how fast time flew. School was starting, and she was amped about getting finished. She decided against working while enrolled in school. She was taking a full load, and she wanted to ace all of her classes. She was enrolled in Cultural Diversity in Criminal Justice; Ethics and Morality in Criminal Justice; U.S. Foreign Policy and Criminal Procedures. She had her some difficult times ahead. So in order to get a jump start Shanae toured the campus in December weeks before school was in session. She became familiar with the university. Shanae was ready to get underway. Now, more determined than ever to succeed, Shanae said a little prayer for reassurance. She had her study in her home setup and was ready to go. She purchased all her books and was in the process of reading them. Learning always came easy for Shanae. Getting an "A" on an assignment without ever opening a book was her motto. However, she enjoyed reading and learning.

Shanae woke up around six thirty to get ready for her eight o'clock class. She decided to dress comfortably because she had a long day ahead of her. Shanae put on her jeans, a brown thermal and her brown and tan designer sneakers, matching backpack and her brown leather jacket. Shanae wanted to leave early so she could find a decent parking space. To her surprise the parking was worst than she thought it would be. She cruised the campus for over twenty minutes looking for parking. She was glad to see a guy leaving a parking space. After parking Shanae headed to her first class of the day. She had three classes today and would be on campus for several hours. She was glad that Tuesdays and Thursdays were a lot easier than her Mondays and Wednesdays. She was glad she did not take any classes on Fridays.

After her first class, she had some down time, so she decided to quickly eat before her next class. She walked to Brady Commons and bought a doughnut and a cappuccino. She sat at a little table in the corner and began to work on her assignment from her previous class. Her assignment was to write an essay explaining the correct procedures of collecting evidence from a crime scene.

After about thirty-five minutes she collected her belongings, discarded her trash and walked to her second class of the day, which was U.S. and Foreign Policy. To her amazement the class as well as the previous one was going to be a breeze. She always stayed posted on what was going on in the world. This class was going to be great. She left that class feeling sure of herself.

There was only a fifteen-minute break before her next class. She was excited because it was the last class of the day. She noticed a lot of the same students from her other classes in this one. She also noticed a handsome man who had been in two out of three of her classes. The first thing she noticed was how captivating his eyes were. His skin was chestnut brown; deep dimples, six foot five, muscular built, goatee and from the looks of it, he had class. He looked like a man who could put in work. Shanae hadn't had work put in on her in a long time. It had been so long that everything she looked at lately reminded her of something sexual. She hoped her hormones were not deceiving her, and he was really fine. Shanae was in a daze thinking about what he could probably do to her when she noticed they were both staring at each other. Embarrassed, she dropped her head and directed her attention on the professor. She continued listening to the professor and wondered if the guy was still staring at her. She refused to look in his direction. No man had ever had her this hot and bothered. She was feeling bubbly inside. She was feeling emotions she had not experienced in a long time.

She checked her emotions quickly. She was here for one thing, and that was to get out of school. She did not have time for a man in her life. Her life was too complicated. The last thing she needed was a distraction. Although he was a fine distraction, she remained focused.

Shanae left class relieved the long day was over. While walking to her SUV, she noticed the guy from class was directly behind her. Her heart started racing and she was nervous. He was getting ready to approach her. She wasn't prepared. She continued strutting down the sidewalk and pretended not to see him. He was less than a few feet from her and her heart felt like it was going to pop out of her chest. Then to her surprise he walked straight past her. Shanae was elated that she didn't have to hold a conversation with him. But, at the same time, she was let down that he paid no attention to her. Immediately her defenses came and she decided to ward off men until she graduated.

When she finally made it to her truck, she spotted him talking to some chic. Shanae started walking with more energy, hit the unlock button to her truck, threw her belongings in the passenger side of the truck and got in on the driver's side. Shanae maneuvered out of the tight space and headed home.

Once at home, Shanae put on some comfortable clothes and decided to relax. However she knew she was not going to be able to relax. She walked over to her nightstand and checked her messages. She had messages from so many of her friends. They all wanted to know how her first day of class went. She called them all back and filled them in on her day. She was concerned because her girl hadn't called. She figured Keya was busy and chalked it as a lost. After giving her family a detailed description of her day, she walked to her study and completed all her assignments she had been given for the day, closed her books and went to sleep.

Shanae slept until noon the next day. Her busy schedule from the previous day had her exhausted. She was so tired. She was also thankful that she did not have class until that afternoon. She decided to head to the spa. While at the spa she relaxed and enjoyed the special treatment she was getting. Once she was finished at the spa she headed to school. A part of her dreaded that she was not a traditional student but she knew it was just a matter of time before she would graduate.

Shanae headed to the bookstore because she was looking for a book she heard was a good read by L.A. Lane called <u>You Have A Pretty Face</u>.

Walking to her class, Shanae prayed that the class was just as easy as the classes from yesterday. She was glad when she went into the classroom because there were not many students. She decided on a seat in the middle of the class so she could blend in. She sat her black leather backpack in the chair next to her and began to read her book. She had about twenty minutes before class started. Deeply into her book and very unaware of her surroundings, she smelled his pleasant fragrance before she heard his voice.

"Excuse me, is anyone sitting here?" questioned the mystery man.

Shanae looked at the seat, which her bag occupied, and all the other available seats around the room and replied, "No."

"Do you mind if I sit here?" The words that came out of his mouth were so sensuous.

Without looking up from her book, Shanae picked her bag up, moved it to the seat on the other side of her and replied, "No, not at all."

Shanae never once looked up from her book. She was getting excited and beginning to feel uncomfortable with his sitting so close to her. She had been staring at the same page for five minutes, and she could not decipher one word on the page. This man had an effect on her that she did not like. Hasaun had had the same effect on her. She decided to stay away from him because she did remember some of the things that had happened to her. She made a mental note to stay far away from this new guy as possible. She also decided she would come to class a lot later so she could select a seat as far away from his fine ass as possible. She continued to play it cool. When class started, she was able to ignore him. She did not care how fine he was. Nothing came before her studies. She noticed him a few times sizing her up. She wore her tight fitting black turtleneck and gray slacks with a pair of leather Prada boots.

Her clothes hugged every inch of her body. There wasn't an ounce of fat on it. She had her hair pulled in a bun at the crown of her head. She was glad she stopped by the spa before going to class. One might have thought she had a busy day ahead of herself. She was dressed so nicely because she and Jade were going to eat and do a little shopping after class. Jade and Shanae had become really close after Victor left.

After class Shanae waited a couple of minutes before she left. She wanted to put some distance between her and Mr. Refined. When she exited the classroom, she saw him walking out the doors. She walked slowly behind him. Her plan was to go the opposite direction of him. Shanae made it to her vehicle without any distractions. It was freezing outside, and snow was beginning to come down. She hated driving in the snow. Once inside her truck she called Jade.

"Hello," answered Jade.

"Hey girl, I was calling to see if we could have a rain check for a snow free day," pleaded Shanae.

Laughing Jade replied, "Once I saw the snow I was waiting on your call."

Embarrassed Shanae replied, "I am glad you're so understanding. Love ya girl."

Happy that she and Shanae had really liked each other when we met, she replied, "Anytime, girl. Love you too. Bye."

"Bye, Jade." With that Shanae ended the call.

In the process of putting her truck in reverse, she heard a tap on the passenger window. She wondered what the hell? Mr. Refined was doing knocking at her window. She opted not to be a snob, but she really didn't want to be nice to anyone and was not interested in being friends with anyone new.

Once her window was completely down Shanae said, "May I help you?"

It must have been pleasing to hear because he started smiling, "I have never seen anyone as gorgeous as you. I would like to know if you would like to go on a date."

Pleased by his interest in her Shanae was still disheartened because she knew she had to turn him down. She had too much to do, too much she wanted to accomplish and was not about to complicate it with a man. So she knew she had to decline.

"I'm sorry. I missed your name."

Xavier thought she was getting ready to turn him down by the look on her face. She was holding a conversation, so he felt he was making progress with her.

Anxious he replied, "Xavier. Xavier Madison."

Smiling, Shanae replied, "Mr. Madison.

Xavier interjected, Please call me Xavier."

Shanae could not believe his name was Xavier. Talk about a classic street name. There was nothing about him that screamed Xavier.

"Well, Xavier. I don't want to sound rude but at this point

in my life I do not have the time or desire to go on a date."

Shanae wanted to slap herself. She wanted to go on a date with him She was just too nervous and scared. Instead of stopping she continued, "I am working on bettering myself. Sorry, but I am not interested."

He never said a word. They sat there looking into each other's eyes. The silence was unsettling. He was looking at her like he didn't understand a single word that had come out of her mouth.

Xavier broke the silence, "Well, thanks for your time Mrs."

Instantly Shanae replied, "Miss Davis."

Xavier walked away from her truck feeling salty. She had turned him down in the nicest way. He wanted to know exactly why. For days, he watched her every move. She moved with finesse and poise. Never in his life had he seen anyone like her. He made a mental note to not give up on her.

Shanae continued her rigorous schedule for months. She was sitting in her study cramming for semester midterms. She was currently holding a 3.9 GPA and was doing great in all of her classes. She was all about her studies and nothing else in life mattered to her.

Xavier did not take the hint. He spoke to her on a daily basis with small talk. Besides school, there was nothing else going on in Shanae's life. Dena and she were still in family counseling, and she saw Ma Rose every Sunday for dinner. She had not seen Keya in a while.

Shanae was glad to be done with her midterms. She knew she passed them all. She was walking to her truck and talking on her phone.

"Momma, I passed all of my finals!"

"I knew you would. School has always been easy for you." Dena was proud of her daughter.

She stopped in midsentence when she saw him. He was sitting on the hood of her truck. She had no idea her day could go from sugar to shit in a matter of seconds. She wanted to turn around and walk the other way but he was waving for her to come over. Opting not to cause a scene, she continued walking to her car. *What a way to start my weekend.*

"Shanae, did you hear me?" yelled her momma on the phone.

"Yeah. No, what did you say?"

"Baby, are you okay? You sound distraught."

Shanae stopped walking and said,

"Momma, Hasaun is on my truck waiting for me."

What! Shanae turn around to go back on campus. I am on my way."

Dena was concerned Hasaun had not been himself lately.

Shaking her head as if her momma could see her Shanae replied, "No, Momma, I have had enough of him. I am letting him know something today."

"Shanae! Shanae!"

Shanae took a deep breath and headed towards her enemy. She could hear her hysterical momma on the phone when she pressed the end button and shoved the phone in her bag.

"Get away from my truck!"

Hasaun just stood there with a smirk on his face.

Shanae continued, "We have nothing to talk about. You and I are over. Why won't you leave me alone?"

After the girls' funerals, Hasaun had begun acting bizarre. He was always ranting and raving. Hasaun was on some bullshit every time she ran into him. He was a major wound in her life that she wished would heal and go away. But Hasaun continued to re-open the wound with his crazy antics. Shanae despised him and everything about him.

"Shanae, we need to talk. I want you back," croaked Hasaun.

The look on her face was pure disgust. She didn't have the energy to even confront him. Shaking her head and walking past Hasaun was the only energy she could muster up. Walking past him was her first mistake.

He grabbed her arm with so much force he snapped her neck. Then he yelled, "Bitch! I see you still think you're the shit. You ain't going to be satisfied until I stomp a pothole in your ass."

Shanae couldn't believe how deranged Hasaun was acting. She hadn't spoke to him in months, and now he wanted to be lovers again. It was not going to happen.

Shanae snatched her arm away and pointed her finger in his face and yelled, "If you put your damn hands on me again I will fuck you up! You better stay far away from me, or your black ass will be sorry!"

The veins in Hasaun's neck protruded, and he clenched his fist. Shanae was scared, but she would never let him know it. She wasn't stupid. She began to back away from Hasaun when she backed into Mr. Madison.

"Mrs. Davis, you okay?" questioned Xavier.

Hasaun was thrown off guard when he heard the nigga's voice. He wanted to know about their relationship and why he was so concerned. *Something else to talk about at a later date.*

Shanae didn't know what to do. She was about to piss her pants. From the look on her face, Xavier knew she was scared and was far from okay. When he saw dude put his hands on her, Xavier became enraged. Shanae didn't want to put him into her business, but she was paranoid and starting to fear for her well-being. She refused to be left alone with Hasaun.

Shanae grabbed Xavier's arm. He could feel her trembling. Then in a not so sure voice he heard her say, "No. No I am not okay. I am terrified, and he has threatened me."

Shanae refused to look Hasaun's way because she knew he

was upset. Xavier had him beat in height and weight. Every inch of his body was muscle, which Hasaun was lacking.

Xavier cleared his throat and said, "You like putting your hands on women?"

Looking at Shanae, Xavier continued, "How could anyone want to hurt a woman, let alone a woman as beautiful as her? You would most certainly have to be a fool." Xavier stood in a challenging stance daring Hasaun to do something but Hasaun never took the bait.

After sizing up Captain Save a Hoe, Hasaun decided he did not want any problems. He never answered him. He just turned around and walked off.

Shanae was so relieved. She thought for sure he was going to pound her face in. She also knew that this was not over. It was so unlike him to just walk away. She knew he would be back and the next time she would be ready for him.

Facing Xavier she said, "Thank you so much. I do not know what I would have done if you were not around," Shanae was truly thankful.

"You do not have to thank me. I was just doing my civil duty."

Xavier wanted to hold her tight and calm her down. He wanted to let her know it was okay. She was trembling. He also wanted to know what role this man played in her life. If only she would let him in.

Releasing his hand, she replied, "Thanks so much. I do not think I can ever repay you for that."

Smiling Xavier replied, "Just being friendly and speaking to me every now, and then. That can be a start. I just hope you stay away from old dude."

Walking to her truck she said, "Trust me, I will. Again, thank you so much."

"Well, I guess this is where we go our separate ways."

Shanae turned towards him and said, "Well, I guess I will see you around. And Xavier."

"Yes."

"It is Miss Davis but you can call me Shanae. Once again thanks." And with that said she hopped in her truck and drove away.

Xavier watched the complicated woman drive off. He wanted to be in the truck with her to make sure that asshole did not come back. Xavier knew that he and Shanae would meet outside of campus.

28

Lounging in a chair on the terrace of her home with her hair blowing in the cool spring air, it was a beautiful day. The sun was shining brightly, and the sky was an amazingly blue. Shanae sat there taking in the view. She noticed how the wind had the leaves moving from left to right on the trees. The ducks abandoned the jerky lake and resided on the bank. She watched the mothers and their children feeding the greedy ducks. They were enjoying the beautiful spring weather.

She used to find this time of year irresistible because it was a time when the weather changed. She loved to see the signs of life. She no longer cared for spring because it was a constant reminder to her that who she had given birth to no longer existed. Her girls were gone, and there was nothing she could do about it

She was so lonely after losing her girls within days of each other. At this point in her life, she did not understand the work of God. As a child, she always heard her momma say that God would not put more on you than you can bear. She begged to differ. He had broken her down over the months. She felt as if she was on the verge of dying. She still had not totally recuperated from the loss of her children. She didn't know if she would. Shanae felt that she was wasting her money on a shrink who continuously answered her questions with questions. Shanae felt she never answered any question, just gave her more to think about. With determination, she was able to function on a daily basis but there was not a second in the day that went by that she did not think about her children. Shanae was going through some trying times. She felt so alone.

There was no Ma Rose across the way to lift her spirits. She was in a gated community where there was total silence. She felt as if she was isolated from the real world. She loved her home and enjoyed the peace and quiet, but she just felt alone. She was so grateful for the people she did have in her life. Her brother was a huge support for her. Yes, he had bought a house for her but the shoulder and ears he offered her were far more important to her. She consistently thanked God for him on a daily basis. The thought of her brother brought a smile to her face. She practically had to make him return to Chicago. He refused to leave her alone. She promised to take care of herself and to visit him soon.

Shanae stood up and walked over to the railing, leaned

over and let the wind blow against her face. The soft touch of the warm breeze relaxed her. Closing her eyes and inhaling, the warm spring air let her release some tension. When she finally opened her eyes, tears were streaming down her cheeks. There were so many tasks she still needed to complete. At this point in her life, she was not happy with the outcome. She had unfinished goals she needed to achieve; she wanted more out of life. On that spring day, she promised herself she would have her life together in a year. She wanted to obtain her bachelor's degree and enroll in graduate school before next fall. She figured this would keep her mind off her issues if she stayed busy.

She usually spent the majority of her time at school and working out in her personal gym. She found herself working out two and three times a day to relieve stress. She had noticed that her body was banging and she had her six-pack back. She was an attractive woman and she turned down men daily. Her justification for turning them down was that she needed to improve Shanae. She did not have the time and the energy to waste on a relationship. Walking slowly inside her house, she sat on the custom-made Italian leather sofa. She found herself crying for no reason. This was the time of day that she enjoyed. The days always went by quickly while the nights seemed to drag.

The ringing of the phone jarred Shanae from her much-needed rest. She walked into the foyer and retrieved the phone.

Half asleep, Shanae uttered, "Hello."

"What's up, girl?" Keya's loud boisterous voice rang through the receiver.

Holding the phone away from her ear Shanae groaned, "Keya, please stop yelling."

Ignoring Shanae, Keya replied, "Do you have any plans tomorrow?"

"No. Why Miss Loud Mouth?"

"Girl, they are having a party and you have been cooped up in that huge fancy home for too long. I was wondering if you would go with me."

Shanae never understood how Keya could say so much without taking a breath.

"Girl, that was too much for me to absorb at once."

"Shanae, have you been sleeping all day?"

Walking over to close her French doors Shanae said, "I came in earlier to sit down. I must have dozed off. What time is it, Keya?"

"It is eight o'clock in the evening. How long have you been sleeping?"

Shanae couldn't believe how fast the time had gone by.

"I came in the house around noon. I don't even remember falling asleep. Girl, I am just so happy to be off from school for the spring break. Midterms kicked my butt."

"So what is up? Do you want to party with your girl or not?"

There was a long pause "Keya I really don't feel like going out. Thanks, but no thanks."

Shaking her head Keya replied, "Shanae, you cannot stay crammed up in your house for the remainder of your natural born life. Please, Shanae, go with me. It could be like old times. We can go shopping for gear during the day, have lunch, get dressed at your house and hit the streets. PLEASE!"

It wasn't a bad idea and Shanae hadn't been out in a long time. She didn't need to go shopping because she also kept busy by spending her money on the latest fashion.

"Shanae!"

"Keya, I hope this ain't no ghetto ass party. What kind of party is it anyway?

"Girl, it is a masquerade party."

Laughing, Shanae replied, "You act like it was a ball, girl. Where is it located?"

"Shanae, stop being so stuck-up. We can have fun! It is at the Tiger Hotel. Big Dave is giving the party."

Shanae knew Big Dave from school, and she knew how he rolled. Against her better judgment, she decided to go with Keya.

"I guess," mumbled Shanae.

"I do not need you guessing. I need ya yessing!"

demanded Keya.

"Keya, what the hell is yessing?"

"Yessing is you saying yes!"

"Yes, Keya, I will go!" yelled Shanae.

"Damn! I never thought you would say yes," laughed Keya.

Rolling her eyes in her head, Shanae said, "Whatever! I do not need to go shopping, but I don't mind going with you. Do I need a costume?"

"Costume is optional. Sounds like a plan. You can meet me at the mall around noon. Let's meet at Mandarin House. We can have lunch first."

"See ya then. Love you."

"Love you too."

Keya knew she could get her girl back on track. She was happy. Shanae agreed to go out. She had never seen her girl so down before.

Shanae sat on her sofa wondering what the hell she had gotten herself into. She hoped Keya remained on her best behavior and didn't pull any of her famous stunts. Keya and Shanae used to party all the time. Shanae found out that Keya was wild and partied a little too hard at times. She couldn't believe she agreed to go. She had not heard from Keya in months, and when she did, she called demanding her presence at a masquerade party.

Shanae climbed the stairs and walked to her closet. She

had turned one of the bedrooms on the main level into a closet. She had shelves built into the walls and all of her clothes, shoes, accessories, belts, and undergarments were color coordinated. The room looked like a color wheel. She was a little excited about the party. She had not set foot in a club for a long time. She knew she wanted to turn heads when she stepped in the club. She was going for something sleek and sexy but still not exposing everything. She wasn't trying to pick anyone up, but she did enjoy inquires.

She walked around the 20 by 20 foot closet and started looking for something nice to wear. She figured with the type of party it was; she could go ghetto fabulous or fabulous. She decided on fabulous. She wanted to stand apart from the rest of the females at the party. After some time of walking around the room, she decided on a white pair of hip hugger Prada slacks with a white and pink Prada blouse. She loved the blouse because of its plunging neckline that stopped at her navel. She decided on her white Prada clutch and white Jimmy Choo peep toe stilettos. She knew she was going to be fierce. Shanae decided she would spice it up by buying some white wings, a white halo, and a white facemask.

Looking in the mirror Shanae decided she needed her hair done. She picked up the phone and called Tasha, picking the phone up on the first ring.

"Hello."

"Hey, Tash, this is Shanae."

Surprised Tasha replied, "And to what do I owe this pleasure?"

Shanae was laughing because she hadn't spoken to Tash in forever. It had damn near been a year.

"Tash, I need my hair done for tomorrow night."

"Where you think you ain't going?" joked Tasha.

"Keya and I our going to some party at the Tiger Hotel tomorrow," replied Shanae.

Tasha thought about how shady Keya could be. Shanae was the only one jaded by her.

"Shanae, are you sure you are ready to hit the club scene?"

"If I do not go now when is the right time, Tasha?" Shanae sounded as if she was unsure herself. She just wanted to be back to her normal self.

Tasha could hear the frustration in Shanae's voice, so she changed the subject. If Shanae wanted her hair done, she would do it.

"What do you want me to do to your hair, sweetie?"

"For starters, I have not had my ends trimmed in a year. My hair is longer than I like it so I want it cut some. I was thinking about some tresses. Shit, Tash I have no idea. You can just hook it up because I have a bad outfit."

Laughing, Tash said, "I'ma do something fresh on you because I know you going to be clean. What time do you want to get your hair done?"

Excited Shanae replied, "Whatever works for you?"

"If you come at three o'clock you will be my last client and your wait time will not be long," explained Tasha.

"Sounds good. I will be there at two forty-five. Love ya!"

Tasha replied, "Feeling is mutual."

Shanae wasn't sleepy so she ran a tub of hot bath water and decided to rest in her jetted tub. Shanae turned down the lights and lit the cucumber melon candles placed haphazardly around the tub. She was actually in a good mood.

After cleaning her taut body, she rubbed down in Shea butter. This always made her body feel like silk. She put on her nightclothes and crawled into bed.

Shanae pranced across the street to the spa. She was thrilled about going out tonight. She figured she could catch up with Keya and have a good time. Once she entered the spa she was greeted with nothing but love. She was getting the deluxe package. She needed a facial, pedicure, manicure, Brazilian and under arm wax and a full body massage. The massage was just what she needed.

Feeling like a million bucks as she left the spa, she headed across the street to the party store. They had just what she needed. She had over thirty minutes to meet Keya at the Columbia Mall. She could take her time because it wasn't that far away.

Traffic was backed up. There was a huge wreck on I-70. Looking at her watch, she realized she was going to be late. She was going to have to hear Keya's big ass mouth. After an hour, she was pulling into the mall parking lot. She was searching for parking when she heard her phone ringing.

Answering her phone, Shanae replied, "Keya, I am looking for parking."

"Hurry up, girl!"

Walking towards the mall entrance Shanae asked,

"Where are you, Keya?"

"Don't have a damn attitude with me because you are late," laughed Keya.

"I can see this is going to be an eventful day."

Annoyed Keya replied, "I am at the damn Mandarin House. I done had my lunch, and now I am waiting on you. We were supposed to have lunch together."

Shanae didn't reply to Keya's statement. She decided that hanging up the phone would really piss Keya off. Arguing with her would make her day. Keya loved to have a heated argument over nothing. She would argue to the end even if she knew she was flat out wrong.

When Shanae found Keya they hugged and discussed how the evening was going to go. Shanae told Keya she had to leave around two thirty because she had a hair appointment at three.

Keya was upset because she couldn't find anything she

wanted at the mall. The mall never had anything she liked. So she didn't understand why was she complaining. She saw several outfits, but she was worried that someone else might be wearing the same one. That was one of the reasons why Shanae went out of town to buy her clothes. Half the time she went to New York to buy her clothes. Keya ended up buying a skimpy outfit out of Express, which could have been a few sizes bigger and some shoes out an expensive department store.

Because Shanae had an appointment, Keya just decided to pick Shanae up from her house. Shanae could see that Keya had an attitude. She had been over thirty minutes late, and they did not have the opportunity to talk over lunch.

29

When Keya picked Shanae up, she was floored. She had deliberately left out the fact that you were to dress in a costume. Shanae took it upon herself to dress up. Keya still laughed because she did not tell Shanae to wear all black. Shanae was an angel in all white.

Shanae was surprised when she saw Keya dressed as a black cat. She never told Shanae she was wearing a costume.

"Heifer, you did not tell me you were wearing a costume," Shanae joked.

"I changed my mind at the last minute," lied Keya.

"Well, we both look good. So let's head out."

The party was packed from wall to wall. There wasn't enough room to maneuver in and out of the crowd. There was a wide array of people in the club. Everyone was wearing a costume. Shanae was so glad she decided to put one on. There were pimps, hoes, hustlers, ballas, clowns, cats, nurses, doctors and everything in between wearing masquerade masks.

When Shanae and Keya entered the club all eyes were on them. Shanae turned around to say something to Keya but she was gone. Shanae saw Keya mingling in the crowd. Shanae was praying she could find a table. After a while she chalked that up as a loss. There were so many people who approached Shanae to say hello. Shanae started talking to people she had not seen in years. She searched around for Keya and after about fifteen minutes she gave up. After mingling, Shanae headed to the bar and ordered a glass of Dom Perignon. Since there was still no sign of Keya, Shanae decided to find a seat to see if Keya popped up. Shanae couldn't believe Keya ditched her. Keya was a breed of her own, but she never had treated Shanae like this. She had not seen her since they stepped foot inside of the party. Shanae could only imagine what she was up to. Knowing Keya, she was somewhere getting it on in a broom closet.

Shanae located a secluded table in the back where she could see the entire room. Shanae was glad she came. She had seen many people. It felt good talking to people. It was nice to be out and not crammed up in her study doing her schoolwork.

Shanae had never seen this many people in one place acting cordially. Then again, she had not been out in years. She was sure many things had changed. Shanae was sitting at the table moving to the beat of the music when a tired looking waitress approached her. She was smacking her lips and popping gum like a low-class slut.

The waitress placed a napkin in front of Shanae and said, "Whatcha drinkin'?"

Considering she had a full glass of champagne in front of her Shanae replied, "I am fine right now."

With a shitty look on her face, the waitress said,

"Baby, you don't understand. I have about six different niggas in here who want to buy you a drink. I am busy as hell, and I do not have time for this."

"I am drinking Dom Perignon," replied Shanae

The waitress rolled her eyes and uttered, "Gurl, what do you want to drink?"

Vicki had worked as a waitress for years and the females never ceased to amaze her. Here it was; she had people wanting to buy her drinks, and this woman picked one of the highest items on the bar.

After looking around the club, Shanae said, "I will have a bottle of Dom Perignon."

The waitress looked at Shanae as if to say, who in the hell do you think is buying you that.

Reading her mind Shanae replied, "If they can't afford it I will buy it."

In about twenty minutes the rude waitress returned to her table with the champagne in hand. She had a smirk on her face.

"Gurl, you ran five of them off with the quickness. But the one who bought it was the finest and a good tipper."

The waitress left her with her expensive bubbly and without any more clues.

After about three glasses of expensive French champagne, Shanae had the urge to dance. She had seen several of her classmates earlier. Now her task at hand was to locate one of them.

She finally saw Delvon Westcott, a former basketball player from her high school. Since he was nice looking she decided to see if he would dance with her

Approaching him, Shanae said, "Come on, Delvon let's dance."

He grabbed Shanae's hand and led her to the packed dance floor where they danced. After about five songs Shanae stopped dancing. She thanked Delvon for dancing with her and went back to her table.

Vicki, the waitress, said she'd make sure no one sat at her table. When she sat back down, she noticed a note on the table. It said,

"Never leave your drinks unattended. I am sending you another bottle."

Shanae looked around the club and was curious as to who was spending so much money on her and not showing his face. Shanae's interest was piqued. She wanted to know who was being the gentleman. He obliviously had his eyes on her.

She continued to look around the club. She had seen half

of the football team from her graduating class and they spotted her. All of the guys came over to speak to Shanae. They were excited to see her. She found out they were in town for her class reunion. Something she had no idea about. She had been wondering why it was so many Kewpies in the house.

She prayed Hasaun was not in the club. Several of the fellows gave her their condolences. That was the only time that night that she thought about her girls. After they had said their good-byes, she sat there wondering who was sending her drinks. After perusing the party, she came to the conclusion there was no way she would ever figure it out.

She also wondered if she would ever find Keya. She still hadn't seen her friend; that made her angry. Tasha and her momma warned her not to go with Keya. After all, Keya had invited her out. She decided it was Keya being Keya. Deciding not to let Keya rain on her parade Shanae decided to keep enjoying herself.

From her bladder, Shanae noticed that she had drunk almost the entire bottle of champagne. She had to use the restroom. Using public restrooms was not something she liked. She got up and walked towards the restroom.

While walking to the restroom she noticed all eyes were on her. She decided for two reasons: one being her never got the memo that it was a blackout costume party. Everyone had on black except her. She had on all white. Two being they thought she had fell apart after her loss. She had run into several people at the party who told her they were surprised she looked so classy. They said they heard she had been through a lot with Ryder and the death of her children. Sure, she was hurting but she had vowed to herself to never let anything ruin her. Her children's death was a tragedy, but it was one of life's lessons she would have to learn from.

Shanae walked to the restroom. She finally arrived after pushing her way through the crowd.

Once inside the restroom, to her dismay, she found out the line was too long. She noticed after looking at the long line she didn't have to use the restroom. She decided to freshen up and head back to her table. The wings and halo were getting on her nerves, so she decided to get rid of them in the restroom. She kept her mask on and exited the restroom. Shanae couldn't believe her eyes. She literally had to stop herself from laughing. The sight she saw was so comical she had to take a double take of the lip locked couple in the corner. They were dressed as a basketball player and cheerleader. She could not believe Hasaun and Jalisa was an item again.

After that kiss in school she figured they would be the last two to be a couple. Shaking her head, she knew she better get back to her table before he saw her, which would not be too hard in all white. She did not want any drama with Dr. Jekyll and Mr. Hyde. She knew it was going to be hard in her all white outfit on. *When I see Keya, I am going to kill her.* As she was rounding the corner, he caught a glimpse of her. Shanae was walking in her four and a half inch stilettos but she was not moving fast enough. Hasaun didn't have to take a double take. He knew those hips from anywhere. *Damn she looks good.*

Shanae was in such a hurry to get as far away from Hasaun as possible, in her stupor she ran directly into Zorro and dropped her damn clutch. Apologizing she bent down to pick up her clutch. The man that she bumped into took that time to admire her beautiful body. He also apologized and offered to help. When Shanae stood up, she was in disbelief. In front of her was Xavier Madison. Shanae's heart was racing, and she was becoming flustered. Seeing him made her lose all composure. She couldn't think. She couldn't talk. She stood there like a lovesick teenager. She wanted him, and there was no denying it.

Shanae decided to break the awkward silence.

"Small world."

In a deep sexy baritone he replied, "I would have to say so myself."

His deep baritone voice sent chills down her spine. She was attracted to him. Now wasn't the time for a number of reasons; the number one reason was Hasaun's crazy ass was in the club. She also knew she needed to stay focused on her priorities, and she could most definitely see herself getting in some serious trouble with Mr. Madison

She looked over her shoulder to make sure Hasaun was not on her heels. She had to get away from the restroom.

A little nervous Shanae replied, "Well, I don't mean to be rude but I have to get going. See ya around."

Shanae felt horrible for being rude and short with him. She just had too much going on in her life.

Before Shanae was able to take a step away from Xavier he bridged the gap and whispered in her ear, "Please don't leave any more of your drinks unattended and your third bottle is on its way."

Shanae was dumbfounded. She had been searching for the responsible party all night. She was attracted to him, but she had to play it safe.

"So, you're the mystery man?"

Smiling he replied, "That would be me."

Xavier wanted her very much. He had wanted her since the first time he laid eyes on her. She was stunning. Never in his life had he met anyone as intriguing as her.

His smile captured Shanae's attention and had her in a trance. She didn't know God invented men like this. He had a body that put L.L's to shame and he looked ten times better than Billy D in his prime. *Damn, he is good-looking.*

"Thanks for the champagne. I really enjoyed it. However, I cannot handle anything else to drink. I have reached my limit." She was so nervous.

"You are welcome. Well, I wanted to share a glass with you but since you have reached your limit, I will have to drink by myself."

His smile had her in a stupor, and she couldn't believe the next thing she said, "It would only be right if I at least sat with you while you enjoy a drink."

Music to his ears he replied, "I think that is a great idea."

Shanae and Xavier walked towards her table.

Hasaun was in the cut looking at the entire scene. He was so mad he wanted to beat the shit out of her and that square ass nigga she was with. He was going to make sure that they both paid for this. *How dare her to disrespect him.*

Once at the table, Shanae saw Vicki the waitress looking at her. Shanae smiled, and Vicki gave her thumbs up. Shanae winked, and they went their separate ways.

In a deep sensual voice Xavier said, "Thanks for inviting me over. I have been captivated by your beauty ever since I laid eyes on you."

Shanae was rendered speechless. *Captivated by my beauty.* She didn't know what to say. She wondered how many times he used that line. Instead of telling him that, she opted to be nice.

"I should be the one thanking you."

His voice and finesse was taking a toll on Shanae. He was so amazing. She was happy that they crossed paths again. The sound of his voice mixed with the soft fragrance he wore had her nothing less than impressed.

"What brings you out tonight?" questioned Xavier.

The sound of his voice had Shanae's womb pulsating. She hadn't been intimate since forever he was making her feel way too good, and he was only talking to her. She just knew he could handle his business in the bedroom.

"I am out with a friend who practically dragged me out. But get this I have not seen her since we stepped foot in the club."

"She just disappeared? Did you drive?"

Shaking her head, she replied, "Actually, I didn't drive. If she doesn't show up soon, I will just have to call a car service."

I'll be your car service. I will drive you anywhere you like if you let me. "I can always give you a lift if you need one."

Flattered, Shanae replied, "I'll keep that in mind."

After discussing her riding situation. Shanae poured her a glass of Dom.

"I thought you said you had enough to drink?"

"My riding situation is bringing my buzz down."

Shanae was feeling giddy after that last cup. In fact she was more than giddy. She and Xavier sat at the table and had great conversation. She could actually talk to someone who understood her. They talked about the penal system and the biased laws. Some topics they agreed on and others they agreed to disagree on. Shanae thought it was safe to talk about subjects she knew about so they would not be sidetracked. There were many topics they could be talking about but she wanted to avoid any topics that might lead to something else.

Shanae and Xavier ended up polishing off the third bottle of Dom. They both were feeling tipsy when they heard the smooth, sultry voice of Teddy Pendergrass blaring throughout the club. The alcohol had an effect on Shanae and before she knew her hands were in the air, and she was singing, "Before you turn off the lights—"

She remembered the song because her parents always played it when she was a little girl and she loved it. She had forgotten that she was sitting at the table with Xavier. It seemed like everyone in the party including Shanae loved this song.

Xavier sat across the table from Shanae admiring her stunning physique. Not only did she look good but also she knew how to move her sexy body. Hearing the slow music let Xavier know the party was winding down. He realized he didn't have much time left with Shanae. After regaining his composure, he asked her to dance.

Holding him on the dance floor was even better than Shanae had imagined. Holding him felt so right. She hadn't felt that way in a long time. Shanae and Xavier danced through several songs. They were oblivious to the fact that Hasaun had been watching them the entire time, and he felt like killing both of them. Once they noticed the crowd dispersing they decided to leave the dance floor.

Shanae had a worried look on her face. Xavier assumed it was because she still hadn't seen her girl and did not know how she was getting home.

Xavier said, "I'll stick around to see if she shows up."

Smiling, Shanae replied, "Thanks, Xavier."

She loved how his name rolled off her tongue. Walking around the party looking for Keya, Shanae continued repeating his name. Xavier. Xavier.

Everyone had left the party, and there was still no sign of Keya. After getting no answer when she called Keya's phone she gave up. She was told to leave the party because no one else was inside she left. Outside of the club she continued to look for Keya. She was heated when she saw the parking space empty. She could not figure out why Keya pulled some ol' slick shit. She could not come up with any reason to treat a friend like this. *What could go on in your mind to leave your friend high and dry?* Shanae wanted to whoop Keya's ass.

Pacing up and down the street Shanae just gave up. She pulled out her phone and called Black Knight's Car Service. It was going to be three hours before they could pick her up. She called a few more car services, but she still didn't have any luck. Shanae was frustrated, but she refused to call Bob's checkered cab. Those drivers look too scary.

"Ugh!!!" yelled Shanae.

She had no clue as to what she was going to do, if she had only listened to her momma and Tasha. As she turned to walk back towards the club, she spotted him. He was leaning against a black Denali looking as handsome as ever. He had a huge Colgate smile plastered across his face. She was a little tipsy and her stagger showed it. Everything she was doing was breaking her cardinal rules. Never be drunk in public, never ride with a stranger and not have a plan B.

Bridging the gap between them and taking a deep breath, she asked, "Xavier, can I please get a ride? I have been looking all over for my friend and I n-need—"

Xavier cut her off in mid-sentence and replied, "I never thought you would ask."

Xavier opened the passenger door to let Shanae inside and walked around the front to get in on the driver's side. She had one foot inside the truck when she was unexpectedly yanked from the vehicle. Her purse went one way, and her masked fell on the passenger floor of Xavier's truck. She was shocked. Her head was pounding. When Shanae turned around, she was looking in the eyes of a mad man. By looking in his eyes, she could tell he was on something heavy, and it was not legal.

Hasaun yelled, "Bitch, what the fuck you think ya doin'?"

"Hasaun get your damn hands off of me!"

Shanae was scared of Hasaun. He had been doing odd shit for some time now. She did not know how to take him. He was belligerent, and he was shaking her so hard her head was jerking back and forth. Before Hasaun had a chance to utter another word Xavier scurried over to the commotion and hit Hasaun in the eye. When Hasaun hit the ground Shanae took that opportunity to break free from Hasaun's grasp and she jumped in the truck and locked the doors.

She could hear Xavier yell, "If you ever put your hands on her again your family will be wearing black!"

Shanae was thankful to have Xavier around. She had never seen this side of Xavier before, and it frightened her a little.

Shanae was rattled from the drama that was happening this evening. Two people that she used to care so much for had let her down. Keya and Hasaun had lost the best part of their minds.

Xavier left Hasaun on the pavement and jumped in his ride after persuading Shanae to unlock the doors. As they pulled off, Shanae looked over her shoulder out of the rear window to see Hasaun holding his eye, yelling and screaming. Shanae could not believe how disturbed Hasaun was acting. Their relationship had been over long before she called it quits.

She was becoming more and more afraid of Hasaun. She did not know what she would have done if Xavier would not have been there. Both Keya and Hasaun were on her shit list.

"Sorry, I didn't mean to get you involved in this BS."

Xavier chuckled and replied, "You don't have to apologize for someone else's stupidity."

However, he did want to know what was going on with her. She was entirely too sweet and beautiful to be putting up with that knucklehead.

Feeling safe, Shanae replied, "Thanks so much. You can't begin to understand how thankful I am."

Without saying a word Xavier placed his strong hand on her fragile hand. She was shaking, and he detected that she was more afraid than she was willing to admit. He finally let her go when they pulled into her drive way. He got out of the truck and opened her door she was a little nervous about him knowing where she resided.

Xavier was adamant about walking her into her house and checking it out for her. Scared and not wanting to be alone Shanae didn't think it was a bad idea. Breaking another cardinal rule, she obliged and let him come inside her home. Xavier was speechless once he entered her home. The house looked like it was taken from a spread of Home's Digest. It was so eloquently decorated. Xavier immediately thought she was into some illegal shit or had ties to the mob. That would explain why ol' dude was tripping.

Xavier gave the house a thorough search and said it

was safe. Shanae walked into the kitchen grabbed her ice bucket, placed a bottle of Dom and filled it with ice. She grabbed two crystal flutes and sauntered into the living room.

A little nervous she asked, "Would you like something to drink?"

Mesmerized by the home, Xavier was still looking around. He felt out of place. Shanae cleared her throat.

Xavier replied, "No, I still have to drive home."

Then he asked, "Shanae, what is it that you do for a living?"

Shanae had noticed Xavier checking out the house while he was making sure it was safe. She knew he would want to know what she did for a living. Smiling she answered, "I am a full-time student. I am also spoiled by my little brother."

"Must be nice."

Xavier's eyes had also seen a picture of a beautiful little chocolate princess. He wondered if she had any children. Before he had a chance to ask any more questions her phone rang. While Shanae answered the phone Xavier poured her a glass of Dom.

"Hello."

"Shanae, where are you at girl? I am still at the club. I have been looking for you."

Keya lied. She was sitting in her living room. She had met a fine brutha who she had to take home. Even if she hadn't met him, her plans were to ditch Shanae in hopes of her flipping the fuck out. She knew Shanae hadn't been out in a long time and she knew for sure being around many people would throw her out of her element.

Shanae could not believe her ears. "Look, bitch, I have not been out in years and your shady ass leaves me at the club."

Shanae tried to control her anger, but she couldn't. She prayed Xavier could not hear her rage.

"I hope the dick was worth it and I hope you got more than just a wet ass. Keya do me a favor and lose my number."

"Shanae, I am sorry."

Keya was trying to hold her laugh in. She was glad Shanae's night was a night from hell. As soon as they entered the club all eyes were on Shanae. It had been like that for as long as Keya could remember. She was tired of getting numbers and hollas for Shanae. All she ever heard was "Hook me up with ya girl."

"Keya you can save it. Not only did you leave me but you are also lying. You know damn well you were not at the fucking club looking for me.

Xavier was in the background snickering.

"You left me by myself all damn night. I never saw you from the time we entered the club. Then I run into Hasaun's psychotic ass. He flips the script on me. Key, I am so mad at you right now. I have to go besides I have company and talking to you while he waits is rude."

Keya could not believe how Shanae was acting. Keya wanted to know who was over at her crib, but Shanae had hung up on her before she had a chance to ask.

Looking at Xavier Shanae said, "Once again sorry. It really bothers me that you have to keep witnessing this crap."

Xavier could not believe half of the foul words that were coming out of such a beautiful lady's mouth.

"No problem. So your girl said she was still at the club looking for you?"

Shaking her head, Shanae replied, "I cannot believe her or this horrible night.

"It's wasn't that bad. Look at the bright side of it we got to know each other a little," stated Xavier.

Shanae picked her flute up and drank the entire glass. She did not try to savor the flavor. She wanted something to help her calm down and forget about Hasaun and Keya at the same time.

"You are so right about that. I have had a great time with you tonight," laughed Shanae.

Trying to make light of the situation Xavier said,

"Remind me to never get on your bad side. I hope this does not offend you, but I am glad she left you at the party. Because I would not have had the opportunity to enjoy your company."

Shanae did not want him on her bad side she wanted

him on her backside.

"I am usually not like this."

Walking over to the chaise Shanae kicked off her stilettos and continued talking.

"You probably think I am mental. I can assure you I am sane."

Xavier didn't know what to think of her. He knew for sure that she was an interesting lady.

"I don't think you are a basket case. At least not yet; but I do think your friends are basket cases."

They shared a laughed. Shanae was rubbing her pretty feet together. She was a little nervous.

Xavier noticed her rubbing her feet together. The sight of her feet moving back and forth was doing something to him. He knew it was time for him to go.

Shanae could not believe that she had a stranger in her house. Sure she had seen him at school the entire semester but she didn't know anything about him. They were both at a loss for words as they were both taking in the sight of each other.

Shanae broke the silence, "Thanks again for all that you have done for me. Next time I will drive."

"I am sorry that you had to go through all this mess tonight, but I am glad I had the opportunity to give you a ride. Even though you have been playing a brutha for months," joked Xavier.

Not knowing how to respond to his statement, Shanae poured her another flute of champagne. Shanae knew he was telling the truth. He had been going out of his way to be polite to her, and she had been a rude bitch. Shanae could not lie.

"Sorry for being so mean. I just do not have the time or energy to devote to a relationship and for some odd reason I believe you are looking for something serious. Yes, I could be selfish and get what I want from you, and call it quits. But I know how that feels and I do not want to do that to you."

Taking a deep breath Shanae continued, "I just have so much to do and think about that it would be unfair to bring someone on the bumpy ride with me."

Xavier could see the sadness in her eyes when she was talking. He wanted to know how such a sincere lady could be in so much pain.

Xavier broke the silence and replied, "Who said it has to be bumpy?"

He never gave her a chance to answer he kept talking, "You shut a brutha out quickly," laughing Xavier said, "Lady, I think you even lowered my self-esteem."

Shanae walked to the sofa where Xavier was sitting and sat next to him.

"You would not be able to even understand all the drama in my life. It's really bad that we have to cross paths right now. My life is just so busy and complicated."

Placing the palms of his hands on Shanae's checks and looking into her eyes he replied,

"Try me. You would be surprised. When I want something really badly, I am willing to work hard for it. Let's talk over lunch tomorrow."

Tomorrow wasn't a good day. She had a lunch date with her momma. *Damn!*

"I know you're going to think I am avoiding you, but tomorrow is not a good day. I have prior engagements."

Xavier knew she would say that. He also thought she needed to let go of her past.

Then Shanae said, "But I would be delighted to go to lunch with you on another day."

It took a lot out of her to utter those words.

Xavier could not believe his ears. "Are you serious? Just pinch me, so I know I am not dreaming."

Shanae did exactly what he asked her to do, and she pinched him.

"Shanae, I never expected to hear those words come out of your mouth."

"Why not? You have heard worse. I know you think I am stuck up, but I am really down to earth."

Shaking his head, Xavier replied, "You do have a man on point when you are around, and looks can be deceiving. You seem so sweet and quiet. But after hearing you on that phone with your girl I am still trying to figure you out."

Shanae's mouth was wide open. She could not believe he said that to her. Closing her mouth, Shanae said,

"They sure can be deceiving. Because when you told me your name was Xavier I was confused. Nothing about you screams Xavier."

"What is that suppose to mean?"

"Xavier is a hood name; something you are obviously not. Look at with you Armani slacks, and tailored shirt. There is not a thing about you that screams hood. You're soft spoken."

Shanae was laughing. She could tell she hit a nerve.

"Girl, your comments are something else. But do not let my clothes fool you."

"Likewise."

30

It had been a long time since Shanae and her momma actually hung out together. They had a busy day planned. They were going to the gym, the spa and shopping. Dena was so excited. Dena finally had peace in her life. She had been incomplete when she and Shanae were not in each other's lives. Now that she had her daughter back in her life, she was content. Her divorce being finalized was a huge blessing for her. When her lawyer told her it was over, she was drawn to tears. She still could not understand how she allowed herself to stay with such a cruel and coldblooded person. She wanted to keep her house, but there was too much negative energy in the house. She sold the family home and bought a smaller one that would only hold good memories.

Dena called Shanae and told her she did not feel like working out, so they met at Spa Sensations. Dena wanted to relax instead of working out. They chatted about school, their new homes and life in general. While at the spa, they had facials, manicures, pedicures and full body massages.

Dena wanted to eat before they went shopping. Shanae's mind was elsewhere. Shanae suggested eating in Café Court. Dena refused to eat in Café Court. Shanae didn't feel like eating in a restaurant, but her momma was not having it any other way. After several minutes of disagreeing, they ended up at a restaurant. Dena and Shanae both ordered steaks and steamed vegetables.

Shanae wasn't feeling good because of all the bubbly the night before. Shanae was forking her vegetables, her mind drifting to Xavier. She could not believe how nice and polite he was. He even opened the car doors for her. She was ignoring her momma, and she hadn't even realized it.

Shanae had filled her momma in on the stunt that Keya had pulled at the party, and her momma was not happy about the ordeal.

"Shanae, I have never cared for Keya. But over the years you guys have continued to be friends. You guys were joined at the hips, never any problems. I thought I had misjudged her. But after this last fiasco she bears watching. Sounds like she is losing her mind or has lost it." Dena continued to talk, "With friends like that baby, you don't need enemies."

Dena knew something was wrong with Shanae. Dena had been talking a mile a minute, and Shanae hadn't said one word to her. Dena snapped her fingers in Shanae's face and said, "Earth to Shanae. Honey, I don't know where your mind is, but it sure as hell ain't with me. What is going on?"

Dena just prayed it had nothing to do with Hasaun's crazy ass.

Shanae played dumb.

"What are you talking about?"

Shanae was trying to avoid this topic with her momma. She already knew what she would say. "It is too soon for you to be courting. Are you ready baby?"

"Shanae don't play dumb with me. You know exactly what I am talking about. If you don't want to discuss it then say so. I just know that Keya's latest stunt doesn't have you so disoriented you can't think."

Shanae felt bad for shutting her momma out but at the same time she did not want to hear her momma's nagging. That's one of the reasons she avoided the conversation about Keya. She refused to waste any more energy on Keya. She for sure wasn't going to tell her about Hasaun.

Shanae took a deep breath and replied, "Momma, there is nothing going on."

Shanae couldn't hide her enthusiasm. She was excited about her upcoming date with Mr. Madison.

Dena observed the smirk on her daughter's face. With a smirk like that, Dena knew it involved a man. She hoped he would put some joy in her daughter's life. She also hoped he was a decent man. God knows Hasaun ended up being a royal pain. Dena felt Shanae needed a companion.

Shanae said, "I might as well come clean because you are not going to drop it."

Dena looked at Shanae and replied, "I am glad you know your Momma."

The ladies shared a laugh and Shanae was still beating around the bush. Then her momma blurted out, "Shanae who is he?"

Excited, Shanae replied, "Momma, I met him at school, but I decided to steer clear of him. But everywhere I went I was bumping into him. Momma he is so polite. I cannot think straight when I am around him."

Taking a breath Shanae continued, "Then I saw him at the party I went to with Keya. He kept me company all night and waited around to see if I found Keya or could get car service. Well, to make a long story short he was the one who gave me a ride home. Momma, he puts your man, Billy D to shame."

She left out the two episodes where Hasaun hassled her and, Xavier rescued her each time. She did not need her momma worrying.

"Does the mystery man have a name?" questioned her momma.

Shanae couldn't believe how calm her momma was.

This was not the reaction she was expecting from her momma. In fact, it was the total opposite.

"His name is Xavier Madison."

"Xavier?" Dena facial expression was priceless.

"Momma, you know better. You always said not judge a book by its cover."

"Baby, I am just saying Hasaun took you down through there. Now you got a Xavier. Can you find a Jack or Steve? You better watch out."

"He is different, Momma. So much different than Hasaun. He even opens doors for me."

Shanae sounded like she was reassuring herself more than her momma.

"Just kidding, baby. I have one question for you. If he is so handsome what the hell are you sitting here with me for?"

Shanae had thought about that all night. She had wanted to call her Momma and cancel.

"He asked me to lunch today, but I had plans with you. So we set a date for next week."

She wiped the crumbs from her mouth in hopes of hiding her smile.

Dena was happy for her. She had been waiting for Shanae to meet someone nice.

"I hope everything goes well and baby, if he looks better than my Billy D, you should have canceled your plans with ya momma," laughed Dena.

"Momma, thanks for being so supportive."

Gripping Shanae's hand, her momma replied, "I do not know why you didn't want to tell me. Let me tell you something, Shanae, don't live your life according to how people judge or support you. Live your life how you want to live it because in the end the same people who judge you don't give a hoot about you. If they did, they wouldn't be judging you. We know there is only one who can judge. So keep Him in your heart and you can't go wrong.

31

It seemed like Monday took forever to come. Who is happy to see Monday? Not many. Monday is the most dreaded day of the week. Now here it was. Shanae was counting down the minutes and couldn't wait. She'd done everything she needed to do. She was so impatient about her date that she could not enjoy spring break. She wanted to see Xavier badly. It was killing her. They were certain where and when to meet but they neglected to exchange phone numbers. How could they forget something so significant? They were both praying the other didn't cancel because then the other person would be sitting waiting with no clue. Worse of all, they would think they had been stood up.

Shanae was anxious. Today was the big day. She was having lunch with Xavier. She was trying to act calm, but she had tried on five outfits and still could not decide on which one to wear.

When she finally decided on what to wear, she put on her cream linen tube top jumper. She wore a chocolate leather belt around the waist and matching stilettoes. She grabbed her brown Jackie O bag and left her house.

Shanae had never been to the restaurant that Xavier selected. She hoped she could locate it without any problems. Within thirty minutes she pulled in front of a very elegant restaurant. The name Diovanni's was engraved on the wall outside the restaurant. The valet parked her truck and she proceeded to the entrance of the restaurant. Shanae was a little apprehensive about the date. She had never been on a date where she was not paying for it.

Xavier saw Shanae at the entrance before she saw him. Breathtaking came to his mind when he saw her. She was an intriguing woman. He was happy she agreed to have lunch with him. The maître d' escorted her to their secluded table towards the rear of the restaurant. The setting was romantic. The dimly lit lights, and the candles throughout the restaurant gave it an intimate feeling. Shanae was impressed with Xavier's selection.

Upon approaching the table, Xavier stood while she was seated. They both sat there for a few seconds one not knowing what to say to the other. They sat there looking in each other's eyes. Shanae could feel her guard letting down, but she thought it was too soon to be head over heels for him. She had just met him.

Breaking the silence Shanae said, "This place is impeccable."

Smiling Xavier replied, "I'm glad you're impressed. It's nice to see a smile on that beautiful face of yours."

"I know I was a mess the other night, once again, sorry. I really do have manners."

Shaking his head Xavier said, "Like I said, I hope I never get on your bad side."

"Xavier, I know every time you are in my presence there is drama. Let's put everything behind us and start fresh. I need to introduce you to the drama free Shanae."

Xavier enjoyed seeing Shanae so feisty. It actually turned him on. Hell, everything about her turned him on. He had never been a one-woman man, but she had him reevaluating his player status.

He still wanted to know what skeletons she had in her closet. He had picked up that she was really uptight about her past, and it weighed heavily on her heart. His goal was to show her that she could move forward and leave the past behind her. He wanted her to know she could count on him.

The waiter placed their butter and bread on the table and returned shortly with their spring salads.

Shanae was nervous for the first time. She hadn't eaten in front of a man in a long time. She remembered starving for weeks when she first dated Hasaun because she was too scared to eat in front of him.

"I hope you do not mind but I ordered the salads before

you came," explained Xavier.

"Not at all." *I like a man who takes charge. He's what I need right now.*

"It smells great in here," stated Shanae.

"Yes, this is one of my favorite restaurants. The atmosphere is great, but the food is even better."

"Do you come here often?"

"Whenever I find time in my busy schedule."

Shanae wanted to know how many women he had brought to this place. She decided to leave well enough alone. This was just their first date.

"Shanae, why did you play me?"

Caught off guard Shanae choked on her iced tea.

Concerned, Xavier asked, "Are you okay?"

"Yes. Yes, I am good."

Scrunching her face up, Shanae replied, "Why do you think I played you?"

"Shanae just stop. You knew I was interested in you and you never gave me the time of day."

Shanae knew he was telling the truth. She did not know what to say.

"Do you remember the drama at school and at the club? That is the mess I have been dealing with since high school. I just do not have time for drama anymore."

Shaking his head in agreement Xavier said, "I

understand. You had a bad experience but to put all men in the same category as that chump is not fair to us good men. All men are not like him."

Shanae could see the sincerity in his eyes. "I am not saying that all men are like him. Nor do I believe they are. I am just not willing to put myself through any unnecessary drama and men seem to bring me just that."

Xavier knew she had been hurt. Living with three older sisters, he felt her pain. That's why he had vowed to never hurt a lady. He would always feel bad for his sisters when they were crying and moping around the house, heartbroken over some man.

"Shanae, you are too smart to limit yourself."

"Xavier, who said I am limiting myself. I have considered my options. This is just our first date. It's not like we are talking marriage. Yes, I was rude to you but I didn't know you either. And I still do not know you. Do not ruin something that could have the potential of being good with your persistence."

Xavier was speechless. From the first time he laid eyes on her he knew, he just knew she would be his wife. He wondered how long it would take her to figure that out.

Xavier just nodded his head, "You're right."

Shanae and Xavier both enjoyed a rack of lamb garnished with vegetables. Over the meal, they had a very interesting conversation and Xavier's nose was wide open.

Shanae broke the silence, "Penny for your thoughts."

"You caught me," laughed Xavier.

"Caught you doing what?"

"I was just sitting here thinking how you have disrupted my plan of action. I am here trying to finish my degree. I had it all mapped out and then you walked into class, and I lost all composure and my mind. I know you keep telling me to chill, do not push. Girl, you do not know how hard that is. One thing is for certain, I know I want you in my life."

Shanae was blown away. She was attracted to him, and he made her feel safe. The only problem was the wall she had around her heart. It was going to be very hard to break.

"And how many times have you used that line?"

"Including saying it to you?"

"Yes, including me."

"I have only said it once."

Once again, Shanae was speechless, not knowing what to say or do. She just sat there trying to figure out this handsome man.

She was happy when the waitress brought the bill over. Xavier handed him what she thought to be a black American Express card. Shanae played it cool. Now she wanted to know what he did for a living.

Shanae and Xavier were not ready to depart ways. They decided to go to Les Bourgeois in Rocheport. The winery had a great view and some good wine. Once they were at the winery, Shanae and Xavier began to loosen up telling each other about their lives. Shanae found out that his parents were together and had been married forty years. She also found out that his parents were both attorneys and had a law firm in Chicago. He was born and raised in Chicago. Xavier was only in Columbia to finish graduate school. He was the youngest of four children. He had three older sisters all of whom had graduated from college. He came from a strong family. He had been in a little trouble when he was younger and took for granted the value of an education. Now he was on the right path and couldn't wait to finish school.

"Is there a special someone in Chicago?"

"You don't beat around the bush do you?"

"Why should I? I want to know."

"Well, since you insist, I guess I will just come clean. I am divorced and have four children. My ex-wife is no longer in the picture."

Shanae could not believe what he just said. What in the world could she do with a man with four kids? All she could think of was baby mama drama.

Clearing her throat, Shanae whispered, "Wow. How many baby mommas?"

Laughing, Xavier said, "Just kidding. I have never been married, and I have no children. And to answer your question, no there is not a special someone in Chicago. I never really had time to settle down with anyone."

"What about here in Columbia?" probed Shanae.

Xavier shook his head and said, "I have only been here for about nine months. I have not had a serious relationship."

Xavier wanted to be honest, and tell Shanae the truth.

"However, when I first came here I did hit the party scene, and took a few women out every now and then but nothing ever came of it. Since I have been here, I have only been with one woman, and she doesn't even know my name."

Taking a sip of her wine Shanae replied, "Interesting."

"What is so interesting?"

"That you bedded a woman, and she doesn't know your name," explained Shanae. "For that matter did you know her name?"

"Shanae, you are something else," joked Xavier.

"No, it sounds like you are something else. The dating game is new to me. I am just curious," replied Shanae.

"I do not mean to sound like a dog, but I wasn't looking for anything more."

Xavier wanted to change the subject. "Do you have any brothers or sisters?"

"Yes, I have a younger brother named Victor and a twin sister named Janae. Mom and dad divorced when I was seven. Dad took Janae with him. We have not seen them in years."

"What do you mean you haven't seen them?" questioned Xavier.

"When Dad left, Mom remarried, and Dad never looked back. To tell you the truth, I still do not understand it. I could have never left my children. I have—I mean had so much love for my children nothing could keep me from them."

"You have children?"

Xavier instantly noticed Shanae's sadness. The mention of her children made her eyes turn cold.

"I mean not that it matters. I was just curious."

"I had two children. They died last year. Sherrice was two, and Shay was stillborn."

Shanae tried to hold back her tears. But she couldn't. It felt good to talk to someone.

She told Xavier about Keya, Dena, Hasaun, Ma Rose, and Bernard. After listening to her trials and tribulations, he was in a state of disbelief. How could one person have so much turmoil in her life?

Shanae was drawn to tears. Xavier placed his arms around her fragile frame and held her. She felt safe. He reassured her that it was not her fault. As he wiped her tears away, she apologized for being a crybaby on their first date.

"Shanae, stop apologizing. You are only human and guess what? Humans cry. I can't begin to understand or feel your pain because you have been through more than I can even imagine. But I do know if you let me I will help you deal with your pain. I will. I think you are a remarkable woman. I do not know too many women who would be as strong as you. Stop beating yourself up, and stop pushing me away. I promise if you let me walk down this path with you, when you run into bumps and think you can't make it. I will be there to carry you along the way."

At a loss for words, Shanae placed her head on his bulging chest, and he held her tightly. She never wanted him to take his hands off her. It felt so right.

Xavier walked Shanae to her truck and made sure she was safe. He had insisted on her riding with him, but she wouldn't have any part of it because of the incident at the club with Keya. They said their goodbyes and Xavier headed towards his truck.

Before he could make it to his truck Shanae called his name. "Xavier?"

Music to his ears he turned around. "Yes?"

"What if we take it slowly? Do you think you can take it slowly?"

"Yes. I know I can," answered Xavier.

"Just friends right now?"

"Yes," replied Xavier.

Shanae grabbed his hand and said, "I am new at this. Thanks for being so understanding."

She walked closer to him and kissed him on the cheek.

Xavier was stuck on stupid. His words were gone. He could not say anything. Just from a kiss on the cheek. He could not believe she kissed him. He pulled her closer and kissed her on her forehead. She hated to be kissed on her forehead because Hasaun always kissed her on the forehead.

Xavier picked up on her uneasiness and asked, "Did I do something wrong?"

"Please don't kiss me on the forehead. Hasaun always kissed me on the forehead when he was up to no good."

"I am not Hasaun, and you will appreciate my kisses on the forehead because they will always be genuine. Do me a favor. Do not compare us. I am cut from a different cloth," stated Xavier.

"Well, I guess you told me," joked Shanae.

They both went their separate ways and were feeling good. Shanae hadn't been happy like this in a long time. She wanted to tell somebody. Keya was out of the question, so she decided to keep her happiness to herself.

32

Keya couldn't believe her eyes. She almost ran into the

car in front of her. She was hoping her eyes were deceiving her.

Keya pulled over and continued to watch Shanae, and this

familiar yet unfamiliar man from her car. Keya was straining her

eyes trying to figure out whom the man was that Shanae just

kissed. Shanae seemed comfortable with him. Keya wondered

just how long Shanae had been dating this mystery man. Keya

assumed Shanae wasn't ready to date at this point in her life.

After all, she claimed to be so stressed out. Well, if she was

dating that meant Hasaun was up for grabs. The smile that was

on Keya's face was huge. She couldn't wait to sink her claws

into Hasaun. What she planned to whip on him would have him

begging for mercy. Keya had wanted Hasaun long before Shanae

came into the picture. When her pretty ass showed up at

Hickman, Hasaun Ryder never looked another girl's way.

Keya decided to watch Shanae and this mystery man from

her car. Hell yeah, she was nosey, but she had nothing better to do. So, she decided to spend her time infringing on Shanae's privacy. For starters, she wanted to know who this man was. She knew he had to be fine because she always had the cream of the crop. Keya sat in her car for over twenty minutes meddling. She watched them talk, laugh, hug, and enjoy each other's company. Seeing Shanae so happy put a damper on Keya's spirit. When Shanae was sad and hurt Keya enjoyed life. Keya envied Shanae for always having everything at her disposal. Especially having men fall at her feet. She wished just once that she had a man who was truly interested in her. Keya was deep in thought when she noticed Shanae and the guy walking towards Shanae's truck. Keya noticed the man was fine, which was no surprise. As the distance between Keya and them shorten, Keya sat straight up and couldn't believe her eyes. The tension crept over her entire body.

Keya neglected all the errands she had planned for the day and returned home. The only thing Keya knew was that she despised Shanae. Keya was irate. She was walking around her little apartment talking to herself. She did not understand. She wanted to know how this could have happened. Keya went into her room and retrieved her photo albums and immediately started to cut Shanae out of the pictures. Keya had had enough with Shanae. As far as she was concerned Shanae was a callous bitch. After about thirty minutes of destroying years of memories, she walked into the kitchen, grabbed her bottle of bumpy face, a glass and began her voyage down memory lane.

Keya wanted revenge. She wanted to hurt Shanae badly. She wanted to come up with a plan that would devastate Shanae. Shanae was going to pay, and Keya was going to see to that. After hours of moping around and three-fourths of the bottle of bumpy face, Keya's head began to throb. Her voice was hoarse from yelling and crying. She prayed her neighbors were not at home because she had lost complete control. Keya was let down. She could not believe Shanae would deliberately hurt her. Keya felt as if her back was against the wall. She had no one to turn to. Her family didn't give a damn about her and now Shanae had turned her back on her. What was she going to do? Keya was tired of fighting for everything in her life. She felt like Ms. Sophia in The Color Purple. She had been fighting all her life. She grew up poor and decided she would never live like her family did. No one had broken the generational curse. Family member after family member lived on welfare and in the projects. Keya fought hard and graduated from high school. Then she went on and graduated from community college. Yes, compared to her family she had come a long way. But for what, she was still living from paycheck to paycheck. She despised her life.

The next morning Keya was jolted from her sleep. Whoever was pounding on her door was trying to take it off the hinges.

Every time they pounded on the door it felt like they were pounding on her head. When she stood to open the door she nearly fell back down. The gin from the previous night had taken a toll on her. She vaguely remembered yesterday. Then she started remembering bits and pieces of the events that took place yesterday. She knew whatever happened was bad because she was drunk. She had not been drunk in years. Alcohol was one of the main reasons her family was cursed. Over fifty percent of her relatives were alcoholics. The pounding on the door became louder and more erratic. She heard her neighbors tell whomever it was that she was inside. *Nosy bastards.* The door was less than five feet away, but it seemed like it was a country mile. She had no desire to open the door. However, she knew she had to open the door because with each knock her head did a somersault. When she finally yanked the door open, she could not believe who stood there. He never addressed her. He just barged into her apartment. Keya shut the door and leaned on it for support.

"Hasaun, what is your problem?" Keya inquired.

Just by looking at Keya, Hasaun knew she was not doing to good.

"I came to get some answers. What the fuck is going on with Shanae?"

The mention of her name did something to Keya. The memories from yesterday slowly began to seep back into her mind. Keya got a bad taste in her mouth, and instantly she began to cry. She lost her balance and fell to her knees. Hasaun was lost. He had no idea what was going on and he for damn sure didn't know what to do or say. He hoped she was okay.

"Damn Keya, did I say something wrong?"

Keya could not believe how emotional she was. Hasaun was standing in the middle of her living room looking dumbfounded. He finally walked over to her, stood her up and walked her to the sofa where he sat her down. He walked to her linen closet and grabbed a blanket. After covering her body with the blanket, he decided to make her a hot cup of tea. On his way into the kitchen, he noticed a pile of cut up pictures on the dining room table. He went through the stack and couldn't believe what he was seeing. Hasaun finished making the tea and cleaned up his mess. He took the used tea bags to the trash. He could not believe his eyes. Inside the trash, there were hundreds of pictures of Shanae smiling at him. He reached inside the trashcan and retrieved all the beautiful pictures of Shanae. Keya had cut her out of all the pictures. Hasaun figured whatever had transpired between the two of them was huge. He wanted to know what was going on. Keya was sitting up when he entered the living room. He handed her the cup of tea and took a seat in the chair opposite her. When he handed her the cup, his touch sent a chill down her spine. Her plan to hurt Shanae was simple. She figured she would get Hasaun in her bed. She would make sure that Shanae found out about it.

"Thanks Hasaun, I needed this," Keya said motioning to the cup of tea all the while imagining them in her bed making hot passionate love.

Hasaun didn't beat around the bush. "Keya, what is going on? I saw the photos. What's up?"

"I hate the bitch. She has no idea of what true friendship is!"

Upset, Hasaun replied, "Keya, don't call her out of her name because if she was here you wouldn't do it. What the hell happened between the two of you?"

Keya detected the defensiveness of Hasaun's tone. Laughing she replied, "You still love her don't you?"

He never answered her. He knew whatever had happened between them was serious, and Keya wasn't taking it well. From the looks of it, Keya was on the verge of a nervous breakdown. She looked like shit, and she smelled like a brewery.

Hasaun couldn't imagine what could be so bad that Keya was drinking. They were like the Three Stooges. Now the only person out of their crew that seemed to be happy was Shanae. Hasaun could hear his mother's voice plain as day. *Boy you better stop taking things for granted because when you least expect it; it will be gone.*

So many times he had taken Shanae's love for granted and once again his mother was right. Shanae's love was gone and the scary part about it was he never once saw it coming until it was too late.

Keya's loud voice startled Hasaun. "You still love her?"

Hasaun loved her so much and he was suffering without her. Shanae was the only thought that consumed his mind. Day in and day out he only thought about her.

Stammering he replied, "Keya, you know I still love her. She will always have my heart. It is not that easy to stop loving her. Man, the sad thing about it, is that I will always love her. If only I would have done right by her."

Keya could not believe the pitiful sight that sat in front of her. She wanted to slap the shit out of him when she saw the tears well up in his eyes. The sight made Keya sick to her stomach. She scooted to the bathroom to wash her face and brush her teeth. Once she cleaned herself up she returned to the living room. She decided to take advantage of the situation.

"Hasaun, did you know that Shanae has a new man?" nagged Keya.

Hasaun clenched his fist and the veins in his neck were protruding. He had seen Shanae with this man on several occasions. He prayed every night that she wasn't serious about the chump. He knew his prayers hadn't been answered when he saw them leaving the club together.

"Yeah. That's why I came over here. I want to know who the nigga is," replied Hasaun.

Keya could not believe her ears. He knew she had a new boyfriend, but he still loved her. *He is a sucka for Shanae.*

Shaking her head Keya said, "And how long have you known about this?"

"Shit, my first run in with ol' dude was at Shanae's school. I was mad at her. When I saw her on campus, I lost it on her. And this chump called himself checking me."

"Wait. Wait. Wait! What do you mean the first run in?"

"Man, it hurt like hell. I have seen them together on several occasions. I just always assumed it would be Shanae and me. I feel in my heart that it is over, but I just can't let go."

"Hasaun, sometimes you make me want to slap some sense into you. You have been wagging your tail behind her stuck up ass for years. I know you of all people know that once Ms. It sets her mind to something she never changes it. Come on now Hasaun."

Keya was in straight ghetto mode rolling her neck and smacking her lips.

"Whatever, Keya."

"Don't whatever Keya me. Where else have you seen them?"

Keya didn't want to hear the other bullshit Hasaun was talking about all she wanted was the scoop.

"Man, I saw them at the Tiger Hotel when they had that big party. Man, when I saw them, sitting at the table sipping expensive champagne. I wanted to choke the shit out of that nigga."

"Not true. We were together that night. She rode with me."

"I didn't see your ass. They sipped damn near three bottles and danced about six or seven tracks. You were nowhere to be found," replied Hasaun.

Keya could not believe the words that were coming out of Hasaun's mouth. Her plan had backed fired on her. Shanae did not freak out at the party? She found a man.

Hasaun interrupted Keya's thoughts. "They were at the party together and they got in a black SUV and left together. It was so unbelievable. Keya, Shanae has never been with anyone but me. What am I going to do?"

"Let's not forget her stepfather," proclaimed Keya.

"Damn, Keya. You know he raped her. What is the problem with you two?"

Keya sat there recalling the night she had purposely ditched Shanae in hopes of her having a horrible night. Keya knew she had not been around people in a long time and being in a crowd by herself was sure to send her over the edge. It did not work out how she planned.

She heard Hasaun say, "Keya I never seen you at the party. If she rode with you, where were you?"

Keya wanted to lie down and cry. She continued

ignoring Hasaun. She couldn't believe she missed all the excitement. Hasaun felt this trip was a waste of time. He knew more information than Keya. Keya wasn't paying attention to him, and she had no answers. He figured Keya was just being her normal jealous self. Hasaun always thought Keya had some type of animosity towards Shanae but after today he knew his assumptions were correct. Shanae would bend over backwards for anyone she loved. He also was tired of thinking about Shanae.

"Keya, who is the brutha?" Hasaun was becoming irritated by the one sided conversation.

"He is a guy I used to date." Keya was stretching the truth. He was actually a guy she took home from the club one night and had never seen again until she saw him with Shanae. She felt salty because she had no clue as to what his name was.

"What?" There was no way in hell that Shanae would go behind Keya. He knew she did not have to play second to Keya.

"Yeah, you heard me. She is messing with my man," cried Keya.

Shaking his head Hasaun said, "I just do not believe it. Shanae has never deliberately hurt anyone. Keya, this is so out of character for her."

"Ya ass is so stupid. She blinds you because you love her. She is a whore. When will you realize that?"

Hasaun was mad that she had a man in her life, but he also

knew how Shanae rolled and he knew Keya wasn't telling the entire story. He decided to pull her cards. "How long were the two of you dating? Keya, are you sure Shanae knew you two were an item."

Stunned by Hasaun's questions, Keya became antsy and couldn't get herself together. Keya stammered, "Y-yes she k-knew."

Hasaun knew she was lying. She couldn't get her words out, and she was nervous.

"Keya, how are you going to be mad at Shanae and let a man come in between you guys?" Looking Keya in the eyes and rubbing is goatee. "You know what I bet?"

Rolling her eyes, Keya replied, "No I don't, and I really don't care to hear."

Laughing, Hasaun said, "I bet Shanae has no idea that you are mad at her. I also think this nigga was just one of your many one night stands and has never looked your way since."

Hasaun was upset because Shanae didn't deserve to have people like him and Keya in her life. He knew he had fucked up and would never be able to be a part of her life. He was messed up about that but; he would not let anyone else deliberately bring Shanae harm.

"Who do you think you are talking too?" Keya was furious.

"What is his name, Keya? Do not forget I know how you roll."

With tears streaming down her face, Keya replied, "You bastard. Yeah, I know you know how I roll."

Keya thought back to the time she tried to have Hasaun sneak off with her, but of course he was not having it. He could not hurt his precious Shanae.

"You're right. I fucked him, and I do not know his name. Shanae has no idea we were together. Are you happy!"

"Keya, you're never going to change. I can't believe you are mad at Shanae over some nigga she has no idea you fucked. Keya, do you know how you have limited Shanae when it comes to men you have fucked. You're bound to bump heads. But do not act like she took him from you."

Laughing and standing to leave, Hasaun gave her a look of pity.

"Where are you going?" Keya didn't want him to leave. She needed the company.

Trying to hold his composure, Hasaun whispered, "What difference does it make? We can't do each other any good. We both are in our feelings."

Keya knew it made a difference to her. This was the man she wanted to spend the rest of her life with. "I was just wondering," replied Keya.

Hasaun felt bad for going off on Keya. He tried to lighten the mood. "Keya, I just have to go some place and clear my mind."

"Hasaun, I don't want to be alone. Can you at least finish your cup of tea?" pleaded Keya.

Nodding his head, Hasaun replied, "Keya, as soon as it is gone I am leaving."

"Thanks, Hasaun."

Keya and Hasaun sat opposite each other both in a world of their own. Keya could not believe how much Hasaun still loved Shanae. Sitting on the other side of the living room, Hasaun could not believe how Keya could treat such a sweet lady so mean. Hasaun knew if you never betrayed Shanae she would have your back no matter what.

Breaking the silence Keya said, "Hasaun, I do not know why I am so upset. For years, it has always been about Shanae. When I am not around her, I feel like nothing."

Confused Hasaun asked, "Keya, does Shanae make you feel like nothing? Does she humiliate you talk down to you or behind your back? Please let me know what it is that she does to make you feel like nothing."

Keya wiped the tears from her eyes and replied, "No, she is always so nice. Hasaun, the sad thing about the entire situation is that she thinks we are best friends, and I cannot stand her."

" Sounds to me like you are the one with the problems Keya," replied Hasaun.

Tears were streaming down Keya's face. Hasaun felt sorry for her. He walked over to the sofa and sat beside her. He hugged her because she needed it. They were only friends because of Shanae. Keya loved the way her body felt against his strong body. She hugged him back. Hasaun assured her everything would be all right and would eventually get better with time. He knew Keya and Shanae's relationship still stood a chance unlike his relationship with Shanae.

Hasaun took Keya by her shoulders and held her at arm's length looking her in the eyes. For the first time, he noticed that she had beautiful eyes and that she was beautiful. He could not understand why she was so jealous of Shanae.

"Keya, you have to let this go. Tell Shanae how you feel and why you feel like this. She will understand, and you will still have a best friend.

Shaking her head, Keya didn't want to deal with the situation. "I've called it quits. I have caused too much unnecessary pain. I do not have the time nor energy for this anymore."

Hasaun wanted to continue the disagreement, but he decided against it. He figured Shanae was better off without Keya in her life. He hugged Keya one last time and stood to leave. Keya wanted him so badly she could not think straight.

"Hasaun, do you have to go?"

Hasaun felt sorry for Keya, and he didn't know what to say.

"I am afraid so. But I will stop back by and check on you in a couple of days."

Keya was happy. She jumped up and gave him another hug. She intentionally pressed her breast against him and held him a little longer than usual. Hasaun was oblivious to the provocative behavior. He only had one person on his mind, and that was Shanae.

Keya walked over to the window and saw him get inside his car to leave the apartment complex. There was only one thing on her mind, and that was Hasaun. She would have him no matter what, and she would hurt Shanae in the process.

33

Shanae and Xavier spent the majority of their spring break with each other. They were constantly on the go. They went out to eat, to the movies and visited several local museums. They were inseparable. They enjoyed each other's company. Once they went back to school there was no denying their relationship. They sat next to each other in the classes they shared. In order to spend time with each other, they had study sessions after classes. Shanae was growing attached to Xavier. The bond they had was starting to alarm her. She hadn't been attached to a person in a long time. She was so confused because she knew how complicated relationships could be. For the weeks, they had been an item she prayed daily for strength. Every day she had to push the thought out of her mind that Xavier would hurt her. His actions showed otherwise. He was so nice and polite. He was a dream come true. Besides all that, he was a gentleman. He never pressured her into having sex with him, which was a plus because she had serious issues when it came to being intimate. She felt her life was taking a turn for the better. She was content with the outcome of her life after all she had been through. Her school was going great and she was happy.

Shanae had stayed up too late last night. She was cranky and didn't feel like being bothered with classes today. She needed some rest, so she decided to cut the remainder of her classes. While the professor explained criminal procedures, she doodled on her paper. She laughed when she noticed what she had written. She was acting like a teenage girl. She had written Xavier plus Shanae equals love forever.

When class was finally over, she walked outside to her truck instead of her next class. Shanae felt as if she was going to pass out; she was exhausted. She decided she would call Xavier later to let him know she would not be in class. She wanted him to take good notes for her.

Shanae was in her own world walking to her vehicle. She hadn't noticed Xavier sneaking up behind her. He grabbed her by the waist and picked her up. Without looking, she knew those big powerful arms from anywhere. He turned her around, and she kissed him passionately.

"I was just going to call you," smiled Shanae.

With a puzzled look on his face Xavier replied, "It looks like you're walking in the wrong direction."

"That's what I was going to call you about. I am tired.

So, I am not going to the rest of my classes. I wanted to know if you would take notes for me."

"Well, darn, I was hoping you would ask me to skip with you," joked Xavier.

Laughing, Shanae said, "One of us has to be on point. So will you please take notes for me?"

"Sure, I'll take notes for you," Smiling he continued, "Gives me a reason to stop by tonight."

Smiling Shanae said, "Thanks. But that's why I have been so tired, Xavier."

Defeated Xavier said, "Does that mean I can't come over tonight?"

Shaking her head, Shanae replied, "Have I ever told you no?"

Xavier and Shanae walked their separate ways. Shanae was going to take a nice bubble bath and just relax. When she entered her home, she went to her room and crashed. She woke up to the phone ringing. Shanae reached for the cordless phone. Half asleep she dropped the phone. Once she picked it up she put it to her ear and said,

"Hello."

"Bitch, you need to realize that you are not invincible. You treat people like shit. When I catch you, I am going to break your neck."

He was in mid-sentence when he heard the phone click in

his ear. She looked at the phone and wondered what deranged person was playing on her phone. She sat there in disbelief. There could only be one person who would be playing on her phone. *He had his damn nerve. All this was his fault. He was the one who killed our unborn child and was MIA for days. He started all this bullshit.* Shanae decided she would teach him a lesson for playing on her phone.

Before she did something stupid, Shanae had to calm down. She wanted to seriously hurt Hasaun but knew she needed to stay focused. He was her past, and she needed to leave him in the past. It was so funny how her past kept popping up in her life. Shanae knew Hasaun did not know where she lived, but she double checked all her locks and walked to her master bath. She needed a bubble bath. The only thoughts that consumed her were killing Hasaun or hiring someone to kill him. She laughed. *How am I going to have someone killed? God, please forgive me. Regardless of the situation I cannot cross those lines.*

After her bath, she dressed and headed out. She had some business she needed to take care of. Shanae headed to the Columbia Police Department. She talked to Sergeant Scott. Shanae told the officer all the details and episodes that had taken place regarding Hasaun. She told him about the school incident, the Tiger Hotel incident and the nonstop phone calls. She wanted to press charges on him for harassing her.

Sergeant Scott suggested she get a protective order against him. She had the orders delivered to Francis' house. Shanae knew once Francis saw these orders she would put Hasaun in his place. At least that was what she was praying for.

She wanted to let her family know what was going on, so she called both Victor and her momma. She knew they would worry and want her to stay with her momma, but she refused to do such a thing. She was a grown woman and she could handle her own. Like she said, her momma was upset, Victor was on his way from Chicago. Shanae explained to the both of them that she had taken the needed precautions and the police were aware of the situation. She assured them that she was only a phone call away and she would stop by to see her momma tomorrow. Dena was not satisfied. She wanted Shanae to get her number changed. After Shanae agreed, they let her off the phone.

The minute she made it home, Shanae sank into her sofa, kicked her shoes off and just sat there. She did as her mother told her and changed her numbers, both her home and mobile numbers. She called her momma and brother and gave them her new numbers. She also called Xavier and gave him her new numbers.

Shanae had cleaned and prepared a candlelight dinner for Xavier and her. Shanae had set a romantic atmosphere in the house. She had candles and soft music playing in the background. Shanae wanted to thank Xavier for taking notes for her. Shanae enjoyed Xavier's company. He was someone she could relate to.

Shanae was walking to the door to let Xavier in. He hugged her and set his keys on the credenza in the foyer.

Sniffing the air Xavier said, "What is that I smell?"

Smiling Shanae replied, "Dinner, if you can stay."

"Only a crazy man would turn down a meal," joked Xavier.

"I am almost finished. You can go clean up and then we can eat," said Shanae.

"Sounds like a plan," replied Xavier.

While preparing himself for dinner, he thanked God. He thanked Him for letting Shanae cross his path. He hoped this relationship worked out. He was falling for her and falling fast. Xavier and Shanae had so much in common. Over dinner, they had a great conversation.

"Xavier, did you take good notes?" asked Shanae.

"I think I did. But you may not be able to read them," replied Xavier.

"You need to work on your penmanship," joked Shanae.

"So I have been told," laughed Xavier.

He stood and put his plate in the dishwasher. He helped Shanae clear the table and put the food away. After the kitchen was in order, they proceeded to the deck where they were going to play a game of dominoes. While playing dominoes, they shared a bottle of wine. She was so glad he did not ask her about why she changed her numbers. They had a great evening and finally called it a night around eleven in the evening.

34

Hasaun couldn't believe what he had just done. His intentions were to call Shanae and apologize for being stupid, and he also wanted to give her the heads up about Keya. But no, he flipped the script when he heard her voice. He was realizing he had lost his rabbit-ass mind when he walked into his mother's the next day and saw her sitting at the table looking at some documents crying.

Immediately, Hasaun ran to her.

"What's up, Momma? Why are you crying?"

She never answered him. Instead, she gave him a look that sent chills down his spine.

"Hasaun, why can't you leave her alone? Shanae has been nothing but good to you. You dogged her, and she stayed. You dogged her some more, and she stayed. You mistreated her, and she stayed. You hurt your unborn child, and she lied and forgave you."

Hasaun couldn't believe what his mother just said. How

did she know?

Clearing her throat Francis continued, "Hasaun, for Pete's sake, you killed y'all unborn child. Yeah, you can look silly all you want. I know you put your hands on her. That child was your blood, Hasaun."

"Momma, why you keep listening to Shanae? She is full of it," said Hasaun trying to lie his way out of it.

"Hasaun, just give it up. I know. I just know. Just like I know that you Ryder men cannot handle a strong woman. But guess what? After all you put her through she still covered for your sorry ass."

Waving the papers she was reading she yelled, "What I do know, if you take your ass near her again you going to jail."

With that said, his momma launched the packet of stapled papers at him. Hasaun caught the packet and at the top he saw Order of Protection against Hasaun Ryder. The plaintiff was Shanae Davis. He could not believe his eyes. Shanae was scared for her life. She depicted him as a violent person who would inflict harm on another person.

Crying his mother continued, "Don't just sit there and act like you are so surprised, Hasaun. Stay away from her. If you do something to her, I will not have your back. I raised you better than this. You have potential. Please tap into it."

Hasaun was upset. He walked over to the phone and picked up the receiver. Before he had a chance to push a button his mother said,

"Ya black ass hasn't learned yet. Besides she has changed all her numbers. So don't attempt to call her. Not even on her cell."

Hasaun sat at the dining room table and cried. Francis knew her son was hurting because he never cried in front of her. She refused to comfort him because he had been the one to cause his own drama. He had dug his own grave. Now it was up to him to get out of it or lie in it and die.

Hasaun wiped the tears away. He was at a loss for words. He could not understand how his life had spiraled out of control. He knew he had to get out of Columbia. There was nothing here for him anymore. He knew if he stayed around he was going to be in serious trouble.

"Momma, I need some help. I have to get away from here. I want to move. Please help me," pleaded Hasaun."

Her heart went out to him.

"What can I do? Where do you plan on going?" questioned Francis.

Hasaun couldn't believe how his mother was treating him. He hadn't thought about where he would go. He just knew he had to get out of Columbia. He had two options, Dallas, Texas, or Kansas City, Missouri. He had family in both places. He also wanted to be close to his momma. He wanted a new beginning. He knew he would have to go back to school; he had a year left. He just sat there not knowing what to do. He was in a trance thinking about the events from the last year and a half. He had no clue as to what he would do. He sat quietly.

"A penny for your thoughts."

"Momma, I could go to Dallas with Aunt Faye and go back to school. Momma, I just need to leave."

Francis knew her baby was hurting. She could see the pain and anguish in his eyes. It hurt her to see him like this. She would do all she could do to help him. She prayed he did not let her down.

"Give me one good reason why I should help you."

Hasaun could not believe his ears. He just did not understand his momma anymore. She was being short and to the point with him. He wanted to scream and yell at her. Screaming and yelling had only gotten a protective order placed against him.

"Because I need your help, Momma," pleaded Hasaun.

"Ump," replied Francis. She stood, grabbed the phone off the table and walked into the living room.

Hasaun had no idea what was wrong with his momma. He sat at the table in heavy thought. He had to get away from here. He could hear his momma on the phone with Aunt Faye discussing his situation. They were talking about him as if he weren't in the next room. He heard his momma telling Aunt Faye he was gone. Nose was wide open. He prayed they would help him. If they didn't, he had no one else to turn to.

After about twenty minutes, his momma returned to the kitchen.

"Hasaun, you have a few months to stay out of trouble. You get everything together, and I will put you on a flight to Dallas. Boy, you need to enroll in school before you leave take care of your business."

"Thanks, Momma," Hasaun grabbed his mom and held her tightly.

Breaking away from his embrace, his momma said, "Don't be thanking me. You need to thank Aunt Faye. You get a job and get in school. Do not be freeloading off her. I am going to send you with some money, but I ain't rich."

She just kept running her mouth nonstop. He knew what he needed to do. He knew it was going to be hard for him to leave Shanae alone, so there was only one option he had and that was to leave.

Hasaun drove to Office Depot and bought him some boxes so he could pack his belongings and mail them to his Aunt Faye's before he left. He had a list a mile long of stuff he had to do.

Once he returned, so many memories of Sherrice and Shanae ran through his mind. He was so miserable. He needed to put the past behind him. Hasaun began to place items in the boxes while tears were streaming down his face. With every item, he packed away it seemed like pieces of him was being packed away.

Hasaun had refused to go to counseling and not deal with all the issues he had. He was between a rock and a hard place. He hoped his move to Texas would get him back on track. He knew Shanae would never take him back but if they could just be friends. That's all he wanted to be was her friend.

35

It had been a few months since Xavier and Shanae had been dating. She knew that the two ladies who were waiting on her were not that happy with her. Ever since she had been dating him, she had seen them less and less. She needed to think about something other than Xavier. He would be going out of town in a few weeks; she hated to see him go. She decided it was time for them to be intimate. He had been patient with her, and she was ready. This was a big step for her. She trusted him and loved him more than she would ever let him know. Shanae could not wait for the special night. She could not believe that he had never once pressured her into having sex with him.

Right now, she was meeting Ma Rose and her momma at Tony's Pizza for lunch. She needed to think about something else because if those two caught on to what she was about to do they would never let her live it down. She prayed she would get herself together.

She was running late when she pulled in front of the

restaurant seeing both their cars in front. She put money in the meter and hurried inside.

"Hey, ladies. How are you?"

"Don't hey ladies us. Where have you been? You are late," declared Ma Rose.

"I was getting myself together. I was hoping you guys were not on time," explained Shanae.

Dena and Ma Rose had both plotted on giving Shanae a hard time. They were kicking each other under the table.

"You need to be on time and not hoping," replied her momma.

Shanae could not believe these two divas. She was only a few minutes late. Shanae sat down with her mouth wide open looking at the ladies.

"Damn, y'all I am sorry. Didn't think you ladies would be so upset." Shanae felt terrible for having them wait.

"You ain't that grown where you can be damning us. You better show some respect." Ma Rose glared at Shanae.

"If we were Xavier you would not have been late," joked her momma.

It was hard for Shanae to contain her smile. She wanted to walk back out the door and go home because her company was badgering her.

"Yeah, I done heard about him but ain't ever been formally introduced. What we ain't good enough for him to meet us?"

"Ma Rose, he is cool. It's not like that. It's just that—"

Before Shanae could continue both her momma and Ma Rose replied, "We know you have been busy."

"Close your mouth. You know you have been playing us," said her momma.

"I did not come here for the third degree."

With that said, Shanae waved the waitress over and order their food. She knew what they all ate and drank so she ordered the food and ignored the bickering old ladies. She knew they had the right to be upset at her. She had been playing them for seven months, and their lunch dates had become obsolete. She would make it up to them.

"Dena, this little heifer done got too grown; cutting us off and ignoring us," stated Ma Rose.

"Ma Rose, you know what that must mean," cackled her momma.

Both ladies shared a laugh at Shanae's expense. Shanae could not believe her ears, so she decided to jump in the conversation.

"Listen, I know I have been playing you both but with school, homework and my new man, yes, I have been busy. That does not change anything. I still have much love for the two of you. But y'all are starting to hurt my feelings," pouted Shanae.

When they saw how serious Shanae was they both burst out laughing.

"We were just playing with you, baby. Just wanted to ruffle your feathers," explained Dena.

"Well, I think y'all are plucking them now," joked Shanae.

"Well, how is your relationship going?" questioned her momma.

"You all are so nosy," Shanae could not contain her smile.

"Well, judging by that smile I think we already know," chimed Ma Rose.

Shanae knew she was in trouble today. Her dear friend and momma were on a warpath. They wanted answers, and there was no shame in their game.

Shanae dropped her head and replied, "It is good."

Dena and Ma Rose looked at each other and back to Shanae, and they both replied, "Good!"

Shanae laughed at the nosy duo and took a sip from her cup. She continued ignoring them. If looks could kill, she would be dead.

"Just cause you live out in that fancy house, go to that big university and drive that high priced truck that depreciated as soon as you drove it off the lot you ain't too big to get a whooping," replied Ma Rose.

"Okay ladies! He is the perfect man. I am experiencing emotions I have never experienced."

"I bet you are," joked her momma.

"No, Momma, not like that. He is just so nice and sincere.

315

Oh and he is respectful. He even pulls my chair out at restaurants and he opens the car door for me. He listens to me. We have so much in common."

Shanae had a dreamy look in her eyes.

"Baby, you got it bad. I think you in love," said Ma Rose.

"Love? It has only been a few months. I do not know if it is love. I do like him. I like him a lot."

Shanae was trying to convince herself she was not in love.

"Shanae, I think you are in love. Time does not decide if you are in love or not. I fell for your dad in weeks." Dena could not believe she said that.

"Really. Do tell."

Shanae wanted to know how they fell in love.

With a sad look in her eyes her momma replied, "Another time, baby."

The waitress placed their food on the table. Shanae ordered a gyro with fries and a Greek salad. Her momma and Ma Rose shared a medium sausage pizza. Tony's was the best pizza place in town. She was raised on it.

They talked about Victor. His business was going great, and so was his relationship with Jade. They briefly discussed Hasaun and his psychotic behavior. She told Ma Rose about his crazy outburst and that she had to put an order of protection against him. Shanae enjoyed a laugh when Ma Rose told her she had his order of protection. Shanae knew she was not kidding though.

They discussed Keya. Shanae knew the conversation was going to be biased because neither of the ladies cared for Keya. She told them she hadn't heard from her in awhile, and she kept it moving.

After lunch and great conversation they all headed their separate ways. While heading home, Shanae realized that she missed Keya. She decided to give her a call. Keya's phone rang and rang. Shanae left a message.

"Hey lady just wanted to talk to you. Call me maybe we can do lunch someday. Bye."

Shanae made a mental note to call her later.

36

Never in her life had she been so happy. Xavier was the perfect gentleman. She felt as if she died and gone to heaven. For once in her life everything was positive. She had started praying and spending hours talking to God and everything was falling into place. She was giving God all the glory. Without Him, she did not know where she would be.

Shanae was returning from the gym when her cellular rang. Of course, it was her mother. She invited her and Xavier to dinner tonight at her house. Her momma felt it was time she met the man who was taking so much of her daughter's precious time lately. Shanae hope Xavier would be able to make it on such a short notice. She didn't make any promises.

Xavier had been feeling uneasy ever since he received the call from Ja. She wanted to rekindle their never existing flame. Xavier could not believe she had the audacity to call him. It had been months since he spoke to her, let alone seen her. He had been avoiding her calls, and he hadn't written her in eons. He figured after all those months she would have chalked it as a loss. He didn't want to risk losing Shanae because of her ignorant ass. He had made plans to go to Chicago and end whatever it was she thought they still had once and for all. She was a sweet girl, but her elevator didn't go all the way to the top. He had finally found his soul mate and he for damn sure wasn't going to lose her.

His plan was to leave tomorrow and be back for class on Monday. He didn't want to be away from Shanae over the weekend, but he knew he had to handle the situation. He would most definitely make the lost time up to her.

He was home packing for his weekend trip. He felt bad for leaving. While packing, he thought about how happy he was with Shanae. He promised himself he would never do anything to hurt her or break her trust in him. While thinking about Shanae, he decided to give her a call and break the news to her.

On the third ring, Shanae answered the phone, "Hello." Her voice was music to his ears.

"How you doing, sexy?" asked Xavier.

"Better since you called, handsome," stated Shanae.

Shanae and Xavier were so into each other it was pathetic.

"I was just calling to let you know I have some unexpected business I need to take care of. Unfortunately, I have to go out of town to handle it this weekend."

As soon as the lie rolled off his tongue, he felt bad. Here he was lying to the person he wanted to spend the rest of his life with. He vowed to never have a relationship based on lies. After the lie, he tried to justify it because he *was* handling some unexpected business. He knew he would never lie to her again because it didn't sit well with him.

"Wow. The entire weekend?"

She had grown accustomed to having him around. His going away for the weekend was going to be hard. At that moment, she knew what she never thought would ever happen again had happened. Shanae Davis was in love.

Xavier had thought the same exact thing.

"It won't be that bad. I will call you every day and give you all my contact numbers. Before you know it, I will be back home," promised Xavier.

"I only have one request."

Smiling Xavier replied, "Your request is my command."

Xavier admired how flexible Shanae was. She never complained and she always went with the flow.

"My mother wants to meet the guy who has swept her daughter off her feet; tonight over dinner at her house. What do you say?"

Shanae slid it in fast hoping he didn't feel put on the spot.

Taken by surprised Xavier replied, "I would love to meet the woman who created such a beautiful young lady."

Smiling, Shanae replied, "Pick me up from my house at six-thirty tonight."

Dinner went great. Dena and Xavier hit it off right from the gate. She gave Shanae the thumbs up when Xavier was leaving. He had been the perfect gentleman. He charmed Dena and Shanae was relieved they got along. Although she was happy about this meeting, she prayed that it went as smoothly when Victor met him. She knew it would be harder, but she decided to cross that bridge when she came to it. Right now, the only thing on her mind was getting home and pleasing her man.

37

When they arrived at Shanae's, Xavier pulled into her driveway, put the truck in park, got out and opened her door. When she stood outside of the car, he hugged her. The hug turned into a kissing frenzy. Shanae handed Xavier her keys and made up some excuse about running to the store to get something she forgot earlier. While Xavier went in the front door, Shanae snuck in the side door and hid in the dining room.

When Xavier entered the house, he was stunned. Candles illuminated the entire house. As soon as he walked in he found a note that read, "Follow the rose petals."

Xavier enjoyed the fragrance coming from the note. It smelled exactly like Shanae. Xavier was aroused. He immediately kicked off his shoes and did as he was told. The smooth voice of Gerald Levert was playing in the background. After following the trail of rose petals, Xavier ended in the dining area. There he received another note that instructed him to sit down. Once he was sitting down, Shanae came from behind him and blindfolded him. After blindfolding him, she gently kissed his face and sucked on his ear. Shanae told him to calm down and began feeding him chocolate covered strawberries. Shanae placed a strawberry in her mouth and fed him. Xavier was devouring the strawberries so he could taste her sweet tongue. After every strawberry was consumed their tongues danced in and out of each other's warm mouths. Xavier was on the verge of losing his mind. Shanae warned him he wasn't allowed to touch her and if he did the game was over. After being told he could not caress her, he wanted to caress her all the more. After feeding him, she escorted him to the master bath. While walking up the stairs, he was allowed to touch her. He had discovered from touching her that she had on a one-piece thong teddy that left nothing to the imagination. Xavier just knew he was going to explode. He had been waiting for this day a long, long time. Never in a million years did he imagine it to be so sensual. He had no idea what Shanae was doing to him, but he was following her every command and it scared him. She had so much control over him and he was like a sick puppy drooling. Shanae undressed him and beckoned him into the oversized jetted-tub. After washing every inch of his body, they walked to her room. Xavier couldn't handle it any longer.

"Shanae, please let me take this damn blindfold off,"

begged Xavier.

Shanae enjoyed having him so gone. It actually turned her on. He was lying in the middle of her bed on top of hundreds of fresh rose petals. Shanae finally gave him permission to take the blindfold off. He looked like a kid on Christmas ripping open presents when he ripped the blindfold off.

When he saw her standing there, it was unbelievable. Her body was perfect, and he planned to touch every inch of her. Xavier was looking at her smiling, imagining all the positions they would be in tonight. He couldn't believe she was going to let him make love to her.

Shanae sauntered over to the bed. With each step, Xavier became harder and harder. Shanae couldn't believe how hung he was; she couldn't help but think that Hasaun was most definitely a snack compared to Mr. Madison. She gently ran her tongue over the head of Xavier's piece. She slowly began to add more and more into her mouth. Shanae relaxed her throat muscles and went to work. She found her rhythm, and it made Xavier's toes curl. Her mouth was warm and wet. She was constricting her jaw muscles. Xavier could not take it. He was gripping the satin sheets, and he felt as if he was drifting away.

She continued to toy with him. She licked his penis and fondled his balls. He jerked at first because of the pressure she was applying to his balls. After the initial pressure it became pure delight. He finally obliged and had never felt so good before. She knew he was enjoying it because he was moaning. It even sounded like he was whimpering. Shanae was ready to ride him and take him to another level. She slowly made her way up his body and straddled her man. Before she had a chance to ride the black stallion, he rolled her over and worked her over with his tongue.

She was the one who was at a loss for words now. The only sounds escaping from her were moans and whimpering. It felt so good. He knew exactly what he was doing. She came twice as he lapped up her juices. She was on the verge of her third orgasm, and Xavier stopped.

He grabbed her and moaned, "I love you so much, Shanae! I swear I love you."

With her eyes half shut she moaned, "Same here."

Once again, Shanae straddled him and this time she inserted his ten plus inches into her warm walls without using her hands. Xavier knew he was dealing with a skilled woman when it came to love making. She had taken him to places he never imagined, and when she slid his manhood into her warm place without using her hands, man oh man. They had a rhythm that was taking both of them to ecstasy. Xavier met Shanae's every thrust. They maneuvered all over the California king. While they were trying all kinds of positions, Shanae thought their lovemaking reminded her of the song by Digital Underground, Freaks of the Industry. "My leg over his back..."

They most certainly worked magic that night in the bedroom. They were so perfect together. In unison, they climaxed.

Xavier knew the first time he saw Shanae she was a special lady. Never in a million years did he think any female would have him sprung. Xavier wanted to be with Shanae the rest of his life.

Out of breath, Shanae moaned, "That was great, Mr. Madison."

38

While driving to Chicago, Xavier knew exactly what he wanted out of his life, and it consisted of being with Shanae for eternity. He planned to put Ja in her place and head back to Columbia by Saturday. He knew coming back early would make Shanae happy.

Xavier checked into the Hilton and unpacked his bags. He took a shower and went downstairs to the bar. After having a few drinks, he looked at his watch. It was one o'clock in the afternoon and Ja was thirty minutes late. He wanted to confront her in a public environment so she wouldn't flip the script on him.

He really didn't have the patience for Ja. He figured there was no way in hell she could possibly think they were a couple. There was only one reason he was even entertaining this meeting. He wanted Ja to know once and for all it was a wrap. He had been praying that she would handle the information with ease and not clown. He couldn't understand why he cared about her feelings. He just knew she could act really insane at times, and he didn't want her harassing him and Shanae.

Ja and Xavier never dated. They used to be really good friends when he worked at her father's firm. However, one night they crossed the boundaries that friends should never cross. He was assisting her father on a very important case and was working late. She showed up at the office with a bottle of the best bubbly and one thing lead to another. As soon as the episode was over, they both knew they had made a huge mistake.

Instead of learning from that mistake, they continued their late night office affair and occasionally went to lunch and dinner. Their friendship had never been the same since. After it was over Xavier continued on as if nothing had happened between them. Ja, on the other hand, took the booty calls as love at first sight and claimed to be madly in love. Xavier didn't have a single ounce of love for her other than friendly love. He knew the situation today could take a turn for the worse. Ja was a fragile lady. Fragile was putting it mildly.

He purposely sat at a table in the mix of everyone by the bar. He knew Ja cared a lot about her reputation so he figured she wouldn't show her ass.

Xavier was nursing his third glass of Hennessey when he saw her approaching his table. Xavier prayed she would keep it together, but something told him she was there for one reason, and that was to claim him as her man.

As soon as she spotted him her face lit up. She had been heartbroken because she hadn't heard from him. It was like he fell off the face of the planet. She was pleased he decided to drop everything and spend the weekend with her. She walked over to the table and sat down. It felt so good seeing him. She made a mental note that he did not stand when she approached the table and for that matter he did not pull her chair out. He always did that. She assumed he was tired from the drive.

"Well hello, stranger. I was becoming a little worried. How are you?"

Ja was giddy and sitting high on her horse. Ja wanted to know what was keeping him so busy, where he couldn't call his woman. But she decided to hold her tongue and see where his mind was at first.

Agitated Xavier replied, "I have been really busy with school. Man, how long has it been since we last talked or saw each other?"

He was trying to make it as easy as possible without leading her on.

Ja didn't particularly care for the tone of Xavier's voice. She had been down this road on numerous occasions. From his tone, she knew he was calling it off. She had already told herself if he left her, he would never be happy. There was no way in hell she was letting him walk out her life.

"I know it's been a while since we spent time with each other. But what does that have to do with anything?"

Ja was reciting a silent prayer, hoping he wouldn't leave her. She didn't know what to do if he did. Xavier decided to end the charade before the crowd began to disperse.

Clearing his throat, Xavier replied, "Ja, a lot has happened since I moved from Chicago. We have not seen each other in forever. Ja, I really do not know how to put this, but whatever you thought we had going—I just don't know what to say."

Xavier paused and was met by silence. He rubbed his head and prayed that she would say something, but his prayers were not answered. She sat there staring a hole in him. Just looking through him. She never said a word.

Xavier continued, "Ja, I never meant to hurt you or lead you on. I just can't believe after all this time, with no communication, you would still think there is something between us. I just don't get it."

Xavier waited for Ms. Psycho to respond, but he was met by more silence. So he continued, "I am sorry if I led you on. I had no intentions of stringing you along or hurting you. I hope we can still be friends?" It was more of a question than a statement.

She could not believe this smug bastard. She had been warned about him, but she still fell victim to his lies and deceit.

She sat there in awe. Oh, how many times she had been down this road. She never was the wifely type, just the friendly type. If he wanted to just be friends, why did he ever cross that line with her?

Words finally came to her.

"You bastard! How could you? Who is she?"

Xavier could not believe his ears. He knew she was a little off her rocker but why did she have the nerve to question him. It had been almost a damn year since they had a conversation. Xavier wanted to slap himself for trying to let Ms. Psycho down the easy way. He could be at home with his soul mate.

"Listen woman, there is no need to raise your voice. Like I said, I never meant to cause you any grief, and I am sick of apologizing for no reason."

"Xavier, you have no right to order me around and tell me when and where I can raise my voice."

"I don't understand why you are so upset. You know we were nothing more than booty calls for each other," stated Xavier.

Ms. Psycho gasped, put her hands on her chest and replied, "Booty call? Nigga, you got me messed up. Never have I ever been a booty call."

"Call it what you want. The fact of the matter is that I am here to let you know that there is nothing between us. There never has been." Xavier, sighed a sigh of relief.

"Oh, really, Xavier. Why? Because you say so! You don't control my feelings. I know that I am in love with you."

"Look, the only reason I came to Chicago was to tell you I am in love. I finally found my soul mate. After all the recent calls I started receiving from you, I knew you thought we had something going on, so I wanted to clear the air and set the record straight."

The pain and distress etched across Ms. Psycho's face was obvious. Xavier never imagined he would bring her so much pain. On the other hand, she had to be dense if she thought they were dating.

Xavier broke the silence, "Ja, are you okay?'

Shaking her head and holding back tears, Ms. Psycho replied, "As okay as I can be. Rejection is nothing new to me. Never in a million years would I have ever thought you would hurt me. I guess you live and you learn!"

Ms. Psycho stood, tossed her expensive cognac in his face and left the bar.

Xavier had never been so happy and relieved in his life. He wiped the liquid from his face and smiled. Everyone in the bar was looking in his direction. With a nod of his head, he assured them all was well. He pulled out his phone and called his baby.

"Hey, baby! What took you so long to call?"

Xavier was thrilled to hear her voice. He was happy she had walked into his life.

"I called to let you know that all is well and running smoothly, and I am getting back on the highway tonight," explained Xavier.

"You handled all your business?" questioned Shanae.

"Yeah."

Xavier could not wait to get back on the highway. His family would kill him if they knew he was in town and had no plans of visiting them.

Concerned, Shanae replied, "As much as I miss you, I don't think it's a good idea. I think you should get some rest and head back in the morning."

"But baby, I am cool, I will be back in no time. Must not miss me?" pleaded Xavier.

Smiling, Shanae replied. "We stayed up late last night and you left at the crack of dawn this morning. Please rest and then come home. I want you in one piece."

Xavier was blessed Shanae was a part of his life. She was sweet and understanding. He admired that about her. She never gave him the third degree or second-guessed him like the other women he had dated.

"Then I guess I will see you in the morning. Please have breakfast ready," laughed Xavier.

"And I love you too," laughed Shanae.

"Shanae, I love you."

Xavier was in a trance. He walked to the bar, settled his bill and walked to his room with nothing but thoughts of Shanae.

Xavier hadn't noticed Ms. Psycho outside the bar. She was watching his every move. She noticed how happy he was while on the phone. She assumed he was on the phone with his "soul mate." Ms. Psycho was hell bent on revenge.

39

Shanae received a call at two o'clock in the morning from Xavier. His truck had been vandalized, and he wasn't going to make it home until later that afternoon. Shanae was let down, but she knew he would make it up to her once he returned.

Xavier was furious. He knew Ja's name was written all over the truck incident. Four tires and a windshield were not cheap for a Lincoln Navigator.

After the call, Shanae could not sleep. She decided to go jogging. At close to five miles, she decided to call it quits. After cleaning her house and getting dressed, it was a little after eleven in the morning. Shanae decided to call Keya. She hadn't heard from her in a long time. She decided it was time to put the club episode behind them. Besides, if she hadn't left her she would not be in love.

Keya ran to her phone and was shocked by the name that was displayed across her handset. She had no intention on answering it. But she knew that Shanae would stop over if she didn't pick up.

"Hello," uttered Keya.

Shanae instantly detected an attitude from Keya.

"What's up, Key?"

The sound of her voice made Keya nauseous.

"And to what do I owe this pleasure?"

"Keya, stop acting so shitty. We are girls. I haven't talked to you in, like, forever. I was wondering if you wanted to go have lunch today, so we can catch up."

Forever would be too soon. Keya wished she had not answered the phone. She did not want to have lunch with Ms. It.

"I will have to take a rain check, boo. My funds are low. But thanks for the offer," lied Keya.

"Keya, I got you. This will be my treat," pleaded Shanae.

Keya and Shanae agreed to meet at Olive Garden for lunch. Shanae and Keya made it to the restaurant at the same time. Excited to see her girl, Shanae walked over and gave her a hug. She instantly noticed Keya's being withdrawn. They proceeded into the restaurant and within minutes they were seated.

"Keya, what's up?"

Shanae was a little concerned that Keya seemed standoffish.

Keya hated Shanae. Looking at her sitting across from her

with her Gucci handbag and matching loafers made Keya sick to her stomach.

"What do you want to be up? I haven't seen or heard from you since forever, and now you think we are best buds? Shanae, I am not your flunky anymore," murmured Keya.

Keya was way past being rude.

Shanae was baffled. She had no idea why Keya was so upset. She was the one who Keya had left at the club.

"What are you talking about?" asked Shanae.

Keya sucked her teeth and never answered Shanae.

"Keya, where is all of this coming from? I have always treated you with the upmost respect. We are like sisters."

Shanae had so many mixed emotions, and she was silently praying she would keep her temper under control.

Keya wanted to take her fist and ram it into Shanae's perfect little nose, but she knew Shanae would whoop her ass in a heartbeat.

"First off, we ain't shit. You, always talking about how we are sisters and all the so-called love you have for me when you don't know shit about me. I had always been in the background when it came to you. You are so fake."

Keya was saying so many hateful things that Shanae tuned her out. Shanae had no idea where and when Keya's hatred towards her had manifested. Shanae had finally heard enough of the bull.

"Keya, please tell me that this is some kind of joke. As long as we have been friends, you cannot possibly feel this way towards me."

Shanae could not believe the look of contempt on Keya's face.

Laughing, Keya said, "Shanae, kill your pretentious bullshit. You make my ass tired always acting as if you don't know what is going on around you. You had to know how you made me feel."

Shanae was silently crying inside. She had never tried to hurt Keya. In fact, she would move heaven and earth for her if she could. Shanae had her face inside her palms when she heard Keya say,

"Bitch don't cover that pretty face now. You took him from me and acted like you didn't know. You knew! Hasaun was supposed to be mine, but you came along and messed everything up!"

What was Keya talking about wanting Hasaun? She had to be hearing things.

"What did you say?" questioned Shanae.

"You heard me. You took him from me!" yelled Keya.

Shanae looked around the restaurant to make sure they were not drawing too much attention. This was the only time she was thankful for the loud lunch crowd.

Whispering, Shanae said, "Lower your damn voice, Keya."

Annoyed, Keya replied, "You do not tell me what to do."

Keya was on some real bullshit. Shanae had never seen this storm approaching. She just always assumed that they would always be friends. Yeah, they had disagreements, but nothing of this caliber.

Dena had always warned Shanae about Keya, but Shanae never wanted to believe her momma. But she should have known that momma always knows best.

"Keya, be glad you didn't have to put up with Hasaun's lying ass. Besides, I never knew you had any interest in Hasaun. How was I supposed to know any of this if you never told me?"

Shanae was way past being angry. She was heated. She continued talking,

"I talk to you about everything. I am sorry you feel like I betrayed you, but I will not take the blame. I have been nothing but good to you and if you do not like it, you can kiss my ass."

Shanae refused to be nice any longer. Keya was on some other type stuff.

"No, Shanae, I will not kiss your ass. I have been doing that for way too many years. So why don't you kiss your own ass," steamed Keya.

Shanae had to control herself. She wanted to drag Keya by her hair outside and whoop her sorry ass. She decided against it. She knew Keya didn't have any fight in her, so she gave her a pass.

"Keya, like I said, I am sorry you feel this way about me. However, I refuse to sit here any longer and listen to this nonsense."

Shanae tossed a fifty-dollar bill on the table and stood to leave.

"How is your relationship going? When were you planning on telling me?" questioned Keya.

Shanae ignored Keya and walked outside the restaurant. She had no idea how Keya knew there was someone special in her life. Keya stormed out behind Shanae.

"Shanae, we are not finished!" protested Keya.

Shaking her head, Shanae replied, "Keya, we most certainly are. You have embarrassed me enough today to last a lifetime. I have nothing else to say to you."

"Shanae, when will you realize that it is not always about you? Besides, you never answered my question."

Agitated Shanae said, "And what is that, Keya? I have had enough of your BS today. What do you want me to answer?"

"How are you and Dee doing? How long have you been dating him?" smirked Keya.

Confused, Shanae replied, "Who the hell is Dee?"

"Shanae, don't play stupid with me. I saw you with him. I hope you know I have already been with your man. Doesn't that make him off limits for you?" laughed Keya.

Shanae had no idea what Keya was talking about,

"Keya, I have no idea who Dee is. I'm starting to wonder who you are."

"Well, let me jog your memory. The day when you lost your child you called me. I was getting busy. The guy I was getting busy with was Dee, who happens to be your man now."

Keya was talking to Shanae as if she was slow, in short sentences that took her too long to say.

Dee? Xavier? Shanae thought could they be the same person. What were the odds of this? Shanae looked at Keya with hatred in her eyes. She could not believe that Keya was actually happy to see her unhappy.

Laughing and shaking her head, Shanae asked, "What is Dee's name? What is his favorite color? How does Dee like his eggs? What does he do for a living? How does he hold you after he finishes making love to you?"

Keya knew she should have left well enough alone, but she was trying her best to break Shanae. Keya knew absolutely nothing about Dee. The only thing she knew was that she took him home one night after the club and never saw or heard from him until she saw him and Shanae together that day. Keya was just looking at Shanae. She didn't know any of the answers to the questions, and she felt really trivial at this point.

Shanae decided to break the silence, "Just like I thought. You don't know a damn thing about my man. Besides that, who the hell told you I was in a relationship?"

Keya was the one on the verge of crying now. Shanae's heart still went out to Keya. She had to stop herself from consoling Keya. She knew she had to cut ties with her. A person as jealous as Keya could be a serious threat.

"I saw y'all together one day and followed y'all. Shanae, I have been with him. How can you stay with him?"

If she wanted sympathy, Shanae was not about to give her any. She had no clue as to what Keya was talking about. She made a mental note to ask him to see if there was any validity to this psychopath's story. Right now, she just wanted to get as far away from Keya as she could.

"You followed us? So you're a PI now? Why didn't you come over and speak?"

How could someone once so close to her hate her as much as Keya did? She felt as if she was in the twilight zone. This was most definitely some weird shit. Shanae never saw this coming. Not in a million years would she ever think Keya and she would be at each other's throats like this.

On the other hand, Keya was upset for a number of reasons. But the main reason right now was that Shanae was so calm, and Keya's act was not fazing her. Then again, Keya thought Shanae was always able to keep her composure under pressure.

"You can't possibly stay with him? He was mine before

he was yours," pleaded Keya.

"Make up your damn mind! You want Hasaun? Now you want Dee? You need to really grow up Keya!"

Crying, Keya said, "You have to have it all don't you? Don't you!"

"Whatever you are talking about happened way before we started dating. You and I are no longer friends, and we will never be, so I don't see the problem with it. I am happy, and we love each other. Sorry. He is my man now, and I don't care if you did sleep with him!"

Shanae was doing her best to hold it together. She wanted to slap the shit out of Xavier. What were the chances that the one girl he slept with was her ex-best friend? Shanae decided to leave. She was about to lose it.

"How can you do this to me?" questioned Keya.

Shaking her head, Shanae replied, "Keya, you did this to your damn self. You have had half the damn town, and now you're worried about who I'm with. If that's the case, I need to move to another town, so we don't bump heads."

"That wouldn't be a bad idea, you moving out of town." Keya thought that was the best damn thing she had heard Shanae say all day.

"You know what Keya, all of this could have been nipped in the bud if you would have spoken that day instead of sneaking around and following us. That was our first date. If you had told me what I know now, I wouldn't have touched him with a ten-foot pole. The damage is done now and I am in love with him so get over it," explained Shanae.

"Just remember, I had him before you," stated Keya.

Shanae couldn't believe how immature and gullible Keya was so she decided to fight fire with fire.

"Oh, now I remember! You must be that slut he said he bumped into at the club," laughing, Shanae continued, "You let him fuck you and you gave him some head. Yeah, he told me about you and how nasty you were. The following morning you expected him to kiss you but he left you standing naked in your apartment. Keya, I never would have thought that girl was you. I thought you had way more game than that. I do not have any problems getting a kiss after we make love. Keya, love is the operative word. Oh, and one more thing. I know his government and it sure in the hell ain't Dee. Go on somewhere with this BS, Keya!"

Shanae jumped in her truck, and sped off. She was crying so hard she had to pull over on Providence to get herself together. How could she go from being happy to being miserable within a heartbeat? What was that old saying, "misery loves company" she was glad Keya wasn't a part of her life anymore, but it hurt. She loved Keya. She just couldn't figure out what went wrong. For that matter, she wanted to know why Keya wanted Hasaun. Some strange shit was most definitely going on. She could not wait to go home and lay down. Her head was pounding.

She didn't know how to play her cards, or who to be upset with. She didn't know if she could stay with Xavier after what Keya had told her. She had so much on her mind and then Keya had brought up that dreadful day. Now she was thinking about her children. She could feel herself sinking back into a state of depression.

40

Xavier's truck was fixed sooner than he had predicted. He was back in Columbia around noon. He entered her code to her garage, and let himself in. He was surprised to see that she was not at home. On the way back from Chicago, Xavier decided on coming clean with Shanae. He didn't want this lie to come back and haunt him. He had learned from previous relationships that it took more lies to cover the original lie. One thing he did not want to create was a web of deceit.

Xavier was sitting admiring the lunch that he had cooked for Shanae. The house had a romantic scene, and lunch smelled delectable. He could not wait until Shanae returned. He wondered where she was. She hadn't picked up her cell phone when he called her. He hoped she didn't take too long to walk through the door.

Xavier was interrupted from his thoughts when he heard the door slam. From the loud thud of the door, Xavier could tell she was in a sour mood. Shanae's face was strained and looked troubled. Xavier started bridging the gap between the two of them. Before he made it to her, she ran in the opposite direction.

He had no idea what could be wrong with her. He hoped she was okay. There was only one way to find out what was going on. He walked into her bedroom, and found her sprawled across her bed weeping. Xavier felt helpless. He didn't know what was wrong. He hated seeing her in so much pain. He sat on the bed and placed his back against the headboard. He tried lifting her, but she pushed his hands off and scooted away. Xavier grabbed Shanae, and put her between his muscular legs. Her back was against his chest. He held her hands, and placed his chin on the top of her head. He wasn't letting her go until she calmed down. He didn't know what had her so upset. He had a feeling Hasaun played a major role in upsetting her.

Once she calmed down, Xavier released her hands. He took his hand, pulled her hair back, and kissed her on the cheek. Shanae's body tensed when he placed a kiss on her cheek. She couldn't believe he had been with Keya. Out of all the men in the world, why did they have to bump heads with the one man she truly loved? She didn't want to lose him, but she didn't know if she could get past this. The only thing she knew was that he made her happy, and she didn't want to lose him.

"Shanae, what's going on?"

Silence and more crying met Xavier. Shanae was staring in

space and ignoring him on purpose.

"Did Hasaun do something to hurt you?" Xavier was upset by the tone of his voice.

"Did he hurt you?"

Shanae still hadn't responded to Xavier. She could tell he was concerned.

"Where have you been? What is wrong? Will you please answer me?"

Shanae felt awful for putting him through this torture. He had no idea as to what was going on. She figured it was time to call it quits with him. It was beginning to get complicated. If she turned her back on him, she would not have to think about Keya and his being together.

"I just don't know where to begin."

He was happy to hear her voice, and he replied, "Start from the beginning."

Crying, Shanae explained the scenario that transpired between her and Keya. She let him know that it hurt her to hear Keya say so many mean things about her. He was supportive. He consoled her and tried to give her some sound advice. She finally began to calm down. He also told her she needed to remember this was the "same best friend" that left her at the club.

"Shanae, with friends like that you don't need enemies. Sometimes, friends grow apart. What I can't figure out is how someone you've known for so many years could be so cruel," said Xavier.

Shanae was glad she had him in her corner.

"I don't know either. I guess I am more hurt than surprised. My momma has always told me she is not to be trusted. I always saw more in Keya. But I guess I was wrong," explained Shanae.

Shanae thought about not telling him that she knew he had slept with Keya, but then she knew she would always be thinking about it in the back of her mind. She hadn't decided if she was going to stick it out with him or not. A part of her prayed it was a lie, but she could remember the smug and confident look on Keya's face when she told her. She knew it was true.

"Xavier, there's more," sighed Shanae

She stood and walked to her closet, and retrieved a photo album. Shanae opened the book, and it handed it to him. He was lost.

"Shanae, what's going on?" Xavier had no idea what she was up to. He never looked at the photo album. He wanted to know what else there was. He knew it had to do something with Hasaun.

Closing her eyes and shaking her head, Shanae replied, "You have slept with her."

After she had uttered those words, she felt sick.

"Is this some kind of sick joke?" Xavier appeared upset.

"Oh, how I wish it was. But she said she has been with you. Imagine how I feel."

"There is no way in hell I slept with this Keya person." explained Xavier.

"Baby, I'm just telling you what she told me."

Xavier threw the photo album across the room and yelled, "Yeah, fucking right, Shanae. She is just a hateful person. She doesn't want to see you happy."

Laughing, Shanae replied, "Is that one of the male species famous lines? Do you know how many times I have been told that? Everybody ain't hating on little ol' me."

Shanae walked towards the center of the room, picked up the photo album and handed it back to Xavier.

"I told you, you are the only person I have been with since I moved here. Besides, the one female I told you I left the clu…"

Xavier stopped in mid-sentence and his piercing look held Shanae's concerned gaze. He shook his head in awe. *How could this have happened? Could it be? No way!*

Shanae shook her head, yes. For the life of him, he couldn't even remember what she looked liked. Shanae pointed to the photo album in his hands. He looked at the pictures, and slowly began to recall the female in the photos with Shanae. Sure enough it was the female he left the club with.

"Unbelievable!" yelled Xavier as he tossed the photo album

on the floor.

"Why do you say that?" questioned Shanae.

With wrinkles in his forehead, he replied, "What?"

"I mean, you leave the club with a woman you don't even know? Anything is possible."

"I had no idea I would fall in love with her best friend almost a year later! It's not something that I planned."

"I didn't say you did plan it. Sounds to me like you need to be more careful."

"What the? What is wrong with you? You're acting like I did this shit on purpose. I would never do anything to hurt you. You have to believe that."

"It just hurts."

He had no idea why she was hurting like she was or why she was giving it so much of her energy. They were not even dating when it happened.

"How did she know we were dating?"

"She followed us one day."

Throwing his hands in the air, and shaking his head he replied, "Oh, that's normal."

"Why are you so angry?"

"I am not angry, just stunned nonetheless. You keep asking me all these questions like I knew, and it does bother me a little to know that I have been with your best friend."

"Tell me about it."

Xavier could see where this was going. She never wanted to be in another relationship because she didn't want the problems or heartache. He vowed never to hurt her and now something from his past had done it. He knew she was trying to backpedal out of it and save face. There was no way he was letting her walk out of his life because she was scared of her emotions. Yeah, she had been through hell and back, but she had to know he had her back.

"Now what, Shanae?" questioned Xavier.

"I don't know. I really don't know?" whispered Shanae.

"You know what I know. For the first time in my life, I am truly happy. I am in love, and something from my past wreaks havoc in our lives. It's out of our control. I told you I had been with someone since I've been here. Yeah, it sucks that it's your best friend, but it never was my intention to do this."

He felt he had to explain this to her. He knew it was going to be even rockier once he told her about Ms. Psycho.

Shanae wanted to believe him, but something wouldn't let her. She wanted to understand. She wanted to still be happy. She knew deep in her heart she loved him. Would it be so bad if she tried to stick it out with him?

"I don't blame you. I am upset for a number of reasons, but the blame is not to be placed on you. I guess shit really does happen. The important thing is how do we deal with the shit, and what will we learn from the shit."

Shanae had a faint smile on her face. Shanae cared for Keya, but she refused to be miserable because she wanted her to be. She had a life to live, and she planned to live it, with or without her, to the fullest.

Seeing that smile did something to Xavier on the inside. It gave him a little hope. He looked into her beautiful eyes and saw pain for the first time. That was a look he never wanted to see in her eyes again. He knew he had one more bridge to cross.

"Baby, I have something I need to come clean with, and put on the table. I realize in order to move forward we have to be honest with each other."

He saw concern in Shanae's eyes.

Shanae sat on the bed her shoulders slumped, "What's up, Xavier?"

I want to come clean with you. I don't want a relationship based on deceit and lies. I hope you can forgive me."

So much had happened to her in a day. She didn't know how she would handle any more heartache.

"T-tell m-me what's going on?" demanded Shanae.

With his head down Xavier replied, "I lied to you. I went to Chicago to see an old friend."

"Male or female?" interrupted Shanae

"I hadn't talked to her in months. She still presumed we were an item."

"Why would she?' questioned Shanae.

Xavier was so nervous he was rambling, only giving Shanae bits and pieces of the story.

"I went to Chicago to tell her whatever she assumed we had was over, and there was never any relationship between us."

He was desperate for her forgiveness, but she was not buying it. "Baby, I promise, that's the truth."

Shanae had been through a lot in one day. She was too exhausted to respond. She backed away from Xavier and walked out the bedroom door. When approaching the kitchen, she noticed that the table had been set for two and had candles on it. The food also smelled good. She hadn't noticed any of this when she first stormed into the house.

She could not understand why Xavier lied to her. The truth she would have understood. She despised a liar. She couldn't stand the sight of him. She wanted him out of her house. She noticed the bottle of DP chilling. She opened it and poured herself a flute. Within seconds, she poured herself another one. She kicked her shoes off and curled up on the sofa. She figured she would deal with her problems tomorrow. Right now, she needed peace of mind.

Xavier walked into the living and said, "Please say something. Don't leave me hanging."

Swallowing the liquid in her mouth, she replied, "What

did you do to me this weekend? You left me hanging on your lies!"

Shanae walked back over to the table and filled her flute once again, and drank the expensive champagne. She began to pour another glass, and decided against it. Because of the way her day was going, she grabbed the bottle and walked over to sofa. No sense in continuing to pour glasses when she had plans to drink the entire bottle.

"Shanae, I know I was in the wrong. I assure you, nothing happened this weekend."

She wanted to believe him, but she couldn't understand why he lied. *Was he trying to hide something? Men were so stupid. Always saying they lied to protect us. When we find out about the lie? Aren't we still hurt?*

"I just can't stand being lied to."

"I know I was wrong. I decided to come clean, and deal with it. I just want you to know that I love you."

Taking a huge swig from the bottle, she replied, "Do me a favor and leave."

He walked over to her grabbed the bottle out of her hand, walked to the kitchen, and poured the contents down the drain. It was obvious she'd had too much to drink. She was slurring her words, and her eyes were glazed over. Xavier was kneeling between Shanae's agile legs. He lifted her head up. "I am sorry for lying to you," he said, "I love you, and I don't want to lose you. I am only guilty of lying. Shanae, will you please say something?"

She stared a hole in him and never said a word. *I can't believe you had the nerve to dump my drink out. Who the hell are you?* She didn't care. She had plenty more where that came from.

He saw her looking at the bar.

He replied, "If you open another bottle of it, I will break every bottle. Because when you're done, we've still got this mess to deal with."

"So you're a mind reader now? We really don't have any mess to deal with. You just need to leave."

Shaking his head, he replied, "I don't want to lose you."

"You should have thought about that when your lying ass was gallivanting down the highway."

"Call me if you need anything and if you still want to work this out. Come hell or high water, we will be together."

"You think so? You think it's that easy because you came clean? Earth to Xavier! You should have never lied in the first place."

"You are absolutely right. Now look at this big mess I have caused. But you're to bullheaded to know when someone is truly sorry."

He walked over to Shanae and kissed her on the lips, and left.

She placed her hands on her moist lips and thought about that kiss. She enjoyed his kisses. Now she was alone and had no one. It took everything in her not to stop him from walking out the door. When he left, she lost her backbone. That night she nursed another bottle of champagne, and cried herself to sleep.

41

It had been three long weeks since she spoke to Xavier. However, she saw him on a daily basis considering they shared three classes. She had contemplated changing her classes, but decided against making such an irrational decision. Instead of changing classes, she always made sure she arrived to class late so he wouldn't have a chance to sit by her. She really missed him, but her life was back in order and free of drama.

Shanae noticed that Xavier was dressed perfectly each day. She couldn't help but wonder what his plans were for after class. She also wondered if they included a female. No matter how much she tried to convince herself to stop wondering if there was another woman in his life, she couldn't get over not knowing. Not knowing if he had given up on them was eating her alive.

She was in heavy thought, and unbeknownst to her she was staring at him. When she snapped out of it, they were both staring at each other. The heat that radiated after their gazing left Shanae hot and bothered. Immediately, she turned her head. She was focusing on the words on the page, but she hadn't read one. God forbid, if the professor asked her a question. She was lost.

She knew that she still had strong feelings for him. Shanae decided not to let her emotions cloud her judgment. Her emotions had landed her in hot water on numerous occasions. She decided to take her emotions, stick them deep into her pocket, and never stick her hand back in it.

Every time she glanced away from her book, she noticed he was staring at her. His staring made her uncomfortable. She was uncomfortable because she couldn't deny her feelings. She was afraid to admit the truth. She was in way too deep. She loved him. She decided not to look up until class was over. She was so deep in thought when she finally looked up, class had been dismissed, and she was the only one sitting in class.

Walking to her vehicle with her head hung low, she felt defeated. If her momma had seen her walking with her head down she would have reminded Shanae that Davis women held their heads up high. She wished she had the strength to hold her head up, but it seemed as if her life was on a never-ending roller coaster.

She knew what she needed to pick her up. She needed

to get out the house, and do something different. She had been going to school and going home for the past three weeks. Every now and then, she would go to the gym to release much need frustration.

Shanae ended up at Yaz, an upscale Jazz bar that she frequented every now and then. She loved the atmosphere and the music, of course. Before she exited the car she freshened her makeup, and entered the bar. The relaxing environment immediately took the tension out of her shoulders. She asked to be seated in the back away from the crowd. She had a lot on her mind, and she wanted to think and drink. She was thinking about her life. Within the last year, she had seen major improvements. She still had some kinks to work out; she knew she would be fine. The major thing she needed to decide on was if she wanted Xavier in or out of her life.

Shanae couldn't believe that she was sitting at the table by herself. She had some serious hurdles in her life, but they weren't all bad. She knew that before she could focus on a man, she had to get herself together.

Damn, she wished she had someone that could hang out with her every now and then. She realized that she had no social life.

Xavier was sitting at the bar inside Yaz moping to Kent about how he messed up with his girl. They practically had to drag him out. He was torn up about his mystery lady.

Kent replied, "Xavier, man if she is this mad about a lie, imagine how she will be if you ever cheat on her."

Xavier looked at Kent as if he was slow, "Man if she takes me back, she don't have to worry about none of that."

Laughing, Kent replied, "Yeah right ain't no pu-"

"Man, this fine ass red bone is over there sitting at a table by herself. She is bad!" interrupted Ray.

Ray was Xavier and Kent's friend who thought every woman he saw was good looking. His short stature reminded you of George Jefferson. He never had any luck with the ladies. Ray was desperate for a companion. However, he was determined too. No matter how many times he was turned down, he remained consistent.

Laughing, Kent replied, "Shit, Ray, they all fine to you."

Both Kent and Xavier shared a laugh at Ray's expense.

Ray was heated, "To hell with y'all. I am going over to spit some game."

Still laughing Kent replied, "If she is as beautiful as you say, she for damn sure don't want your ugly ass."

Again they both laughed at Ray. Ray was their boy, but he thought the unattractive ladies were bad.

Ray walked away from the bar and over to the table where Shanae was sitting. They continued laughing and joking about Ray at the bar. Ray approached Shanae's table.

"Can I get you something to drink?" asked Ray.

Shanae saw him coming. She wished he would have walked past her table, but luck was not on her side today.

Shanae noticed that he was much shorter than she liked. He wasn't hard on the eyes, but he was no Xavier either. Immediately, she stopped herself from giving him the Davis "look over." That's probably why she was sitting at the table alone.

"No, thank you," declined Shanae politely.

"May I sit?" ask Ray pointing at the available chair.

All kind of bells went off in her head. She wanted to know what he was up to. Mentally, she had to tell herself to calm down, and just enjoy the company of someone else.

"Sure," replied Shanae. After much deliberation in her head, she didn't see any trouble in holding small talk with the guy.

Ray jumped right into conversing with Shanae. "What is a lovely lady like you doing dining alone?"

Smiling, Shanae replied, "What makes you think I'm alone?"

Ray replied, "Because I saw you come in by yourself. I also have enough sisters to know that some man has hurt you, and you have a lot on your mind."

Lifting her hands in the air Shanae said, "You caught me. I don't want to talk about it.

Ray thought her smile was beautiful. She was drop dead

gorgeous. Shaking his head Ray replied, "I know I am a stranger, and know nothing about your situation but one thing I do know is that whoever he is, he is a damn fool for letting you get away."

"He's not a fool. We all do things we're not proud of," smiled Shanae.

"You're defending him? That only means one thing; you still love him," replied Ray.

Smiling, Shanae replied, "Right, I am supposed to be mad at him."

"Just shows you have a good heart. Don't let him walk over it," Ray replied.

Shanae didn't have any intentions on letting him walk over her heart. That's why she had been going through the motions for weeks.

Placing her hands over the left side of her chest, Shanae said, "He won't be walking over this heart."

Shanae and Ray continued with their small talk. Ray ordered shots, and they took shots. After the third round of drinks, licks, and sucks of tequila, Shanae decided to slow down. She was feeling the tequila. She knew once she stood the effects would be ten times worse. Shanae realized Ray was a comedian. She hadn't laughed in a long time. He had her mind off her troubled life, and it felt good to laugh.

Meanwhile, Kent and Xavier were trying to see what

the lady looked like. They figured she must have given him the time of day because he never returned to the bar.

Shanae and Ray were having a good time. They were both laughing and enjoying each other's company. Laughing was something she hadn't done in a long time. Ray asked Shanae to dance, and she agreed. Kent caught a glimpse of her when she stood to walk to the dance floor.

Shocked, he couldn't believe how beautiful she was.

"Man, close your mouth. What's wrong with you?" questioned Xavier.

"Man, she is that deal, and she is dancing with the troll," joked Kent.

Xavier turned around to find them on the dance floor, and said, "Where is she?"

Her back was to Xavier he couldn't see her face. Something was so familiar about her thighs, her legs, and her ass. If he didn't know any better he would have sworn up and down that Ray was dancing with Shanae.

"Man, I can't see her face," Xavier was rubbernecking, trying to see who this mystery woman was.

"I can tell you this. She is bad," ogled Kent.

"Kent, that looks like my girl!" Xavier was in killer mode.

Kent noticed how his demeanor changed, and he prayed for Ray's sake that the mystery lady wasn't Xavier's girl.

"Xavier, you would think she was your girl as much as you

miss her," Kent tried to lighten his mood.

Ray and Shanae were having fun on the dance floor. Ray twirled Shanae and dipped her with the fineness of a professional dancer. That last dip and twirl were enough for Xavier to see that Ray was dancing with Shanae.

"I don't think, I know. That is my girl."

Standing up and walking to the dance floor, Xavier was determined to pound Ray's head in.

Seeing Shanae dancing with Ray infuriated him. He quickly got over being mad, and noticed how beautiful she was. She was swaying her hips to the soulful beat.

Xavier yelled, "All hell, naw!"

There was no way in hell he was going to continue to allow Shanae to dance with Ray's sick ass.

Curious, Kent replied, "Do you know her?"

Walking over to the dance floor, Xavier looked back and replied, "Hell, yeah. That's my woman."

Kent spit his Hennessy out of his mouth, and this time he laughed at Xavier.

Shanae couldn't believe who was approaching the dance floor. The look on Shanae's face worried Ray a little. He prayed her man wasn't in here, because he sure as hell didn't feel like fighting; besides his boys were on the other side of the bar.

"What's wrong? You looked like you've seen a ghost?" questioned Ray.

She never took her eyes off Xavier. He was so handsome. Seeing him made her miss her rhythm, and she was no longer on beat. Ray noticed her hesitancy.

Xavier stepped in front of Ray and told her,

"You shouldn't be dancing with this guy," he told her. He is nothing but trouble."

"I am a big girl. I can handle myself."

"Oh, I know you can handle yourself."

"You're being really rude, man. Now, if you would excuse me."

Ray was having such a good time. He hadn't noticed the lust and longing in both Shanae's and Xavier's eyes. They loved each other.

"Shanae, we need to talk."

"I am a little preoccupied right now. Let me check my schedule to see if I have some time to talk with you," smirked Shanae.

Ray could not believe Xavier had the nerve to be pushing up on his dance partner.

"Xavier, man, quit hating. Go call your woman, and makeup. You have been crying for weeks."

Shanae had no idea they knew each other. This was too funny. It made her feel good to know that he had been sulking over her.

"Ray, man, step off," insisted Xavier.

"Look, Xavier. I will get back with you later. Right now, I think you're making my dance partner uncomfortable," stated Shanae.

Ray still hadn't caught on that the two knew each other. He had noticed that Xavier was too familiar with her, but never in a million years did he once think that Shanae was Xavier's woman. He wanted Xavier to go sit down so he could keep enjoying himself. It had been forever since a lady had shown him any attention.

"Like hell you will, Shanae."

"I ain't stepping off. You meddling man," yelled Ray. He felt like he needed to say something instead of looking back between the two of them.

Kent was sitting at the bar laughing his butt off. He prayed Ray stepped off because he could tell from Xavier's stance that he was no longer playing around.

"Well, Ray, I hate to burst your bubble, but this is my damn woman. Now step off and quit looking at her like you want to sop her up with a biscuit. Last warning, man."

Xavier was clenching his jaw muscles and was apparently upset.

Ray looked at Shanae, then Xavier, and back to Shanae. Shanae shook her head up and down letting him know it was the truth.

Defeated, Ray left the dance floor. He thought Xavier

was one lucky bastard.

"So now you're around town dancing with other men?" questioned Xavier.

"I didn't see a problem with it."

"Would it have been a problem if you walked in here, and saw me dancing with another woman?"

Shanae looked stupid. She knew her feelings would have been hurt if it were the other way around. However, she would never let him know that. He was even sexier mad.

"I mean, I haven't seen you in like, a month, so I just assumed it was over." stated Shanae.

"I'm so sick of your games, Shanae."

Xavier didn't get this lady. She was so complicated. She didn't know love was staring her in the face.

Shanae could not believe how upset he was.

"I think I should leave," stated Shanae.

"Shanae, we need to figure out what is going on between us. Or if there is an us. I mean this silent treatment isn't getting us anywhere. We can't keep living our lives in limbo."

Shaking her head, with tears in her eyes, she backed away from him and ran out of the bar. He could not believe she ran out on him. However, he knew she had to be close because she left her Hermes bag on the table. After collecting her belongings, he went over to his boys.

Looking at Shanae's bag in his hand, Ray said, "Does your woman know you're a cross dresser?"

Kent laughed and Xavier shook his head. Ray had an attitude.

"Ray, stop hating. She is my woman, and that's that. But on a serious note, don't ever put your hands on her again," warned Xavier.

Kent knew this situation had the potential to get out of hand, so he intervened. Ray was well past being drunk, and God only knew what was going to come out of his mouth.

"Xavier, he didn't know she was your woman," replied Kent.

Looking at Ray, Xavier said, "He knows now."

"Man, I am out of here. Thanks for listening, Kent. Ray, no love lost. I have to go find her. She left her purse.

Kent gave him a hug and told him to go handle his business. While Ray felt he had been disrespected and ignored him, Xavier left.

"He is one lucky bastard," stated Ray.

"Ray, stop hating and be happy for him," joked Kent.

"Whatever, man," replied Ray as he finished his drink.

Laughing, Kent said, "Stop hating."

42

Shanae was at her truck when she realized she left her bag in the bar. There was no way she was going back in there. The very place she runs to avoid her problems, she runs right into her problems. The night was going great until she saw Xavier. His presence did something to her. Seeing him knocked the breath out of her. Her insides got all fuzzy, and her mind got confused. She wondered what she had done in life to continually be blindsided.

She was in front of Yaz's pacing back and forth. She had been waiting on a patron to leave the establishment to ask them to go back inside to get her bag. With her luck, they all must have been taking advantage of the happy hour. Shanae had never seen Xavier so upset. It scared her. She tried to downplay his remarks. When he was talking to Ray, he was acting like a dog marking his territory. Ray seemed like such a good guy. Xavier made it clear that she didn't need to be dancing with him. Shanae liked Ray, and she wasn't going to let Xavier decide to whom she should be cordial. She chalked it up as him being jealous.

She knew she would have been crushed if he were dancing with someone. They still hadn't hashed out their problems or talked to each other since the incident. She knew it was time to figure out what she wanted out of life. She had so much on her mind.

Shanae began to wipe tears from her face. She was so lonely and sad all because of her pride. She just didn't want the lies to become a constant in their relationship. She needed her bag so she could go home, but she refused to go back inside.

The effect of the cheap tequila was having a huge effect on her. Her head was spinning, and she was so ready to leave Yaz's. Shanae knew the only way to leave was to go back inside and retrieve her bag. She leaned her head on the passenger window. She had to decide what it was she wanted in a relationship. Most important, she had to decide if she wanted Xavier.

Shanae froze when she felt those manly hands touch her shoulder. She didn't have to turn around. She just knew. His touch seemed like it ignited something inside of her. It did something to her on the inside. It took away all the pain she was just experiencing. She wondered how those hands belonged to a person who lied to her. Who had deceived for her for no apparent reason? She wanted to know why he lied. There had to be some reason why he lied.

Shanae turned around, and there he stood. Holding her bag and looking dumbfounded. She reached for her bag, and he gave it to her.

"I would have been out here sooner, but I had to say my goodbyes."

Shanae wanted to run off and leave him standing, but she wanted some answers.

"Thanks for bringing me my bag."

"Shanae, can we go somewhere and talk?"

"Sure. There's a bench right over there."

"Not what I had in mind."

"Take it or leave it. This afternoon is not what I had in mind either, but it happened."

"Calm down. I do not like seeing you out of your element. Get yourself together."

He began walking to the bench, and took a seat. Shanae followed suit. She wanted to get this over with so she would know what she was up against.

For several minutes, they sat there in silence. Xavier was holding on to Shanae's hand like his life depended on it. He kept placing small kisses all over her hand.

She was so stressed out. She wanted to be mad; she wanted him back. His lips on her hand had her hormones doing all kind of things. How could he have this kind of effect on her? Man, she knew what her hormones wanted to do. She had to keep the situation and the issues in perspective.

"Shanae, I miss you so much!" whimpered Xavier.

Shanae ignored him. He missed her so much, he hadn't called her in a week.

"Is that why you don't call anymore?"

"Why should I keep calling? I called for two weeks straight at least fifty times a day, and you never picked up."

He had a point. She had been ignoring his phone calls and ignoring him altogether for the last few weeks.

"I don't know why, but I expected you to keep calling me."

Shaking his head, he replied, "Why did you expect that?"

Shanae was pissed. "Considering you started all this bullshit with your lies. I expected you to keep calling me until you made it right."

Shanae was not good at this. She was coming off as some love stricken teenager. She didn't know if she was mad or happy to see him. She was always in control, but not this time. She loved this man and had no way of telling him. She wanted him to come back to her, crawling and crying. It was not going as she thought it should go.

Breaking the silence she asked, "Why did you lie to

me?"

Xavier had asked himself that for weeks. *Why did I lie? It was a mistake that had caused me so much heartache and time trying to figure out why.*

Defeated, he replied, "I have no idea."

"That's all you have to say?"

"Anything else would be a lie. I am trying to be honest. I told you I lied, and that's it."

"How do I know that's the truth?"

"You don't. You just have to trust and believe that. At this point, I have nothing else to lose, so why lie."

"Point well taken."

"You know why we're both sitting here in pain, and can't eat or sleep at night?"

With a perplexed look on her face Shanae replied, "Not a clue."

"That doesn't surprise me. Well, guess what? Let me give you a clue. Your pride is the reason we are in this boat. You need to get over yourself."

Upset, Shanae replied, "Apparently you have had way too much to drink. Don't put this on me, you're the liar. Not me. You did this to us."

Pointing her finger at him, she repeated, "You did it."

"No, I don't wash my problems away with alcohol. I try to face them like a man."

"What do you mean by that?"

"Not a thing," lied Xavier.

He had noticed that every time she was upset she poured herself a flute of DP. He could tell by her slurred speech that she had tossed back more than a few tonight.

"I can handle my alcohol, and I am not an alcoholic. That is something you do not have to worry about Dee."

"My name is Xavier. Don't call me Dee."

He was getting irritated.

"I can't call you Dee, but other people can? What do I have to do to call you Dee?"

Shanae was pushing his buttons on purpose. She was pissed, and she wanted him to be hurting like she was.

"You're acting really childish. But you know what you have to be to call me Dee?"

"Enlighten me."

"A ho, that's what you have to be," barked Xavier.

He knew he went too far with his last statement. It was evident she was still tripping off the Keya BS. He just wanted to hold her, but something was stopping him.

"Well, I guess I will continue calling you Xavier," joked Shanae.

They both shared a laugh. "Shanae, sorry for being so disrespectful today."

"Oh, I'm just letting it slide, because I know we are both

a little emotional right now. But don't make it a habit."

Her face lit up the block; she was so radiant. If only he had told the truth.

Shaking his head, he replied, "Shanae, what's the difference between lying to you every day telling yourself you don't love me? When you know you do; then lying to someone else."

"The difference is that I am responsible for me. If I want to lie to myself, that's between me, myself and I. But if I lie to someone else, it's involving them not just me."

"Still makes you a liar. You just lie to yourself. Just was asking."

"It's funny how your lie has insinuated that I am an alcoholic. I lie to myself, and it's my prides fault. Xavier, you lied to me. You knew my situation. You know all I been through. You knew dating you was very hard for me. You knew this, and you promised me you would never hurt me. But that's neither here nor there when it comes to you."

"Shanae, I came to you, told you the truth, and you still won't have anything to do with me."

Shanae could tell this was a never-ending battle. They were both too stubborn for their own good. She decided to end the conversation.

"I see you're still lying. This is what you did; you lied, and then told me you lied, and now I won't have anything to do with you. Did I ever give you a reason to ever lie to me?"

That's the messed up thing about the entire situation. If he had told her what he was doing, she would have been like okay go handle your business and get back home. She was the most understanding and poised woman he had ever met. He had no clue as to why he lied. He was so accustomed to lying to females that he hadn't recognized she was a lady that only wanted the truth, and would stand by him. He understood he messed that up.

Shaking his head, he replied, "Never."

Wow, the way he said, "never" tugged at her heart. It was sincere. She could tell he was angry with himself for the lie. They sat there in silence not wanting the conversation to end, but knew it had to. Xavier was holding on to her hand with all the love he could. The love was there, but the trust wasn't. You can't have one without the other.

"Where do we stand?"

He had to know. He couldn't keep holding on to memories. If it was over he needed to move on.

"I don't know. I know that I love you, but the trust issue is a hard bullet to bite. I've got to have it," explained Shanae.

"You know what I think? I think you're so scared to commit that you keep making all these damn excuses up."

"Stop cussing at me!"

"Sorry, Shanae. Didn't mean to cuss at you," joked,

Xavier.

"This is not a laughing matter. Xavier, for crying out loud, you lied to me!"

Xavier had no intentions on making her cry even more. He just felt bad but damn. He just lied. He could see the tears in her eyes. She was doing all she could do to hold back. They were about to flow from her eyes down her soft, beautiful face.

"Shanae, you act like I slept with her. I went to Chicago to tell her there was nothing between us. That's it!" yelled Xavier.

"Did you sleep with her?" Shanae was staring a hole in him. She was trying to read him to see if he was lying. Either he was good at lying or he was telling her the truth.

Shaking his head, he said, "Naw, I didn't sleep with her. I could have if I wanted too. I didn't go up there to sleep with her."

"Oh, that's supposed to make me feel better? If you wanted to you could have. What stopped you?"

He had the damn nerve to tell her he could have if he wanted to. It took everything in her not to slap him.

"My love for you!"

With that said he stood from the bench, and walked off.

He left her sitting there feeling stupid. She believed him the first time he told her, but she wouldn't leave well enough alone. Now she was alone. She sat on the bench thinking about her circumstances, and how she could make them better.

She opened her truck, got her backpack and called for a car. She wasn't going to let Jose have her wrapped around a pole. Cuervo that is. She would get her truck in the morning.

43

Hasaun was packed and ready to head west down I-70. He really wished he could see Shanae. He wanted to apologize to her for being such a jerk. Over the past weeks, Hasaun had thought about many things. There were so many aspects in his life he wanted to change. He knew leaving Columbia was a huge step in bettering himself. He just wished he could share this moment with Shanae.

Holding the heirloom in his hands brought back so many memories. He didn't know how he would give it back to her. When he played ball in high school and later in college, Shanae had given it to him for good luck. While packing, he discovered it along with letters and pictures from Shanae. That was a trip down memory lane he wished he had done differently; there was no way he could give it back to her without being detained by the police. Hasaun considered mailing it to her, but he didn't want to risk losing the valuable piece of jewelry. What he decided on next was the biggest mistake of his life.

"Keya, I need a favor," stated Hasaun.

Keya hadn't heard from him since she opened up to him a while back, "What you need, boo?"

"Keya, kill the boo shit."

He never could understand how Shanae could have been her friend.

She noticed his irritation, "I was just playing, Hasaun."

"I have something of Shanae's I need you to give it to her for me."

The mention of Shanae's name sent Keya off the deep end.

"Hasaun, when are you going to wake up? She doesn't want you anymore. Besides, why don't you give it to her yourself?"

Hasaun was finally beginning to realize how deranged Keya was.

"Look Keya, if you can't do it then its cool."

"I can do it."

Keya was pissed she had do something for him that involved Shanae.

"If she didn't have a restraining order against me I would do it myself. Just this one time Keya," pleaded Hasaun.

"Why is it so important to give it back to her? She doesn't want to see me, so she might not come and get it."

"She will. It's a family heirloom, her grandmother's. She will want it back."

Keya agreed.

Hasaun was on his way over to drop the heirloom off. Keya was ready to implement her plan. She lowered the lights and lit candles. She showered, and put on a revealing crotchless cat suit. However, it took Hasaun longer than usual to arrive at Keya's.

When he finally arrived it was a little after nine in the evening. She could smell the liquor reeking from his pores. From the sight of him, her plan was going to be easier than she imagined.

"Hasaun, what took you so long? I didn't think you were still coming over here."

Hasaun was messed up. He had this stupid grin plastered on his face that he couldn't control.

Licking his lips, he replied, "I've been at my friend's house. They had a going away party for me."

She heard him, but she didn't. The only thing she knew is if he licked his lips one more time like L.L. she was going to explode.

"What are you talking about going away party?"

Keya prayed he wasn't leaving Columbia. They hadn't had the opportunity to make love.

Realizing he hadn't told anyone he was moving, he

explained his predicament to Keya. Keya was livid. He was leaving tomorrow to better his life. She knew she had to move fast to carry out her plan. In her heart, she knew he was leaving because he couldn't have Shanae.

Looking at her outfit for the first time he said, "Did I interrupt something?"

Lying Keya replied, "Well, actually, I thought you were my date but it doesn't look like he's coming. Would you like a glass of wine?"

Hasaun was already drunk and figured one glass of wine wouldn't hurt, so he agreed to have a drink with Keya.

"Only if you put some clothes on."

Hasaun sat on the couch, and watched Keya as she seductively walked into the kitchen. For the first time in his life he noticed that Keya had a nice ass. He had never looked at Keya as anything other than Shanae's best friend. In addition, best friends were off limits.

When he started noticing her firm behind and toned legs, he tried to gain his composure. That's when he knew he needed to leave. He figured it had to be the bud or the Hennessy. Whichever it was, he knew he needed to leave before something happened he regretted.

Walking back into the living room with two glasses in her hands, she noticed the lust in Hasaun's eyes. She smiled at him, and moseyed into the living room where he was sitting.

Hasaun immediately broke his gaze. Keya also noticed the bulge in his pants, which instantly turned her on. She handed the glass to him, and sat beside him on the sofa. She stretched over him to retrieve the box he brought. Keya purposely pushed her double D's against his chest. It had been a long a time since he had been intimate, and Keya was turning him on in a major way.

As he scooted over Hasaun said, "Damn, Keya, give a brutha some space."

In a seductive voice Keya replied, "Why? You can't handle it?"

Hasaun ignored her and demanded, "Go put some clothes on, girl."

"Boy, please this is my house. Besides I ain't worried about you."

Hasaun feeling funny from the wine, asked, "What is this shit you got me drinking?"

"White Zinfandel," laughed Keya.

Trying to shake the feeling from the wine he replied, "This shit is strong."

Laughing Keya replied, "You can't handle a women's drink."

"This ain't my first drink, and it has me feeling kind of woozy. I still have to drive home."

Hasaun opted to put the drink down. He wished he had decided that two glasses ago. He knew it was time to go.

Seeing his hesitancy Keya knew she needed to act fast before he left.

"Hasaun, you want to watch television?"

"Yeah, I need to watch something so I can sober up and head home."

For some strange reason he was hot. He decided to take his shirt off. He was glad he set the wine down because it was having a weird effect on him.

There was no way in hell he was going home tonight. Keya had big plans for tonight, and no one was leaving her apartment until she accomplished what she sat out to do.

Keya walked over to the television bent over, and her thong went right up the crack of her pear shaped derriere. Hasaun couldn't take it anymore, and if that wasn't enough when she turned the television on, a porno was playing.

"Oh, sorry about that," lied Keya.

"Yeah, right, Keya. What the hell do you have up your sleeve?"

"Don't be coming in here giving me the third degree. You should have been here hours ago. I thought you were my date. Sorry, I had already set the mood for a night of love making."

"Well, unset the mood, because I ain't your date. This wine is doing some weird shit to me."

He was trying to pull it together. He avoided looking at

Keya, and wished she would go get some clothes on because she was making him feel uncomfortable.

"Keya, will you please get some clothes on?" begged Hasaun.

"Why you want me to put some clothes on?"

"Foo, you making me uncomfortable. If I was Shanae, you wouldn't be uncomfortable," snorted Keya.

In his stupor Hasaun replied, "That's for sure. I would be breaking her off something proper I wou—"

"I get the picture!"

Hasaun stopped running his mouth.

Keya was furious. Walking back over to him she replied, "I can do things you never imagined. You would not even remember Shanae."

Keya was walking towards him, and he knew she was up to no good. He felt it was time to leave. However, when he tried to stand, he could not feel his legs and he felt light headed. Once he fell back down Keya began to take advantage of him. She began to caress his inner thighs, and slowly began to rub his Johnson, which was at attention. He wanted her to stop but it felt so good. He had been longing for her touch for so long. He closed his eyes and allowed Shanae to take him to ecstasy. She undressed him. When they were both nude, she kissed him. Their tongues danced. The warmth of her mouth sent chills up and down his spine. He couldn't imagine what made her take him back.

He opened his eyes and there she stood, beautiful as ever and so perfect. He held her face in his hands and moaned, "Shanae, I love you so much. Please don't ever leave me again. I will never hurt you."

With that said, he gave her another passionate kiss.

Keya's body stiffened, and her heart was racing. She couldn't believe he thought she was Shanae. Keya was humiliated. She wanted to scream. No matter what, Shanae always seemed to ruin her happiness even when she wasn't around. Because she wanted him that bad, she ignored him and pretended to be Shanae's pathetic ass.

Keya pushed him back on the sofa, and slowly began tracing circles around the head of his penis with her tongue. After massaging his head with her tongue she relaxed her throat muscles, and slowly added more of him into her mouth. She consumed all his manhood, and she quickened her pace. Hasaun couldn't believe how good Shanae was making him feel. He let out a loud moan, and began palming Keya's head as she went to work on him. Keya loved the way his body felt against her. She was in heaven. She knew for a fact after she put it on him he wouldn't be going to Texas. She would make sure of that. She knew he was on the verge of no return so she bobbed her head up and down faster. She couldn't wait to taste his sweet nectar. With his every shudder, she performed faster.

The guttural moans that were coming from Hasaun turned Keya on. She refused to stop. She was on a mission. Mission of ecstasy and forbidden love. Finally, she got what she wanted. Her mouth began to fill with his sweet nectar, and this was only the beginning. She had more plans for him once they made it to the bedroom. That was the task—getting him in the bedroom.

"Shanae, promise me you will never leave again," begged Hasaun.

Annoyed Keya replied, "I promise I will never leave."

Tears welled up in Keya's eyes. She couldn't believe the only man she loved only cared about a selfish bitch who wouldn't give him the time of day. Keya lay there feeling beaten. That feeling was washed away when she felt Hasaun enter her. He was finally making love to her, and it felt so good. She met his every thrust. She could most definitely get used to this. After they both climaxed, and began to see stars after their intense lovemaking, Hasaun fell asleep.

Keya lay watching him sleep. He was so peaceful. She was so thrilled he wasn't like the rest of them who ran to put their clothes on, and leave her by herself. He was the first man to sleep in her bed. She didn't care if he was staying because of the drugs. He was in her bed and she loved every minute of it. She was delighted he was finally hers. She lowered her mouth to his succulent lips, and planted a warm moist kiss on them.

Now she was on her way to implement part two of her plan.

Keya placed a call to Shanae, and explained to her about her grandmother's heirloom. Shanae was a little hesitant. It was late at night. She couldn't understand why it couldn't wait until in the morning. With much ado, Shanae agreed to come over, and pick it up. Keya instructed Shanae to use her spare key to let herself in. She also told her to leave her key when she left.

Shanae had forgotten all about the expensive piece. She hadn't seen it in years. Shanae threw on some sweats, a hooded jacket, and drove to Keya's. Keya told her it was in her room on the nightstand.

Keya brought the wine in the bedroom and, woke Hasaun up. He was feeling funny but he did not care. He was not going to let a headache ruin a great night. He was finally with the love of his life. He drank another glass of wine, and was ready for dessert.

Hasaun was out of it. He was acting like an animal. Keya began to get a little nervous. She was beginning to think she had given him too much of the drug. She hoped he didn't die or fuck her to death. They were in the infamous sixty-nine position when Keya heard the front door open. Immediately, she asked Hasaun to hit it from behind. He did not hesitate because that was his favorite position. He rolled her over and inserted his piece in her hot moist crevice, and was in a stupor. Keya thought her back was going to break.

Hasaun kept telling her to back it up, bounce it up and down, and to toot it up. She was working extra hard to please him. She wanted him to forget about Shanae. If he didn't after tonight she didn't know what she would do. He kept calling her Shanae, which was pissing her off. She just blocked him out, and went with the flow.

When Shanae entered Keya's apartment she noticed she had been getting her freak on. Shanae couldn't believe the mess she had left. For Pete's sake, she knew she was coming over. There was a freak movie on in the living room, wine glasses were on the table; her lingerie and men's clothing were spread out all over the living room. Shanae couldn't believe this mess.

She shook her head and walked towards the bedroom. As she approached the bedroom she heard a lot of sexual sounds inside. She guessed Keya was watching another one of her famous freak movies before she ran off in such a hurry. She turned the knob to Keya's door, and nearly passed out from the sight. She stood in the doorway speechless. She couldn't believe what she saw. They were having a time of their life. She didn't know what to do.

She watched two people that she once loved so much betray her. The only thought that ran through her mind was, *Were they fucking each other the entire time? How long had it been going on?* She could not believe her eyes.

"What is going on?" yelled Shanae.

When he heard her voice, he immediately stopped. He looked towards the doorway and into Shanae's eyes. He was confused. How was she over there when he was still deep inside of her? Hasaun looked down and for the first time that night; he realized he hadn't been making love to Shanae. It had been Keya. He moved quickly away from Keya, and started towards Shanae. Shanae grabbed the jewelry box from the nightstand, and ran out of the apartment.

44

The funny thing about the entire situation was she didn't know why she was crying. Those two people had hurt her over and over. She thought she was so over the both of them. Seeing them in such a compromising position bothered her. Once upon a time they were her life—her best friend, and the love of her life. Never would she have believed this.

Instead of going home, Shanae stopped by the store. She needed something sweet. Shanae was searching the aisles at the local grocery store. She bought brownie mix, pecans and vanilla ice cream. Now she was running around looking for some whipped cream. She was going to pig out, and forget about the events of tonight. Shanae had cried the entire ride to the store until her eyes were puffy

She was walking down the aisle when she heard his voice. She knew that voice, and laugh from anywhere. He sounded so happy, and he was talking to a female. They were laughing and joking. She couldn't believe her ears. Shanae just opted on getting her stuff and leaving. She had had enough drama for the evening to last her a lifetime. She did not want to deal with Xavier, and his lady friend. After all, that's what she kept telling herself she wanted. She hoped Xavier did not see her. In addition, she looked a mess. *What are the odds?* Of all the nights. Her hair was a mess, she had on baggy sweats and an oversized hoody. Not to mention her face was stained with tears, and her eyes were blood shot.

She stood in the center of the aisle debating which way she should walk to avoid running into him and his date. It was killing her to know that he had moved on. She decided to go the opposite direction to the checkout lanes. Shanae walked down the aisle with her head down, and into the checkout lane. In her peripheral she could see him but she refused to look in his direction. She couldn't stand to see him with someone else. Especially not looking like Little Orphan Annie. There was no way in hell she was letting him see her. She put her back towards him and his date, and hoped he didn't notice her.

Just her luck they were right behind her in line. Her heart was racing a mile a minute. She was so nervous. The cashier taking his sweet time didn't help.

She could hear them talking about his family and his parents. About how much fun they all had earlier in the day. Shanae was literally about to lose it. *She's met his family?* The duo was having a good time. They were reenacting how is father was doing the Electric Slide at some event they had just left. They shared a laughed that had Shanae upset. They were supposed to be laughing and enjoying his family together not this stallion he was with.

Frustrated Shanae ran her hand through her curly locks, and took a deep breath. She kept telling herself, *"Pay for your food and leave."* She could have done just that if the cashier would speed up. Just her luck he ran out of register tape, and decided to replace it. She had never been so nervous in her life. She spaced out, and wished she were somewhere else.

Xavier caught a glimpse of her, and thought she looked familiar. When she rubbed her manicured hands through her hair he could have sworn it was Shanae.

Shanae was jarred from her daze when she heard, $20.32 is your total."

He was looking at her as if she had lost her mind.

"I'm sorry. I didn't hear you."

Shanae's hands were shaking something terribly.

"$20.32," he repeated.

Shanae reached inside her purse and grabbed her wallet. When she tried to open it, she dropped it, and all the contents fell to the floor. Her face was flushed, and she felt a panic attack coming on.

She picked up her black card told him to run it and

began picking up her belongings all the while trying not to let Xavier see her.

Then she heard the lady with Xavier say, "Your ID and some change is behind you, miss."

Shanae took a deep breath turned around, bent down and grabbed her items.

"Thanks."

"Shanae, is that you?" questioned Xavier. He knew she looked familiar.

This bastard, thought Shanae. She grabbed her items, and card from the cashier, apologized for taking so long, and walked off. She never turned back around to see him.

"Deb, pay for this. I am going to see what's going on," stated Xavier

"Sure," replied Deb.

Xavier ran after her. He caught up to her near her vehicle.

"Shanae!"

When she turned around. Once he looked into her eyes he knew something bad had happened. She was torn to pieces. Which wasn't new for her. She seemed to always be going through something. She was a piece of work. He felt her pain. He wanted to take it away but she refused to let him in.

"Yes, Xavier. It's me," whispered Shanae.

"What are you doing out this late?"

Shaking her head she replied, "You have some nerve questioning me. You're the one out this late with another woman."

She was trying so hard to hold her tears back, but she could feel her cheeks getting hot, and her vision getting blurry. Before she knew it, they were running down her face. Silent tears. She was always told silent tears were the worst. They resonated in the depths of your soul, and needed no sound behind them. They were powerful all by themselves.

Xavier hated seeing her so sad. He took his thumb and cautiously wiped the tears from her face. The feel of her delicate skin pulled him in.

"You want to talk about it?"

"How about we talk some other time. I have a lot going on right now," begged Shanae.

She didn't want to look too needy in front of his new woman. Shanae refused to wipe her tears. If she wiped her tears then she was acknowledging that she was crying. The last thing she wanted to do in front of this man was to keep looking vulnerable.

"How about we talk now?"

"Maybe because I have ice cream in my bag and I don't want it to melt."

She wanted to say, *because you're out with your woman.*

"Shanae, you look like shit. Are you okay?"

"Well, damn, Xavier! I guess my look matches my mood."

Shanae began to wipe her tears from her eyes as she saw the woman approaching them. She was gorgeous. Shanae had to give it to her. Deb walked towards them smiling, and waiting to be introduced. Shanae gave Xavier a look that spoke a million words. She did not feel the drama. Xavier knew that look and he smirked at Shanae. Meanwhile, this damn Deb kept smiling, and was happy as ever. *Why the hell is she so damn happy?*

Shanae broke the silence and said, "Look, I need to get myself home. See you guys later!"

Shanae had to keep repeating her three C's in her head. Cool, calm and collected!!!

Laughing, Xavier said, "Why are you leaving so fast?"

Shanae could not believe this arrogant bastard. It took everything in her not to knock that smug ass smirk off his face.

Trying to hold her composure, but failing miserably, Shanae replied, "Yeah, I should be going. Three is a crowd."

Walking towards the driver's door, she prayed they would walk away from her. She wanted to punch Xavier in the mouth. She knew she was angry because she wanted to harm him. If he knew how close he was to being slapped he would leave.

Deb felt bad for Shanae's pain. It was etched all over her face. She wished Xavier would stop the BS.

Before she could open her door, Xavier held onto her arm.

"Shanae, I want you to meet someone who is special to me."

Whispering, Shanae replied, "Xavier, please spare me. I am not up for this. You wouldn't be introducing her to me if we hadn't run into each other at the damn grocery store."

"Probably not. Since we're here we might as well be polite," smiled Xavier.

Shanae whispered, "I don't want to meet your freak of the week."

"Shanae, I know you have more class than that. We are all adults here."

Deb felt horrible because they were not doing a good job of whispering.

The pain on her face spoke volumes. Shanae snatched her arm away from Xavier with all her might and said, "Look, Hugh Hefner, I don't have time for this sh—"

Shanae stopped in mid-sentence. He was not going to make her lose her cool in front of his date. She smiled, nodded her head and opened her door. She had to keep coaching herself silently of her three C's.

Xavier realized he might have gone too far with her. He

decided it was time to cut the charade. Deb thought he was insane to keep toying with her emotions. Besides that, she had been called his freak of the week and a playboy bunny.

"Deb, this is Shanae. Shanae, this is Deb, my sister," laughed Xavier.

Shanae let a huge sigh of relief. Deb ran over to her and gave her a hug.

"I feel like I already know you. I have heard so much about you."

Shanae looked at Xavier and back to Deb.

"It's really nice to meet you, too. I have heard a lot about you, also."

Shanae gave Xavier a look that could kill. She stared at him through slits and shook her head with a look of disgust.

Deb noticed her anger and replied, "Well, I hope we get to see each other before I go back home. I am going to the car. Looks like you two need some time alone."

Deb gave Xavier that look telling him to handle his business. He had been talking about Shanae all day to his family. It was obvious he was in love, and she could see why; even at her worst she was still beautiful. She seemed to be nice. Deb hoped they would work it out. She hated seeing her brother troubled.

"Nice meeting you, Deb. Maybe we can hang out before you leave."

Deb smiled and walked away.

Xavier saw all the sugary items in her bag, and knew whatever it was that was bothering her it was bad.

"Xavier, I need to get home."

"I am worried about you."

"I am good. Trust and believe."

"If I trust and believe will you trust and believe?" questioned Xavier.

"Boy, don't start with me. You do not know how close I was to busting you in the mouth," joked Shanae.

"Oh, I knew," admitted Xavier.

"I have to get going."

"The only way I will let you leave is if you call me when you're home safe and sound."

"Okay. I promise I will call you." Shanae wanted to get home and relax.

"Shanae, one last thing. Can I have a hug? You look like you need a hug."

Laughing Shanae said, "You just want to get a free feel. Boy, I am not stupid."

Shaking his head Xavier replied, "And you know this man!"

"That's exactly why I am not letting you get one."

"Naw, all BS aside I just want to give you a hug. Looks like you need one," said Xavier. She wanted to hug him just as bad as he wanted to hug her, if not more.

"Sure, Xavier, you can give me a hug."

She needed it in more ways than one. His strong embrace did something to her. She noticed how vulnerable and weak she really was. When he felt her tremble he wanted to drive her home, and tuck her in bed himself.

He kissed the top of her head, and whispered in her ear,

"I love you more than anything. Don't forget I am just a phone call away."

Shanae had no idea why she was playing so hard to get. She wanted this man, and she wanted him bad. She wiped her tears and said,

"Thanks, friend."

"Friend?" Xavier was not settling for being just a friend.

"We're not friends?"

Xavier wanted to be honest, "Hell, naw, we ain't friends. Shanae, whether you realize it or not, I am your man."

"How does that work? You go with me but I don't go with you?" Shanae had to laugh at that.

"You know what they say about people who laugh at their own jokes."

He walked her to the driver's door helped her in and said, "Make sure you call me when you get home."

"Will do," smiled Shanae.

Shanae knew one thing for sure. She loved this man

more than she was willing to admit. She realized she had to do some serious soul searching, and figure out what she wanted in life.

Ten minutes later Shanae was opening her door and letting herself in. She was so happy to be home. She didn't want to call Xavier because she knew the conversation would more than likely end in a disagreement. Nevertheless, she also knew she had promised him, and if she didn't call he would be knocking on her front door within minutes. She decided to prepare her brownies, and put them in the oven before she placed the call to Xavier.

Licking the spoon, Shanae picked up her phone and dialed his number. "What took you so long to call?"

"What happened to people saying hello when they answer the phone?"

Laughing, Xavier replied, "Just worried about you. Want to make sure you are safe."

"Well, I didn't want to break my promise to you so I called. I am home safe and sound."

"Thanks for calling."

"It's really not that big of a deal. You don't have to keep thanking me."

"I hurt when you hurt. The pain in your eyes tonight let me know something is troubling you. Just remember I am here for you."

"That makes me feel better. Xavier, I am going through a lot right now. Which is nothing new. I just need some time," replied Shanae.

"Shanae, time waits for no one. Stop shutting me out," begged Xavier.

"What am I supposed to do?"

"Trust your heart."

"This old heart has had me in so much stuff I shouldn't have been in. Why should I trust it now?" laughed Shanae.

"What does your heart say about me? Be honest with me?"

Shanae didn't want to answer the question her heart said to give it another try. Stuttering she replied. "My heart tells me to give us another try. My body says give us another try. My mind says give us another try."

"So what's the problem?"

She took a deep breath and replied, "You were so right about me because my pride says hell, naw! And I just can't get passed that pride."

Xavier felt so let down, "Shanae, do you love me?"

"More than you could ever imagine."

"Then what am I supposed to do?"

"I don't know!"

She felt so stupid. Why she was playing this mind game she had no idea. Why couldn't she just let him back in.

"Are you telling me we should move on?"

"I'm not telling you anything. You do what you do"

"You are so full of shit. When you thought I was doing what I do tonight, you cared. Why can't you just be honest with yourself? You want me. You really want me."

Shanae didn't know what to say. He had busted her. The only thing she was doing was breathing into the phone. She had no idea what to say.

Xavier broke the silence, "I guess I have to move on."

He sounded defeated.

He continued, "I want you to know if you ever need anything, I am here for you. I just can't grow old and lonely waiting on you."

"Whoa, not what I expected to hear. However, I don't expect for you to keep waiting around on me. It's cool we can be friends."

Shanae wiped the tears that were flowing from her eyes.

"You don't know how hard that was for me to say. Now, I have to keep telling myself to move on."

"It couldn't have been as hard as it was for me to hear it. It sounds so final."

Joking, Xavier said, "I am glad it was hard for you to hear. You are putting us through all this unnecessary bull. When you know we both want each other."

Shanae refused to take the blame, "No, Xavier. Your lie is putting us through this."

"Ouch!"

Shanae felt bad for being a smart mouth.

"Truth hurts. Like I said I guess its just time to move on."

"If you move on I might have to leave town, Xavier. I don't think I can handle seeing you in love with someone else."

"Who said I would be in love?" questioned Xavier.

"I just figured."

"Besides if you move, I am coming with you. You're not leaving me that easily," joked Xavier.

"Stop contradicting yourself handsome. Besides I have already left you."

"That's the effect you have on me. You stop flirting with me. I don't need these mind games."

"I'm not playing any mind games. You are handsome. That's a fact."

"It's not a fact. That's your opinion. There are some people who may think I am unsightly."

"I doubt it."

"Shanae, what are we going to do about your pride?"

Laughing Shanae replied, "That's a first. I have never had anybody who wants to do something about my pride."

"You know I can't move on. My heart just won't let me. I love you, woman."

"Xavier, I love you too but I cannot stand being hurt again."

"Don't take this the wrong way. Aren't you hurting now that we are not together? So why not just give it another try to see what it is worth."

"Boy, you are something else," laughed Shanae.

Xavier had to laugh himself. "It sounded good."

Both Xavier and Shanae shared a laugh. It felt good to laugh together. Their laughter was met with silence. They both knew what that meant.

"Man, I guess this is where we say goodbye."

"Only if you want to, Shanae. You could say come over."

"If I asked you to, would you?"

"If I told you to open the door, and I was outside would you?"

"If you promised not to ever hurt me again."

She walked to the door and put her ear to the door. She could feel his presence through the door.

Xavier and Shanae were now talking through the door.

"Shanae, I will never lie to you again or hurt you."

"I love you, Xavier."

"I love you, Shanae!"

"You will never lie to me?"

"Never."

"You promise?"

"I promise."

"Will you always take my feelings into consideration?"

"Always!"

"I'm scared, Xavier."

"I will protect you."

"I don't want to be hurt."

"I will never hurt you again."

He could hear her sobs through the door. He wanted to be on the other side comforting her.

"If I open this door, it's forever?"

"Forever it is, Shanae!"

"Forever ever?"

"Forever ever! Ever ever!" laughed Xavier.

Shanae unlocked the top lock before she took the chain off she replied, "No more games."

"No more games, baby.

"Xavier, I also—"

Xavier cut her off in mid-sentence and replied, "Open the door. I can't take it anymore."

45

Dave walked into Keya's office, and couldn't believe his eyes. There were depositions and cases stacked to the ceiling. He hadn't seen her around the office for a few days. He had no idea her work was piling up. He didn't know what to think. This was totally out of her character. She hadn't called in for several days. It was like she vanished. Dave had called her many times since her disappearing act. He now knew her number by heart. He knew there was no way in hell she hadn't heard the plethora of messages he left on the machine. He thought she would at least have the decency to quit face to face.

Keya was the last person he wanted to fire. He enjoyed her in the office plus she was eye candy. He always picked up on her loneliness. It showed all over her face. For years he had been attracted to her, but she was so cold. He wanted to know what had caused her to be so withdrawn and unsympathetic. He knew he had to find out what was going on with her, before he made any rash decisions to fire her.

Dave couldn't believe he was standing in front of her door. He didn't know what he would say or how she would react. The only thing he knew was that she wasn't quitting on him. He admired her. Why? He didn't know but he always saw the good in her, which was the reason why he hired her in the first place even though she was a little rough around the edges.

He pushed the doorbell. No answer. After five attempts he decided to knock on the door. She had to be inside because her car was in the parking lot. Once he tapped on the door it sprung open. Dave looked into the apartment. No sign of Keya.

"Keya! Keya are you in there?" yelled Dave from the doorway. The apartment was silent.

Against his better judgment, Dave entered her apartment. He knew that he could be in serious trouble if her apartment was a crime scene. Considering her door was ajar. He only entered because he had a bad feeling something was wrong with her. He had presumed correctly. Inside, he was bombarded with a horrible stench. He immediately ran to a window and opened it.

Dave walked through the apartment yelling her name. He was met with an eerie silence. Approaching Keya's bedroom, the smell intensified. Dave had a churning feeling in his gut. He pulled his handkerchief out of his pocket and covered his mouth and nose. He prayed nothing bad had happened to her.

Once he opened the door he was mystified. He yelled to no

one in particular.

"What in God's name has happened?"

He couldn't believe his eyes. She was tied to her bed stiff as a board. Her bed had dried blood and other bodily fluids on it. Her face was covered with dried blood. Her eyes were swollen shut, her nose was broken and she had a busted lip.

He ran to her and checked her pulse. Within seconds he had the police on the phone. She had a faint pulse and she was gasping for air. Dave didn't want to touch her but he couldn't stand seeing her lying in that disgusting bed. He pulled his pocketknife out and cut her loose from the bedposts. He laid her on the floor, ran to her linen closet, retrieved a blanket and covered her with a clean blanket.

She was so close to death. He had never seen anyone so close to death. She was on the cliff hanging on by her pinky; at the bottom was death. Something was willing her to hold on. The doctor told him he saved her life. If he had not gotten there when he did she wouldn't be here today.

Sitting in his office, he had no idea what he should do about Keya. He had just finished allocating her workload around the firm. He knew she was going to be off for a very long time. He never told anyone what had happened to her. The last thing he needed was the office gossiping about Keya. He told them she wasn't coming in for a while and that was all they needed to know.

Dave had tried the numbers in Keya's file and didn't have any luck reaching a family member. The one person he heard her talk about had told him to contact a family member. He wanted someone to be there for her when she woke up. He was beginning to feel sorry for her. She had no one. No family. No friends. No one cared about her well-being. It was as if she was all-alone in the cold world. He couldn't imagine why anyone would beat her so badly. He wanted to know what kind of people she associated herself with. Not having anyone to care for you or about you must have been really hard. He heard she was having problems a while back but never in a million years would he ever have thought her life was in jeopardy.

He planned on finding out what had transpired in her apartment and who left her for dead. Right now he had to put this Keya mess to the side and head to court.

After a long day in court Dave decided he would pay Keya a visit. He was anxious to find out what had happened. He wished he could have been there to protect her or prevent the incident from ever taking place. He vowed to always have her back from this day forward.

When he walked into her room her back was towards the door. He entered the room and there was no movement from her. She lay there as still as ever. He walked around the bed and sat in a chair where he could she her once beautiful face. The swelling in her face was going down but she had a long road to a

411

full recovery. Her eyes were closed, however, not by choice. Her nose was bandage and her face was black and blue. Someone really had it out for her.

She couldn't believe he was back. She couldn't see him but she felt his presence and she smelled his fragrance. When her nurse told her who saved her she was speechless. She never knew Dave had a caring bone in his body. This entire ordeal was unexpected; from Hasaun beating the breaks off her to Dave being her knight in shining armor. She would never know how to thank him for saving her life. The doctor told her she would have never made it another day. Dave had saved her.

She could feel his piercing eyes trying to figure out this mess. She wondered what her colleagues thought about her. Keya wished she could talk. She couldn't and there was nothing she could do about it.

Dave questioned if she was sleep. He questioned if she knew he was there or not. She looked one hundred percent better than she did when he found her. However, she still wasn't out of the woods.

Dave decided to ask her a question to see if she responded, "Keya it's me, Dave. Is it ok that I am here?"

Keya couldn't believe the sincerity in his voice. She nodded her head yes.

Smiling, Dave replied, "I am so glad you are okay. I have been worried about you."

Keya could tell he was smiling and she was glad someone had been worried about her. She wanted to thank him but her face and lips were twice their normal size.

"Keya, I tried to reach a family member or a friend to be here with you. Do you have anyone I can call?"

For the first time in years Keya realized she was in this cruel world all by her lonesome. She shook her head no.

Dave's heart went out to her. He couldn't imagine her dealing with something of this caliber by herself.

He said, "I'll be here for you. I'll make sure you are taken care of."

Keya wanted to yell thank you. She was happy he would help her. No one had ever given a damn about her. Now the one person who was helping her was someone she'd least expected. She had always made an extra effort to push his buttons and to piss him off. Now here he was vowing to help her.

When Dave stood to leave, he walked over to her bed and held her hand.

"Keya, you get some rest. I will be back tomorrow."

Keya squeezed his hand as if her life depended on it. She was thanking him in more ways than one.

After Dave left, Keya felt bad. She lied to him. Just like she lied to the police, doctor, nurse and anyone else who asked her what happened. She simply told them she had no recollection of anything. The only thing she remembered was waking up in the hospital. When, in actuality, she remembered everything. She remembered him tying her up, fucking her with no regards to her feelings, beating her with an electrical cord, smashing her nose in and pissing on her. She thought that was bad until he defecated on her and told her to eat shit and die. She knew he was going to kill her. Once she seen all the blood that was gushing from her nose and face she lost consciousness. Never in her life would she think Hasaun would treat her so maliciously.

She lied because she was ashamed to admit it. She wanted to push those horrible memories as far back in her subconscious as possible. She couldn't believe how cold and calculated she had been. Her plan had backfired and she had pushed everyone who ever gave a damn about her out of her life. What were the odds of Dave stepping up to help? She was going to work hard not to ruin their friendship.

46

Hasaun caught the next thing smoking out of town. He couldn't believe he flipped out like that. Now he was afraid CPD was looking for him. He put a number in on Keya. He couldn't believe she played him for a sucka. He was so angry and discombobulated he had no idea what was going through his mind. Whatever she put in his wine had him on another level.

After the fact, he felt horrible for what he did to her. It was some weird sick shit that happened. However, at the time he wanted to teach her a lesson. She was playing with his emotions and she had jeopardized Shanae and his relationship even more. There was no way in hell Shanae would ever associate with him now; all because of Keya's sick ass.

He had been in Texas for a few weeks when he realized he was cool. He called home every day to talk to his momma. He was making sure no police had been by looking for him. He figured Keya never told anyone what happened and he expected she was still alive because he hadn't heard she died. He swore he would never put his hands on another female. He had one thing on his mind and that was getting his life back on track.

Hasaun had landed a job at a local high school and was the assistant basketball coach. He also enrolled in online classes at a local college. Hasaun had less than a year left to complete his degree. He was having a great time coaching the kids and keeping occupied. There wasn't a day that went that he didn't think about Shanae. He had been on several dates but nothing panned out. He decided to stay focused on is job and classes.

Hasaun was working extra hard and his passion for the sport showed at every practice and game. He was dedicated to landing a job as head coach somewhere. He loved basketball and he was letting his fervor show on his job. His head coach was glad he chose him and the players enjoyed having him as a coach. He was cool and laid back but when it came to basketball he metamorphosed into a beast.

After a long day of work and practice, Hasaun had to rush home, study and or do homework. He was getting in the hang of everything and staying out of his aunt's way.

His aunt turned out to be a miserable prune that was always on his back. He paid her every month for staying with her, bought his own food and personal supplies. He even had to buy his own toilet paper. He wanted to get the hell away from her as soon as possible. He never remembered her being so bitter. He knew for sure she was not going to stop him from accomplishing his goals. He was finally feeling good about something in his life since his children died and Shanae left him.

He tried to tell his mother about his aunt but she jumped on the defense and backed her sister. She told him he was ungrateful. After all she was letting him live with her. He couldn't understand how he was being ungrateful. He was paying her. He had a nice chunk of change stashed away and planned on moving soon.

He was in his room working on a paper when he heard a knock at his bedroom door. He walked over and opened the door and there she stood. A short petite, salt and pepper haired beast. Beside her horrible attitude she was a beauty. He knew she was about to complain about something.

"Hey, Auntie how are you?" asked Hasaun as he took a deep breath and prayed she didn't jump down his throat.

She looked at him over her glasses and replied, "I have been better."

"Is there anything I can do to help?" Hasaun did not understand her. He cleaned when he had time. He fixed her porch, doorbell and other things that needed repair around her home and she still complained. He hadn't even been there three months. Three months is usually the time frame people get irritated that you are in their home. Even though they invited you to stay. They start acting funny and rude for no apparent reason at all. He hadn't even reached that three-month period.

"Yeah, stay out of my way," she said with a stern look.

Hasaun knew his aunt's bark was louder than her bite but she was starting to work on his nerves.

Rubbing his chin with a stunned look Hasaun replied, "I will do just that."

He shut the door and walked back to his homework. Before he had a chance to make it back to his desk his aunt burst through the door.

"Boy, don't you ever slam a damn door in my face. Have you lost your damn mind?"

"You told me to stay out of your way. I was in my room, you came knocking on my door and now you're mad for no reason. What am I supposed to do?"

"First off, you don't have a room. I was coming to let you know that I will have a house guest over for the weekend, so stay out of our way."

She walked out his room and slammed the door.

He prayed her friend released some of her sexual tension because she most definitely needed some. He was going to look for an apartment tomorrow. There was no way in hell he could deal with his aunt. He was bound to snap on her. If he snapped on her, his mom would have his head.

Hasaun was happy that it was nearing the weekend.

They didn't have practice or a game. This barely happened and he was going to enjoy it. He was able to use the school gym so he worked out after work, anything to avoid his aunt. She was going to drive him back to smoking weed.

When he pulled up, he noticed a strange car in the driveway. He knew it was his aunt's weekend guest. *So much for staying out of her way.* He eased his key in the door as quietly as he could. He made an extra effort to close the door as gently as possible. He was dressed in a pair basketball shorts and a black beater. He was drenched from his intense workout and his muscles looked like a Hershey's bar.

He heard voices in the main room and was walking as fast as he could to make it to his room before he disturbed the wicked witch. He made it without bringing his aunt any grief. He prayed everything worked out. He was going to look at an apartment in the morning. He sat his duffle bag on the bed, took his shirt off and was thankful he had a bathroom in his room. He was untying his shoes when he heard a tap at his door.

Damn! What the hell. He was convinced she was crazy. She kept telling him to stay out her way but she kept coming to his damn room. He ignored her knocking. Of course it grew louder and more persistent. He walked over to the door and snatched it open just to irritate her. It worked.

Once the door was open his aunt looked at the door then

back at him.

"I know you not snatching doors open?"

He was so mad he hadn't noticed her guest behind her. "No, ma'am."

"I was just wondering because don't nobody snatch doors open around here but me. Boy, you need to put some clothes on."

"I was about to hop in the shower when I heard a knock at the door." *If you stop harassing me maybe I can.*

"Humph, well I just wanted to introduce Lily to you."

His aunt had her nose turned up and was just a nasty old bitty, so much for southern hospitality.

Lily? Damn I thought it was going to be a male friend. Wishing he would keep her occupied over the weekend.

That was the first time he laid eyes on her she was beautiful. Not beautiful like Shanae but a Plain Jane beautiful. He forgot his aunt was there. He just stared at her. He couldn't wait until the day he stopped comparing other women to Shanae.

She had been in awe as soon as he snatched the door open. He had muscles for days. His smooth black skin was to die for and he was handsome. He had her feeling' some type a way. His aunt had told her to steer clear from him because he was nothing but trouble.

Hasaun decided to stop being rude and extended his

hand.   "Hi, I'm Hasaun. Nice, to meet you Lily."

Lily couldn't get herself together. *Damn this man was fine.* Hasaun prayed she said something before his Aunt Faye started jumping to conclusions.

Lily was so embarrassed. She wished he had a shirt on. She heard Ms. Faye clearing her throat and she blushed. She stuck her hand out and replied, "Nice meeting you. I'm Lily."

Her southern drawl had him as soon as she opened her perfect mouth. His eyes lit up and his heart was racing a mile a minute.

Faye didn't like what was going on between the two. She knew her nephew had some issues and Lily was a good girl. She was not letting the two of them cross any forbidden waters.

"Well, you get in the shower. We have stuff to do."

With that said, she slammed her door in his face and walked off with the southern belle.

Hasaun woke up the next morning at the crack of dawn. His dreams were consumed of Lily all night. He didn't get any sleep. He couldn't get her beauty out of his mind. He wasn't going to let her distract him from his Saturday morning ritual. He needed to clean the house, cook his aunt breakfast and run three miles.

He didn't understand why he continued to clean and cook for her mean tail every Saturday. He knew she enjoyed waking up to a clean house and breakfast even if she never admitted it.

He wanted to be the bigger person. He had the house clean

and breakfast cooked. He made sure he cooked a little extra for Lily. He was on his way out the door when he heard his aunt stirring.

Lily watched him in the driveway. He did a stretch routine and was off down the street. She thought it was thoughtful of him to clean and cook for his aunt. He didn't seem as bad as Ms. Faye had portrayed him.

Unbeknownst to her, Ms. Faye was standing behind her and as if reading her mind Ms. Faye said, "Everything that glitters ain't gold."

47

Hasaun had had enough of his aunt. She was starting to wear him slick. All she ever did was complain, complain and complain some more. He could see why she was single. No man in his right mind would want to listen to all her damn nagging. He always felt like he was in her damn way. The last couple of days she had been preoccupied with Lily and hadn't been on his case. He knew that wouldn't last for long. He was in his room getting prepared to go check out an apartment. His aunt was driving him crazy. He broke down and called the apartment complex he drove past every day. He had been praying all week that he got the apartment because he needed to get out of his aunt's house before he ended up cussing her out. He couldn't take her shenanigans any longer. She was one bitter old woman.

He found out that Lily was from Tunica, Mississippi, and she was visiting Aunt Faye because her mother was a close friend of Aunt Faye's. Lily was hiding from an abusive boyfriend. She planned to head back to Tunica as soon as he was arrested. She had been dating the psychopath for two months and he had become jealous and controlling. She called the relationship off and all hell broke loose. Hasaun found all this information out from ear hustling. Once he found out she had just as many problems as him, she didn't seem so beautiful after all. His aunt didn't have to worry about him pushing up on her because she had her own skeletons to deal with. He didn't want to add theirs together. He would stay as far away from the southern belle as possible.

Hasaun grabbed his keys, exited his bedroom and headed towards the front door. His hand was on the doorknob when he heard her annoying voice.

"Hasaun?" The sound of her voice was like nails scrapping down a chalkboard.

Why can't she leave me the hell alone? Ugh! "Yes ma'am," This ma'am shit was getting on his nerves too.

Instead of answering him, she walked towards him. He could never tell what type of mood she was in. He for sure as hell wasn't telling her he was looking for an apartment until he knew he had the damn apartment. If he told her and didn't get the apartment she would call him ungrateful and since he didn't want to live there, he could leave. He was so sick of her games. He didn't want any shit out of her this beautiful quiet spring morning.

Looking him up and down with her nose slightly turned up, she replied, "We're having a nice eloquent dinner tonight and I want to make sure you stay out of our way tonight. We have some important folks coming over and don't need you messing anything up."

She didn't even let him respond before she walked off and dismissed him.

Shaking his head and laughing on the inside he walked out the door and prayed one last time that he would get the apartment.

Important people my ass! I didn't care about her little raggedy stuck up southern wanna be belle friends.

He wondered why his aunt hated him so much. As much as her nose stayed in the air, he was starting to think he was funky. Yeah, he had messed up but damn, she had three boys and they were all in federal prison for drug trafficking. Seems like she would be a little nicer to people who were free on the streets. There was no way in hell he could stay with her any longer. He couldn't complain to his momma because that was her sister. Being the only child, he couldn't relate to their bond. He knew he couldn't go to his momma about her crazy ass sister. He wondered what kind of eloquent dinner she was having. She wouldn't know eloquent if it slapped her in the face.

Lily watched Hasaun as he left the house. She couldn't

help but wonder why his aunt treated him so poorly. From what she had observed he was civilized. He worked every day. He purchased his own food and he even cleaned and cooked for her on Saturday mornings. Lily made the mistake of asking Faye why she hated Hasaun so much. She gave her a watered down speech of being a devote Christian and there wasn't an ounce of hatred in her body. She loved all her brethren. Still, Lily wanted to form her own opinion about Hasaun before she took Faye's information to heart because according to Faye he was bad news and she needed to stay as far away from Hasaun as possible. Lily knew there was no way in hell she was going to be able to stay away from his fine chocolate ass. There was an unspoken chemistry between them and she was willing to find out what it was pulling them towards each other.

Hasaun held on tightly to the apartment keys in his pocket that his fingers were sore and beginning to cramp. He was not going home to deal with the wicked witch. He stopped by Stone Trail Bar and Grill. He had a few beers and ate dinner. He made sure he wasn't going home until after her "eloquent dinner" was over.

Hasaun was enjoying the live band when a shorty walked over to him and asked him if he wanted to dance. He looked at her and noticed she wasn't as beautiful as Shanae.

Damn, why am I always comparing other women to Shanae. I have to close that chapter of my life.

He escorted her to the floor and they danced to a few songs before her man snatched her off the floor. Hasaun shook his head and headed back to his seat. The place was packed and had a mature crowd.

Hasaun seldom had a chance to relax. He was always so tense when he was at his aunt's. Tomorrow he would be moving out of the wicked witch's house. He was going to start packing when he got home. He had boxes and tape in his trunk. He left the bar around midnight and headed to Costco's. He purchased the basic things he needed for his apartment. He was glad he had been saving money. He was able to pay the first and last month's rent and his deposit. He still had enough for a rainy day. He bought dishes, utensils, a trashcan, cleaning supplies, curtains and some blankets. He knew once he told his mother, she would send him a care package. She might even come down and help him find furniture.

When he finally made it home it was after one in the morning. He knew he was breaking the cardinal rule, which was to never come into her house after midnight. All the lights were off and he was pleased he didn't have to deal with the wicked witch. He quietly entered the house with his boxes and walked to his room without any delay. He was extra careful not to drop anything and make any unnecessary noises.

He was glad living with his aunt was almost over. He wouldn't have to walk on eggshells anymore. Once he tiptoed down the hall to his room he sat the boxes down took his shirt off and finally breathed. Then he heard the tap at his door.

His nostrils flared and he wanted to scream. *She's like a fly on the wall. Why can't she just leave me the hell alone?* This was it. He was certain now more than ever he would be moving tonight because he was going to let her despondent behind have it. He yanked the door open and it startled her. Lily stood there in a plain white cotton nightgown that was transparent because of the lighting. Her hair was out of the simple bun she usually wore at the crown of her head. It draped over her shoulders. There was something about her looks that made him want her. They stared at each other both sizing each other up. Hasaun couldn't help but notice her plump nipples through her cotton gown. He had to get her away from his room before his aunt heard them. She would swear he was taking advantage of sweet little Lily.

Lily broke the silence, "May I please come in."

Hasaun was having second thoughts about letting her come in. She was so sweet and innocent looking that it turned him on. Not in a sick perverted way but in an angelic way.

Against his better judgment, he cleared his throat and replied, "Sure."

Moving aside he let her sway those love making hips into his bedroom. She looked sweet, delicate and petite. It was something about a southern woman and her hips and plump derriere.

Lord, help me.

"Thanks," smirked Lily.

Her southern drawl had him going crazy.

"No problem. What can I do for you?"

" I couldn't sleep. I heard you come in so I wanted to meet you."

"The wicked witch already introduced us."

He wanted to smack himself. He could not believe he called her the wicked witch in front of Lily.

Laughing she replied, "Don't worry. I won't tell her what you called her."

"Thanks, she just rides me so hard it drives me crazy."

"Riding you hard drives you crazy," joked Lily.

Hasaun couldn't believe this little southern belle was trying to take it there. He had to get her out of his room before something bad happened. Then the wicked witch would most definitely kill him.

"Lily, what can I help you with?"

"Nothing. I just wanted to get to know you. You don't seem as bad as the "wicked witch" described you."

"Oh yeah, well looks can be deceiving. You already have enough problems back in Tunica you don't need more."

"What do you know about my problems?"

How the hell did he know? She knew for sure Ms. Faye

hadn't told him.

Hasaun had let the cat out the bag. He wasn't supposed to know about her problems. He stood there with a blank look on his face and avoided the question.

"You know it's rude to listen in on other's conversations."

"Thanks for informing me. I know you have your hands full," replied Hasaun.

Poking her lips out and rolling her eyes, Lily took it upon herself to sit on the bed. Once she was seated she eased her legs on the bed and sat Indian style. Her cotton gown rose above her knees and exposed the inner most part of her delicate thigh.

Hasaun was looking at her butter cream thick thighs and was speechless. He had to get her out of his room. He could feel the blood circulating in the wrong parts of his body. Hasaun was in a trance thinking about rubbing that delicate soft skin. He rubbed his hand up and down his face and shook his head. He had to get her out of his room before the witch found them. At this moment he was more scared of himself then any wicked witch. His carnal thoughts were taking his mind hostage.

Noticing the effect she had on him, Lily broke the awkward silence, "What are you doing with all the boxes?"

She wasn't oblivious to the fact that he couldn't take his eyes off her thighs and when he looked at her breasts, he licked his silky chocolate lips.

Hasaun didn't hesitate to reply, "I'm getting the hell up out of here in the morning. I know when I'm not wanted and Aunt Faye doesn't want my black behind in her house, so I'm moving."

" Where are you moving to?" questioned Lily.

Damn, I just built up enough nerve to talk to him and he is moving already.

"I found an apartment not too far from my job. I got the keys today and I'm moving tomorrow," boasted Hasaun.

"That sucks. I wanted to get to know you and maybe hang out. Looks like I'm going to be here a lot longer than I expected."

Lily had been trying to figure out how to approach him and then when she did; she found out he was moving. She really wasn't feeling this. She had wanted him the moment she laid eyes on his chocolate six foot plus easy on the eyes self. In addition, she had an itch and she was willing to let him scratch it.

"Maybe we can hang out some time. I'll give you my address but you can't let my aunt know because I can't handle her smart ass mouth," laughed Hasaun.

"Know your address or that we're hanging out?"

Laughing Hasaun replied, "I don't despise her that much to keep her in the dark about my whereabouts. I just don't want her to know that we will be communicating."

"Ok, that's a deal. Well, let's get you packed."

Lily grabbed a box and began taping it together. She passed it to Hasaun and he began packing it. After about fifteen boxes they both sat on the bed and caught their breath. The room seemed so empty and their breathing was the only audible sound.

Their eyes locked on each other, both taking in the sight of each other. She loved his rich chocolate skin. He loved her deep dimples. They inched closer to each other. They could smell each other's fragrance. She closed her eyes hoping he would kiss her. She wanted to feel those soft succulent lips on her. She could tell he was a good kisser.

Her thoughts were interrupted when he said, "Lily, as much as I hate to say this but will you please leave."

She opened her eyes, stood, pulled her gown down and replied, "You sure about that?"

Hasaun stood and said, "More than sure."

He couldn't help but notice how erect her plumped nipples were and how flushed her face was. For the first time he realized they both had a weird effect on each other.

Inches from him she replied, "You don't look more than sure."

Hasaun didn't like the game she was playing. Sure he could have hit it and quit it but look where that had him. Her sexual taunting had his emotions all over the place. She placed her smooth delicate hand on his chest. He backed away from her electrifying touch.

"Lily, please leave?"

She smiled and said, "On one condition."

She couldn't be serious. He was on the brink of no return so at this point anything she suggested he was willing to do.

"Yes, what is it?"

"Let me taste those chocolate lips before I go to bed?" She thought he was going to pass out.

Shaking his head he replied, "If you put those soft lips on me you will be leaving out of here with more than a kiss."

That was music to her ears. It had be five long months since someone had plucked her guitar. Excluding the pitiful piece she got from her ex, which she wasn't counting.

Laughing, Lily replied, "I don't want anything but a kiss and then I'll leave. Or we can keep the discussion going and stir the wicked witch."

Lily stood there challenging him. He knew for damn sure he didn't want his aunt up. Shaking his head he replied, "What am I getting myself into?"

Explaining her in his room and all the boxes to his aunt was one confrontation he wanted to escape.

"One kiss and then you have to go," sighed, Hasaun.

Smirking, Lily stood her four feet eleven inches self on the bed, bent down and kissed Hasaun. She placed her delicate tongue in his warm succulent mouth. Her gentleness and attentiveness had his emotions all over the place. She continued to massage his mouth with her eager tongue. He was worried about what he would do to her but here she stood manhandling him.

Once she removed her experienced tongue from his mouth she sauntered out the door and down the hall. He stood in his 12x12 room craving her like a junky.

Hasaun lay on the bed wishing he wouldn't have asked her to leave. There was something between them he enjoyed. He hadn't had that feeling since Shanae. Finally, he was able to connect with another woman. He had to play his cards right with Lily. He had Aunt Faye to worry about if he messed it up. Looking at the empty room, he dozed off and was awakened by the all too familiar banging at the door.

48

The swelling and bruising had finally gone away. Her beautiful features were slowly but surely replacing the monstrosity that he had observed previously. No more swollen eyes or lips. Still discolored but she was starting to look like a person again.

Whomever the evil person was that attacked Keya would most definitely pay for what they did. Not only was she attacked but also she was sexually assaulted. She had refused a rape kit apparently for her own selfish reasons. His DNA had been washed away. At least that's what Keya thought. Dave had gone back to her apartment and collected his own evidence. He collected sheets, cups and had a PI dust for fingerprints. Dave was adamant about locating the attacker. Come hell or high water the attacker would be located.

Keya could see the wheels turning in Dave's head. He wanted details while she wanted to put the horrible ordeal behind her.

Yes, you have been heaven sent but your inquisitiveness is alarming.

She had brought the attack on herself. She'd been manipulative and conniving, trying to hurt and deceive Shanae and seduce Hasaun all at the same time. Her plan backfired and she lost the only two people who she ever considered her friends. Not only had she sabotaged her friendship with the both of them she had also caused Shanae to despise Hasaun even the more. Not that he hadn't played his own hand in destroying their relationship. She would never forget the look of disgust on Shanae's face. It was permanently etched in her brain. However, at that time seeing Shanae hurt and run out distraught made Keya happy.

Her happiness only lasted for a brief second. Then it turned to the worst experience she had ever encountered. Urine and feces permeated her nostrils as she slowly drifted into an unconscious state. She had asked herself several times why she had done what she did. She wasn't thinking rationally and she finally realized it was not worth it.

Dave watched Keya wipe tears from her face. He had noticed her silently crying more on a regular basis. He was glad she couldn't remember the horrific events that landed her in ICU. She was finally out of ICU and was looking forward to being released.

"Keya, is everything okay?" Dave asked as he handed her his handkerchief.

Keya cleared her scratchy throat and replied, "You have to ask?"

Dave had witnessed a softer side of Keya while she was in the hospital but every now and again the rough around the edges Keya resurfaced. He enjoyed that Keya. He wasn't accustomed to the sweet and docile Keya. He wished she would find a way to incorporate both personalities into one. There was something about the rough around the edges Keya that turned him on.

Inhaling, Dave replied, "I just want to make sure you're as comfortable as possible."

Keya decided to stop being mean because he was there with her. As a matter of fact he was the only one who was by her side.

"Dave, don't take my mood swings personally. I just got a lot going on."

"I'm not taking anything personally. Keya, my being around doesn't make you uncomfortable does it?"

Keya was not going to make any mistakes that would cause or push Dave to walk out of her life. She had grown attached to him and enjoyed his company.

With a strained genuine smile Keya replied, "Dave you could never make me feel uncomfortable. You've been by my side throughout this entire ordeal and I am truly grateful to have you here."

Dave tried to contain his excitement. He was sure his face was red. Keya saying she was grateful made him blush. He was happy. The nurse walked in and killed the awkward silence.

"Keya, how ya doing today!" asked Melinda, the overweight day nurse whose shoes were screaming "save me."

Keya always heard her before she saw her. She breathes so loudly. She was one of Keya's favorites. Lord knows she couldn't stand those heifers on the evening shifts. Those were some awful wenches. Keya overheard one of them saying, "She knows good damn well who whooped her ass and raped her. There isn't that much amnesia in the world."

Keya remember listening to the smart mouth wench and crying. She never said anything to the nurse but she let Melinda know and Ms. Smart Mouth was nice from that day forward.

"Hey, Melinda, I'm doing good."

"I bet you are. You've had this fine man by your side day and night. I'd be doing good too," laughed Melinda.

Keya wanted to knock some sense into Melinda but she was way past being embarrassed. She looked over at Dave and it looked like someone had doused his face with red paint.

Embarrassed, Dave replied, "I'm her boss and I'm just looking out for her."

Shaking her head Melinda said, "Yeah! Yeah! Yeah! Y'all both keep trying to convince yourselves that y'all just friends. Shoot, Ray Charles could see the chemistry between the two of you."

"Melinda, stop it!"

Melinda stopped checking Keya's IV drip, looked at Dave then back at Keya and replied. "Stop what? Telling the truth? Child' please that's one thing Melinda won't stop. I tell the truth no matter what."

Keya thought Melinda was going to go on forever. Why couldn't she just shut her damn mouth?

Keya and Dave sat there shocked and feeling some kind of way about the truth that nosey nurse Melinda was spewing. Truth or not it was uncomfortable nonetheless she had no plans on shutting her big truthful mouth.

Continuing, Melinda said, "Both of y'all sitting in here like y'all don't have feelings for each other. This circumstance alone shows you how tomorrow ain't promised. So why in the hell y'all acting like there is nothing between you guys?"

Both Dave and Keya knew she was telling the truth. How awkward was this? A complete stranger telling them that they wanted to be more than friends?

Believe it or not Melinda was still running her mouth, "You betta swoop him up before I do."

Dave was crimson now. Shaking her wide hips and round

body Melinda said, "Because baby, once I whip it on him he gonna be talking about Keya who. Don't play ya'self, Keya. Besides all these other hoochies on this floor trying to get his attention. Lucky for you you're the only one he has eyes for. Girl, time don't wait for nobody and sometimes love walks out your grasp."

Melinda put a heated blanket over Keya's legs, gave her fresh water and left the room. Keya wondered how Melinda could say so much without taking a breath. Once Meddling Melinda left the room the silence was so thick in the room you could slice it with a knife. Dave's red face, neck and ears were slowly returning to their natural color.

Keya knew there was some truth to what Melinda was saying but who was she to set them out like that. Keya noticed how handsome Dave was. He had an olive complexion, which led her to believe, he wasn't one hundred percent Caucasian, jet-black hair, six-foot frame and a body to kill for. Besides being handsome, he was a respectable person and lawyer.

They were both afraid to break the silence. Neither one knew what to say or do. Was Melinda telling the truth? How would they move forward? Each of them was hoping that the feelings were mutual. They were both afraid of rejection.

She decided to break the silence, "Dave, you have to excuse Melinda. She thinks she knows everything."

Dave refused to let Keya off the hook that easily. Melinda

had opened the can of worms and there was no way he was putting the lid back on. It was now or never and he decided to clear the air. Standing from the leather recliner, he walked over to her bed, grabbed the stool with the six wheels and sat beside the bed.

Keya couldn't believe how her heartbeat escalated. She continued asking herself where these feelings came from. Was she vulnerable and begging for love or companionship in all the wrong places? She couldn't understand how she could feel anything towards a man after all she had been through.

Something was different about the feelings she had for Dave. They resonated in her heart. She felt emotionally connected to him, unlike all the other men. When she had feelings for them more often than not, those feelings resonated between her legs. What was her boss doing to her?

Dave gently placed Keya's hand in his.

"I don't want you to be alarmed by what I'm about to say I want you to think about it and don't push me away."

Scared, Keya closed her eyes. She didn't like the direction of the conversation. She didn't want his pity.

Shaking her head and against her better judgment she said, "I can't make any promises."

"Keya, I want you know that long before this horrendous incident I had a thing for you. I never wanted to cross the lines. After all I am your boss."

There were so many thoughts running through her head. What would people think about her? What would they say at the office? Keya was thinking about everything except herself.

Dave waited for Keya to respond. She never said a word.

"There is no other way to say this. I want you. I want you so bad that my heart aches. I want your mind, body and soul. I want every delicate and complicated part of you. I realized this once you stopped coming to work. Not having you around was hell. I was miserable without you. I want us to grow together on so many levels. Keya, please give me the opportunity to put a smile on your face, soul and heart."

What the hell? He wanted to put a smile on my what? Lord, help me!

Finally, Keya opened her eyes; the most sincere eyes she had ever gazed into met hers. She had no idea what to say or do. She knew she couldn't leave him hanging. She kept asking herself why he wanted her. She was afraid to move forward. She'd never experienced a man who wanted to be hers. She always played second fiddle. Now she was given the opportunity to be his woman and she was terrified. His mesmerizing eyes pleaded with her.

She knew she had to say something, however the words just wouldn't come. She knew when they did; she would have to choose them wisely.

Clearing her throat she replied, "I have issues with trust. I have issues with fidelity. I hurt people, Dave."

"Anything else?" questioned Dave.

With a crooked smile Keya said, "I'm damaged goods. Why would you want to trust your heart with me?"

He saw her inner beauty and it was something he wanted to work towards.

"Keya, I'll never give you a reason not to trust me. You've never been with the right man to want to be faithful. I will never worry about you hurting me because I'm all yours. You will never have to doubt my loyalty or commitment to you. How can you say you're damaged goods? Nothing about you is damaged or undesirable. Keya, nothing is perfect in the beginning but progress towards perfection can be our destination."

49

The Holy Spirit was moving at First Missionary Baptist.

Shanae hadn't been to the First Missionary Baptist Church or any church for that matter in a long time. She was most definitely getting a word from the book of Acts. The smile plastered across Ma Rose's face was worth a million bucks. She was happy Shanae was in church with her. Ma Rose knew that Shanae had some faith issues after losing both of her girls. It was moving to see her clap her hands and say amen and hallelujah every now and again. It was a major breakthrough. After her children died the mere mention of God's name would send her eyes rolling to the top of her head. Not today. She was enjoying the word.

Pulling into Ma Rose's housing complex Shanae asked,

"Has anything changed around here?" Shanae perused the neighborhood and noticed the people hanging out and doing the exact same thing they did when she lived there. However she didn't recognize any of the faces.

Shaking her head Ma Rose replied, "Same stuff just different tenants."

Ma Rose had lived in the housing complex more years than Shanae had been born. Why she refused to move was something Shanae still hadn't figured out.

Shanae had offered to move her from the housing complex on numerous occasions but she had refused every time. Shanae could remember her saying, *"this is all I know. Been here for forty-seven years. I'm not accustomed to your fancy lifestyle."* Eventually, Shanae gave up on the notion of Ma Rose moving.

Shanae braced herself on the wall and unzipped her four and a half inch heeled boots. After placing them against the wall she walked to the sofa and sat down on the plush pillows. Ma Rose hobbled to the kitchen.

"Ma Rose, you need my help in there?"

As soon as Ma Rose walked in the house she immediately headed towards the kitchen. Her roast, carrots and potatoes had been in the slow cooker since the wee hours of the morning.

"No Suga, you sit there and rest. You're my guest. It's been such some time since I've had you here. Just enjoy your time."

"Awe, Ma Rose. I'm sorry I've been neglecting you. It feels so good to be here with you," explained Shanae.

Shanae sat on the couch and for once was worry free. She made a mental note to spend more time with the people she loved and especially Ma Rose. Her normal hustle and bustle life was nonexistent while she was at Ma Rose's.

Her tired body sank into the plush pillows and she thought about all the tasks she needed to complete. Life in general was a never-ending job. Always doing this or that. In spite of all that had happened to her, she would be graduating soon.

Leaning her head back and looking out the window across the yard she saw her old project. Lord, the stories those walls would tell if they could talk. There were happy, sad, trying, disappointing and lonely times in that project. Thinking about Sherrice running through it screaming and yelling brought a smile to her face. Her smile slowly faded away as she remembered all the horrible things Hasaun had done in the projects. He had caused her or should she say she had allowed him to cause so much pain.

Instead of blaming others she always looked at herself and asked, "What could I have done differently?"

She was mature and over the stage of not owning up to her mistakes or problems. Living in the projects she learned so many things. She met several well-rounded folks.

Contrary to what the stereotypes said about poor people Shanae met some great people. While living there Shanae met some very intelligent people who had been dealt horrible hands in life. They wanted to be better but lacked family support to do better. One thing she noted while living there was that they all looked out for each other.

Shanae had drifted off down memory lane but was jarred from her thoughts when Ma Rose yelled, "Food will be done shortly, Shanae."

Smiling, Shanae said, "Ok."

Looking at 201B she shook her head and wondered how her life would have turned out if her girls were still here. She would never forget what she had done for some of the tenants and she would never forget what they had done for her. They always had her back. She remembered tutoring Serena for her GED, which she passed and was now enrolled in community college. Those memories put a smile on her face. It wasn't all peaches and cream but neither was the other side of the tracks. The only downside was that she wished she could have helped more. At that time she just couldn't help more. She had her own problems to deal with. Hasaun, raped, disowned, knocked up and the list could go on and on.

However, those wasn't the worst of her problems Never in a million years would she have ever guessed she would be considered a battered woman. That was the first and last time any man would ever hit her. That one push changed her life in more ways than thinkable. Opening her eyes, Shanae wiped the tears away, exhaled and stood to go help Ma Rose with dinner.

50

Shanae was at a stage in her life when she was finally getting ahead. For so many years she was lost and at a standstill in life. Not knowing where to go or who to trust. Until recently she had been so naïve. She believed that a person who loved you would never hurt you deliberately. She was proven wrong over and over again. Loved ones had hurt her. She had been hurt. By Bernard. By Hasaun. By Keya. By Xavier. Even by her mother. They all had caused her pain. She still had a long way to go to heal.

Because out of all the pain the only people she forgave were her mother and Xavier. She hoped she could eventually forgive them all. Forgiving was still a work in progress when it came to Shanae. However, she knew they would never be allowed in her circle again if she decided to forgive them.

Shanae was taking her time getting dressed. She really

wasn't in the mood to go seen Carmen. Carmen her shrink felt Shanae wasn't seeing much progress because she was covering up her hurt and anguishes. She wanted her to face her problems head on. She told Shanae that she was never going to be one hundred percent until she admitted to herself she was still hurt.

Her shrink told her she walked around with an, "I'm all good attitude," when she was jacked up emotionally and mentally.

Shanae entered the eloquent building and took a seat in the waiting area. She was counting the lines on the polished hardwood floor when she heard her nerve-racking voice.

"Shanae, darling, I am ready for you."

Shanae could not stand her voice. She hated it because it was so whiney. She couldn't understand how someone was always so chipper. Shanae stood and entered her shrink's office, which was quite comfortable. It made her feel at home. Shanae sat on the plush sofa, kicked her shoes off and propped her feet up.

"Hello, Carmen, how are you?"

Smiling, Carmen replied, "I am doing just great. However, my main concern is you. Have you thought about what I suggested?"

Shanae closed her eyes and inhaled. Carmen never had a problem with getting right to the point.

"Carmen, I can't. I don't want to talk to them. I want to

forget about them."

Doodling on her paper, she replied, "Shanae, it may seem scary but I know it will help the healing process. If you confront your problems instead of running from them it would make your life a lot easier."

Carmen wasn't your average shrink. She had gotten to know Shanae's games and she gave it to her straight up. Shanae always had tendency to make her life harder than need be. Carmen always set her straight. Shanae may fuss and complain but she had mad respect for Carmen.

"Running from them! I am not running from them. I can't believe you keep making me out to be this deranged scared fragile person."

Poking her chest Shanae continued, "I am strong! I am very strong," trying to convince herself.

Tears were streaming down her face and she was shaking. Shanae promised herself after this session she would never come back.

Passing her a box of Kleenex, Carmen replied, "Shanae, I am not sorry if I upset you. My intentions are to help you. If you don't want to face your problems then I will drop it. However, if I drop it your recovery will be nonexistent."

What the hell does she mean she's not sorry for upsetting me? She will be when I don't come back and she stops getting that fat weekly check.

Shanae was glad she gotten it through her thick head that she wasn't going to confront Hasaun, Keya and/or Bernard. Never in a million years. Her life was finally on track and she planned to keep it that way. With them not being in her life she was doing well. She pushed them so far back in her subconscious that she never thought about them. Why drum up old emotions if she didn't have to?

The visit ended on not so good terms and Shanae was scheduled for another appointment next week. She had to figure out a way to address her problems without seeing the people who had caused her so much distress.

Shanae was hauling ass to get as far away from Carmen's building as possible. She nearly knocked a young lady down. She was in such a rush she never even noticed her. When she lifted her head, she could not believe who it was. She looked tattered and tired. She had scars all over her face. She wanted to know what happened but she continued out down the hallway and ignored her.

Shanae pushed the door opened and was glad to be outside. Leaving the building she heard her say, "Shanae, please wait."

Shanae picked up her pace and continued walking towards the parking garage. She could hear the footsteps behind her getting closer. There was no way in hell she wanted to talk to her. She never wanted to hold a conversation with her again.

How could someone you love and care for be fake and a phony?

Keya had made it crystal clear that she never cared for her and they were never friends. Shanae couldn't grasp Keya's reasoning because Shanae felt as if they had been sisters at one point in time.

"Shanae, please wait! I am so sorry!" yelled Keya.

She prayed Shanae would stop and hear her out. Keya knew how bullheaded Shanae could be and never thought in a million years she would stop.

Why she stopped was unknown to her. Something about her voice told Shanae they both needed some closure. Something about the way she said sorry seemed sincere. Something about her weak and fragile demeanor softened Shanae's guard.

Standing in the warm spring air, Shanae slowly turned around. Keya's battered face looked so depressing. Shanae tried to stay mad at her but she couldn't. Something was wrong.

"Keya—"

Keya instantly cut her off, "I am so sorry. I don't know how to explain my actions but I know I am sorry. So sorry for all the pain I caused you."

Shanae didn't hate Keya like she thought she did. For the first time she did what any caring person would do. She put her emotions and feelings aside, closed the gap between them and wrapped her arms around Keya. Keya wrapped her limped arms around Shanae.

"Keya, I am sorry too. I never took time to listen to you. Please forgive me."

Shanae and Keya held each other. So many emotions flooded back into her memory. They were once two peas in a pod. They walked to a bench and sat.

Shanae found out a lot about Keya; things she never knew. She found out Keya had been molested by a close family friend and she had never said anything. She found out Keya despised her family for being addicts and poor. She also found out that Keya had been living a lie. She always worked hard because she knew she was poor and never would amount to anything if she didn't. Shanae realized for the first time how bad Keya had it growing up. For the first time, she listened to Keya. Shanae wished her the best and they parted ways.

Shanae cried as she drove out the parking lot. She cried because she would never have her girl in her life again the way it used to be. She cried because she was happy to know Keya was still alive. She had been worried about her when Keya's boss had phoned her. They had settled their differences once and for all. Shanae felt at peace.

She thought about what Carmen said, *"You can't keep running forever because eventually you're going to hit a brick wall."*

Maybe if she confronted them she would be better off.

51

Shanae wasn't up to cooking tonight. She promised Xavier she would cook him a home cooked meal. Now she wished she would have kept her big mouth shut. She despised grocery shopping. She figured while she was there she might as well get everything she needed. She was tired and school was beginning to take a toll on her. She couldn't wait to walk across the stage. She had about four more weeks until she graduated and then she would have a short break before she started law school. She was taking summer classes so she could get it over with. Her mother told her she needed to take the summer off to regroup. Shanae refused to.

Now she saw why people made grocery lists. They knew what they wanted and they had a plan. Her on the other hand, she was walking in circles. Forgetting certain items and then remembering them. She felt as if she was on a scavenger hunt. Her cart was overflowing and she made a mental note to never let her pantry and refrigerator get empty. A trip every two weeks was better than spending over and hour in the store.

She was standing in the produce section. She needed lettuce, tomatoes and green onions. Shanae also wanted a watermelon. She never knew how to pick a good sweet one. The ones she picked were never ripe enough. She picked a small one and knocked on it. She knocked on a few more. All the knocks sounded just alike. She couldn't tell the difference. Hell, she didn't know if you knocked on watermelons anyway.

Then she heard a familiar voice, "Chile, you don't knock on watermelons."

Shanae turned around and there she stood. Not sure what to say so she replied, "Hello!"

It had been a long time since she saw or heard her voice. She didn't know what to think.

"Is that all I get is a hello. Chile, you betta get over here and give me a hug!" yelled Francis.

Shanae hadn't seen Hasaun's mother in a long time. She prayed things would remain cordial. She remembered their last encounter and it had not been good. Francis held her ever so tightly. Shanae had been close to Francis at one point in time. It's funny how two people can grow apart and not even know it.

"Well, it's good to see you. How have you been doing?"

Smiling, Francis replied, "I can't complain."

"Tell me something, Francis, just how do you pick a

watermelon?"

"Chile, you just pick one. And hopefully you get a good sweet one," exclaimed Francis.

"Will you please do me the honors of picking one for me because I never get a good one?"

Francis placed a nice size watermelon in Shanae's cart and was in mid-sentence when Shanae heard his voice. Chills instantly radiated through her body. She gripped the shopping cart.

Francis immediately noticed Shanae's apprehensiveness. She wanted to reassure her that everything would be ok. She wanted to let her know he was a different person. Before he had a chance to utter a word Shanae said bye and walked off.

She didn't look back and she hauled tail getting away from the Ryder's. She wasn't ready to face Hasaun. The last time she saw him he was in the bed with Keya. She despised the ground he walked on.

Francis knew as soon as she heard his voice that Shanae was going to react in a negative way. Hell, she couldn't blame her. Hasaun had weaved a deceitful and abusive web with her and she refused to put up with it. So many nights she prayed they would work it out and get back together. However, once she found out their issues she knew their relationship was beyond repairing. Their being apart had worked out for the both of them. Shanae looked good and was almost done with college.

Hasaun was doing well and Texas had matured him.

"Ma, was that Shanae?" He didn't have to ask. He knew those hips anywhere.

Francis saw the excitement in his eyes. She prayed he didn't do anything stupid.

"Yes, baby that was Shanae but that isn't for you to worry about. Let's finish shopping."

He walked off before she could finish her sentence. Hasaun walked away from his rambling mom. He walked in the direction he saw Shanae going. There were so many things he wanted to explain to her. He finally had started to man up. He wanted to apologize. He had done so many mean and disrespectful things to her. Some he was responsible for. He wished he had never stepped out on her because he would still be with her. The incident at Keya's he had no part in it. He wanted her to know that.

Shanae wished she had gone with her first instinct, which was to leave the store. Shanae maneuvered her cart and walked in the opposite direction. She felt nauseous and her hands were shaking. She made a mental note to find a different store to shop at. When she rounded the corner of the aisle there he stood. Looking at him brought back so many memories. She remembered him pushing her down, cheating, lying and having sex with Keya and his violent outbursts. The sight of him made her sick. She abruptly turned her cart around and headed the other way.

Hasaun refused to let her leave without him speaking his peace. He ran down the aisle and yelled, "Shanae, please listen. I need to explain!"

She stopped walking, turned around and glared at him.

"What do you want to explain? Why in the hell do you think I care? You fucked my life up and if I never see you again it will be too soon."

She was pissed. She couldn't figure out why in the hell she was crying. She knew he wasn't worth her tears. She turned her cart in the opposite direction and began to walk off until she heard his voice again.

Hasaun wasn't disputing anything Shanae was saying. He just wanted her to know he was so sorry. He didn't want to fight or argue with her.

"Shanae, I just want you to know that I am sorry for everything I have ever done to you. I am sorry for being so stubborn and downright cruel at times. I hope you can find it in your heart to forgive me."

Hasaun paused and continued, "There isn't a day that goes by that I don't think about you. There are a few things I want to say to you. I never meant to hurt you. That stuff with Keya was foul. I want you to know that I never touched her before that day. She drugged me and set me up so you could walk in on us. She is not your friend so stay far away from her. I am sorry.

Sorry for everything. Sorry for the loss of the girls, harassing you and lying to you. Please find it in your heart to forgive me. Sorry." With that being said he walked off.

Shanae stood there speechless not knowing what to say. She didn't know what had happened to him but whatever it was it was for the best. He was nice and concerned about her. In fact he was acting like the old Hasaun. She wanted to say something but her mouth wouldn't let her.

When she finally turned around he was out of sight. Shanae finished her shopping in a daze and headed home. On the entire drive home she thought about Hasaun. He was so sincere. She was happy for him. She figured something was finally going right in his life and he was headed in the right direction. She prayed he stayed on that path.

52

Shanae couldn't believe where the time went. Hasaun had consumed her every thought. She wanted to know what was going on with him and why he had vanished. She had tried everything to stop thinking about him. She needed a clear head when Xavier walked into the house. She didn't want him noticing her drama once again. Shanae was adding the finishing touches to dinner when she heard his keys in the door.

Xavier greeted Shanae with his warm mouth. Shanae always enjoyed being around Xavier. They were inseparable and could not keep their hands off each other. Shanae and Xavier were perfect together.

Blushing, Shanae said, "Baby, you haven't had dinner yet."

Smiling, Xavier replied, "I usually have my dessert first." Planting kisses on her neck he slowly began to lift her shirt. Shanae was enjoying every minute of it.

She finally stopped him. "Xavier, stop."

"Why?" Xavier moaned as he slowly massaged her soft firm breast.

"I worked hard on dinner. I say we eat then pick up where we left off," replied Shanae.

Smiling at him Shanae realized just how much she really loved him. On the other hand, she couldn't figure out why Hasaun was on her mind. She was determined to push him out of her mind and concentrate on her man, the man she loved.

Shanae made both their plates and they sat at the table. Xavier was eating like there was no tomorrow and Shanae was playing with her food. She wasn't eating much.

The conversation was short and to the point. Xavier sat and watched Shanae play with her food. She kept drawing designs in her pasta with her fork. Garlic bread was her favorite and she hadn't touched it. Xavier prayed she was okay. There was always something going on with her. He wanted tonight to be a drama free night but he couldn't resist the temptation. He had to know what was up.

"Baby, are you on a diet?"

He knew she wasn't. He just wanted to find out what was on her mind. Shanae was deep in thought and she hadn't noticed Xavier watching her.

With her lips slightly turned up Shanae replied, "No, should I be?"

Holding his hands out in front of him as to ward off evil

spirits Xavier replied, "Whoa, I didn't mean to offend you. I was just asking because you haven't eaten anything on your plate. No, you don't need to be on a diet. You are perfect."

"No one's perfect, Xavier."

"I didn't say 'no one' was perfect I said you were perfect."

Shanae felt so stupid. She was being rude for no apparent reason. She didn't want to tell him she saw Hasaun earlier. She knew that would open up a can of worms. Not that Xavier had anything to worry about or did he? Seeing Hasaun today did something to her. He looked better and at peace. He looked like the old Hasaun. However, why did she care?

Shanae didn't want to lie which was one of the many reasons she wanted this conversation to end. Meanwhile, Xavier wanted to know what was taking her so long to answer.

"What is it baby?"

Shanae blew out air and in a frustrated tone replied, "There is something bothering me but I rather not discuss it tonight. I need some time to sit on it. I don't want to ruin the mood."

Xavier couldn't believe it. She just did not want to tell him what he thought. Offended, Xavier replied, "Baby, the mood is already ruined. Conversation is dry and it is apparent that you are miles away from me. You haven't touched your food and you seem so out of it."

Shanae didn't want to have this conversation, at least

not tonight when she was so confused. She wished she could lie but nothing good ever came from lying. Lying usually brought more heartache and pain. One thing for sure she knew, she loved Xavier and nothing would ever change their love.

God, why do you make my life so complicated?

"Please drop it. I just don't want to talk about it!"

Shanae walked over to the sink and dumped her food. Leaving Xavier sitting at the dining room table Shanae walked out of the dining area and into the living room and sat on the sofa.

Xavier sat at the table totally lost. He knew what was going on and he knew it had to do with Hasaun. He saw the bastard a few days ago. He knew it would only be a matter of time before he wreaked havoc on Shanae's life. He prayed she was smart and didn't fall for him hook, line and sinker. He had seen so many women fall for no good men. His sisters were prime examples of choosing no good men. He couldn't understand why some women were so weak.

Xavier emptied his plate and walked into the living area. He wanted to know what was going on but he decided against badgering her anymore. If she wanted to shut him out then so be it. He was tired of playing her damn games. He wasn't a kid and he had stopped playing games years ago so she could play her games solo he was leaving.

When Xavier entered the living room Shanae was lying

across the chaise looking at the ceiling. She avoided eye contact and didn't acknowledge him. For her to treat him like a complete stranger; it hurt. In hopes of getting her attention he cleared his throat. Still no response from her, Shanae was way too dramatic.

"Well, Shanae, dinner was great," faking a yawn and a stretch he continued, "It's been a long day. I'm going to get out of here. I'll see you tomorrow. Thanks again."

With that said Xavier grabbed his keys and left.

Shanae faced the terrace and continued ignoring him as she heard the door close. Shanae felt so bad. She hadn't planned to hurt his feelings. She was trying to spare him. Shanae stood and walked out on the terrace. Shanae enjoyed the warm breeze. Sitting in her chair, she thought about life and how it had once spiraled out of control, back into control, back out of control and now was it in or out of control. She wanted to know what control really was.

Shanae didn't have the energy to go chasing after Xavier. She wanted to but she fought back those feelings. Maybe she should give up on him as well. Eventually he would hurt her like all the others. For so many years she felt she needed someone to have her back. Now, as a mature lady, she knew she didn't need anyone to have her back. She was a strong intelligent woman who had her own back.

Shanae stood up and yelled, "I don't need anyone!" I have

my own back!"

Pointing into the black night she continued, "I don't need you! You! You or you!"

Deeply consumed in thought, she hadn't heard Xavier come back into the house. He was upset and he wanted answers. She played him like a sucker and he wanted to know if it was for her old flame. Now looking at and hearing Shanae he wished he would have left and stayed gone. Xavier kept hearing her repeat it over and over, *"I don't need anyone!"*

Shanae was still on a rampage yelling she didn't need anyone she was oblivious to the fact that Xavier was listening to her.

Walking closer out on the terrace, hearing her harsh words further pissed him off. Each time she yelled she didn't need anyone it felt like the wind was getting knocked out of him.

"Does that include me?" He was on the verge of breaking down but he would never let her arrogant ass see him break down especially if what he thought was true.

Startled, Shanae turned around and gazed into the eyes of a wounded man. She didn't know what to say or do. There was so much she needed to explain.

"Xavier, how long have you been standing there?"

"Long enough! Now, will you please answer my damn question?"

Scared for the first time in a long time she had to make a

choice that would change her life forever. She had to answer him but she was confused. Her life was chaotic. She could be strong and face the drama head on or she could push everything and everybody out of her life and start over. Mentally she was exhausted it would be much easier to just walk away.

"Shanae, please answer my question!"

Shanae figured it was easier to run away from her problems or was it? If he could have given her the evening to think about the situation she knew it wouldn't have taken her a second to answer his question. At least that's what she thought.

"I love you. How can you question that?" pleaded Shanae.

"I never questioned your love. I asked if you needed me. Do you need me or are you wasting my time?"

Shanae wished she were in a faraway place that was drama free, unlike her life. Drama always followed her she was beginning to wonder if she was a drama magnet.

"There is a fine line between needs and wants. I don't—"

Xavier cut her off in mid-sentence, "Stop with all this psychological bullshit. A need, essential, necessity, obligation. What is more important to you a need or want?"

"A need is more important Xavier, because—"

"Okay. Shanae, now answer my question. Am I a need or a want?"

He could see her squirming. He had set her up and was he

slick about it. She wanted to dig a hole and crawl in it.

"Xavier, that was a trick question. I don't want to answer," whined Shanae.

Xavier was growing tired of the game. Shanae could tell by the look on his face he was becoming frustrated.

Without any emotions at all, Xavier replied, "Shanae, please answer my question."

"A want! I want you. I don't need you," yelled Shanae.

Xavier felt like shit. He had bent over backwards, sideways and every other way for her. Naturally, he was hurt but he wanted her to know he knew Hasaun was back.

Wounded and grasping for hope he asked, "Do your wants ever become needs?"

Shanae felt awful. She walked over and wiped the lone tear away that fell out of his eye.

"Sometimes I want them so bad I think I need them. Xavier, it's a hard question to answer. I love you and I don't want to lose you I need oxygen and good health."

He had one last question he wanted to ask and then he would leave for the evening.

"Shanae was I a—"

Ring. Ring.

"Just one second."

Picking up the phone Shanae said, "Hello,"

No answer. Again she said, "Hello,"

When Shanae heard his voice, she almost blacked out.

"Shanae, it's me. Hasaun. Can you talk?"

"I'm sorry you have the wrong number," Shanae lied and hung up the phone.

Edgy Shanae said, "You were asking me a question."

"Yes, I wanted to know if I was a need or a want before Hasaun came back to town?"

Shanae's entire demeanor changed. She was nervous and fidgeting with her hands. Her palms became sweaty. She could not understand why this was happening to her. Most of all, she couldn't understand why she was giving Hasaun so much of her time. She could tell that she was hurting him and he was getting tired of her shenanigans.

She played dumb, "What are you talking about?"

How in the hell did he know about Hasaun?

Laughing, Xavier continued, "You should really practice what you preach. Who was on the phone?"

Shanae didn't know what to say or do. Why was she lying? She hadn't done anything wrong. She wanted to be honest but lies just kept rolling off her tongue.

"I believe you heard me say it was the wrong number," yelled Shanae.

Too much was going on. Her patience was running thin. Hasaun had questions. Xavier had questions. She had questions. It was too much.

Shaking his head he replied, "Yeah, I heard you say wrong number but your eyes said something else. My mother told me that the eyes never lie and your eyes, my dear, tell me you are hiding something. What it is and why you're acting like this has Hasaun's name written all over it."

Shanae didn't utter a word. She refused to talk. She was afraid of the lies that would continue to roll off her tongue. She sat silently which was pissing Xavier off.

"When did you see him?"

Shanae ignored the question.

Again Xavier said, "Shanae, when did you fuckin see him? Why are you acting like this? What are you hiding?"

Shanae couldn't explain her feelings. She wasn't hiding anything but she was afraid that Xavier would hold this moment of deceit against her.

Whispering, Shanae replied, "Today at the grocery store."

He knew it. The only thing she had to do was tell the damn truth.

"So that explains your actions and why you have been so distant over dinner."

He couldn't explain why he was so calm. Inside it felt as if his heart was mush.

"Xavier, I didn't want to upset you. The reason I was so out of it was that Hasaun was pleasant. He even apologized. It was really weird and yes, I was thinking about that, but not how you're thinking I was thinking."

Upset, Xavier replied, "So now you're a mind reader? You're just a jack-of-all-trades. Tell me what I'm thinking now?"

Stunned, Shanae replied, "I didn't mean it like that."

"Well, how did you mean? I still want to know who was on the phone," yelled Xavier.

As if on cue the phone rang. Shanae didn't want to answer the phone. Xavier was looking at Shanae with doubtful eyes. The phone continued to ring, Shanae refused to answer it.

"It's probably just the wrong number again," lied Shanae.

Shaking his head, Xavier laughed, "Or Hasaun."

Shanae walked over and picked up the phone, "Hello."

"Shanae?" whispered Hasaun.

Stunned Shanae asked, "How did you get my number?"

Hasaun knew it was against court orders but he had to speak with her.

"It was on my mom's caller ID. I guess you called earlier."

Shanae had forgotten about her earlier attempt to contact Hasaun.

Xavier was stunned. He couldn't believe he had her telephone number. She had to have given it to him. He wondered why their relationship was so complicated. Xavier hoped she ended the conversation soon because he couldn't stand to listen any longer.

He walked out to the terrace and sat in one of Shanae's

fancy chairs. Xavier put his face in his hands and took a deep breath. He was afraid. Afraid because he didn't know where he and Shanae stood. He hoped they could work things out. Never in his life had he been so let down. Shanae was playing entirely too many games. She would most definitely have to figure out who she was and what she wanted.

"It feels good to hear your voice. I have never stopped thinking about you. I know I did you wrong and I am sorry."

So many emotions were running through Shanae's mind. She was glad he had finally started to mature but there was too much from their past for her to overlook. For some reason it felt good to know he was in a better place.

"Hasaun, it was good seeing you also."

"I really want you to know that I never deliberately tried to hurt you. Please tell me you accept my apology." Hasaun sounded like he was pleading.

"Hasaun, we were young and we both made some mistakes, some worse than others but I do accept your apology."

"Shanae, that means so much to me."

Hasaun was elated that she accepted his apology. Her being upset with him and them never having any closure was wearing him slick.

"You don't have to toot my horn. It's time we both move pass this hurdle and get on with our lives. I hate to cut you short but I have company and talking to you is somewhat rude, if I do say so myself."

"My bad. I didn't realize you had company. I guess I'll get off this phone. Shanae, it was good seeing and talking to you."

Hasaun didn't want to get off the phone.

"Same here. You make sure you take care of yourself."

"You do the same. Bye, Shanae."

"Bye, Hasaun."

And with that said Shanae placed the phone in its cradle. She knew he was a better person and because of that she had to push him away. After all he was still her first love.

Shanae turned around and to her surprise Xavier was no longer in the room. She instantly became scared. She prayed he hadn't walked out on her.

How could she ever consider being cordial to Hasaun again? While she had found it in her heart to forgive him there just wasn't a place for him in her life. How in the hell was she going to explain this to Xavier?

Her chest was pounding and her nerves were taking a toll on her. She ran around the house looking for him. There was no sign of him.

Shanae walked into the living area. At that moment she felt all alone and abandoned. She had pushed the one and only man out of her life that loved her unconditionally. Why had she been so stupid? Shanae tried to hold back her tears but they took control of her. Her cries echoed throughout the house.

"Xavier!" yelled Shanae, frantically perusing the room.
"Xavier! Xavier!" again Shanae yelled with urgency.

Hearing Shanae's frantic scream, Xavier ran back into the
house. Her back was to him and she was on her knees. She was
so beautiful even in her brokenness. He stood in the living room
watching her. His feelings were all over the place because of
this drama filled woman.

Oblivious to the fact that Xavier was in the house Shanae
whimpered, "Xavier, I am so sorry. Please come back. I love you
so much."

Shanae wiped the tears from her eyes and continued, "I am
so stupid. The only man who ever showed me love. I have
pushed you out of my life. Please, God, send him back to me. I
love him. I love him so much. I need him in my life."

Her last statement shocked him. There was no way in hell
she needed him. Not big bad Shanae Davis, the Shanae that
didn't need anyone.

"I need you too."

Startled by his voice. She thought he had left her. She
leaped up, turned around and sure enough there he stood
looking as handsome as ever. Shanae ran to him and he
wrapped his muscular arms around her slender body holding
her ever so gently.

"Baby, remember we have to always be honest with each

other or this relationship won't last based on lies."

"I know. I am sorry.

53

Victor was becoming tired of the same outcome. His PI had been looking for his father and sister for two years now. Every time he met with him it was the same song and dance. We're getting closer. At this point Victor thought the guy was banking off of him. He was considering hiring someone else. He loved his family and wanted them together. He hated not living in the same town as his mom and sister. Not knowing where his dad and other sister relocated to was worse. Missing his family always gave him an excuse to go home. Victor was homesick and he missed Jade.

At the spur of the moment he decided to go home. He didn't exactly know where he would stay since he didn't know where his mom's house was. He decided to crash at Shanae's. He couldn't wait to see Jade. He talked to her every night. He wished she would move to Chicago.

Once Victor got home, he was going to let his family know

that he was looking for his father and sister and that he needed their help. He hoped Dena could give them some help. Victor was beginning to want more out of life. He wanted a family and he planned to have one.

After a long day's work Victor entered his walk in closet and began packing a carryon bag with everything he needed. He didn't want to be bothered with baggage claim. He would just purchase any items he forgot. He was headed to O'Hare airport.

Victor used his key to let himself in. When he entered Shanae's house he immediately felt at home. He went to the guest bedroom and put his belongings away. Victor freshened up and headed downstairs to fix something to eat. Victor decided on a BLT and chips. He was sitting at the table devouring his sandwich when he heard Shanae's keys in the door. It made him sit straight up in his chair. His sister was laughing. He hadn't heard her laugh in a long time. What also caught his attention was a male's voice. Victor sat quietly and eavesdropped. They sounded happy. Victor was relieved his sister was getting her life back on track.

Victor eased from the kitchen table and walked into the foyer. In the foyer, Shanae and some dude were lip locked.

He prayed this dude was legit. She had been through a lot. He was overprotective of her because he didn't want to see her hurting again. Witnessing the chemistry they were sharing, he wished he had made other arrangements. There was no way in hell Shanae was going to welcome his intrusion with open arms. They were deeply enthralled with each other they hadn't even heard him approach, the love-struck duo. He made sure not to get too close to them because he didn't know if they would be scared and end up beating him down. Clearing his throat finally caught their attention.

Immediately they stopped swapping salvia and looked up. Both startled. One face was excited and the other was perplexed.

Xavier, seeing the happiness on Shanae's face, figured he wasn't an intruder. She let go of Xavier and ran over to her handsome baby brother. It had been awhile since they saw each other. Xavier was puzzled. He didn't know who this man was or how in the hell he got into Shanae's house. Whoever he was, he meant a lot to her because her smile never left her face.

It was Xavier's turn to clear his throat. He was starting to feel like the third wheel.

"Excuse me for being rude," stated Shanae. She walked over to Xavier and replied, "Vic, this is my friend Xavier. Xavier, this is my little brother, Vic."

She was happy to have two of the three men in one room that she loved with all her heart. Even though she was nervous. She could tell Victor was sizing Xavier up. She knew she had deliberately not told Victor she had a boyfriend and she was very vague about Victor to Xavier. It seemed to be some tension in the room, which made Shanae antsy. The two alpha males were fighting for their territory.

Victor had to realize she was his big sister. After a brief standoff, Victor offered his hand to Xavier. They said their hellos and remained cordial. Each man noted the firmness of each other's handshake. The silence was too much for Xavier and his being introduced, as a friend wasn't sitting well with him either. He figured he would give Miss Drama Queen some time with her brother. He wasn't feeling the energy anymore.

"Shanae, since you have company I'm going to head out. I will get with you tomorrow."

With wrinkles in her forehead she replied, "Why so soon? You and my brother haven't even met. I can cook dinner as planned."

Shanae was borderline begging. They had plans for the evening and she didn't care if Victor was there or not.

Xavier hated when she begged. Any other time he wouldn't be able to resist her considering, she had just stepped on his toes and called him a friend. It wasn't going to be hard at all tonight. I guess you could say he was in his feelings.

He never could stay mad at her long; she was just so damn adorable She looked at him with pleading eyes.

He placed her chin in his hand; kissed her ever so gently on her lips and replied, "I will see you soon." Just give me a call when you have time."

Xavier said goodbye to Vic and walked out the door.

Shanae could not believe how rude he was acting. This was not how their evening was planned. She should have been somewhere in that house getting it on by now. But her brother had to show up unannounced.

"Vic, hang on. I have to see what's wrong with him." With that being said she ran out the front door.

Before he stepped into his vehicle she yelled, "Xavier! Hold on a second!"

She ran up to him and put her arms around him.

"Why are you leaving?" She gave him a concerned look but he was staring straight through her. "What's wrong?"

Just a few moments ago you was acting as if I weren't anything to you. Now you have the audacity to question me.

He needed to get away from her and think about some things. They hadn't been dating that long and every time he turned around they were faced with drama. It was starting to be too much.

"Nothing, Shanae. Just nothing."

"I just don't get it. Why are you upset?"

"I am not upset. I just need to get home and relax."

"What the hell did I do now?"

Shaking his head he answered, "Are you really that naïve? You should think before you speak."

"So, now we're insulting each other? What the hell did I

do?"

With a smug look on his face he said, "Listen, your being out here with me is being rude to your guest. Why don't you just let your "friend" go home and we can discuss this tomorrow or whenever you have time for your friend."

Wow, she didn't realize her calling him a friend would really bother him. She just wanted a chance to discuss it with Victor. How could she be so smart and so dumb at the same damn time? She was always getting in heated situations that could have been avoided.

"We had a great night planned. Please don't bail on me."

He couldn't believe her. She had her priorities all wrong. She thought just because he loved her, he was to act like some puppy madly in love wagging his tail behind her. She was sadly mistaken.

"Shanae, it's been a long day. I just need to go home. We will see each other tomorrow.

He was madder than she realized. "I'm sorry. Seeing him shocked me. I'm sorry if I hurt your feelings. It was not intentional."

Shaking his head he replied, "It's never intentional with you. The shit you do is ridiculous. Everything you do is to make sure you stay looking good in others eyes. You never think about anyone but yourself. Introducing me as a friend or talking to your psychopathic ex on the phone while I'm at your house.

You're too smart not to think. Just think some damn time. You're not the only one with feelings. You're too damn smart to act so simple."

He was upset. He made some valid points but she was not going to continue to let him insult her.

"I understand. I hurt your feelings. I'm sorry for hurting them. I didn't realize calling you a friend was going to piss you off so bad. I am truly sorry. I'm taking ownership of hurting your feelings and I'm genuinely S-O-R-R-Y. I'm sorry. Yes, I know my saying sorry doesn't make you feel better at once but I want you to know I'm sorry."

Shanae took a deep breath and continued, "You calling me naïve or simple isn't making you feel any better so let's stop with all the sly ass comments. This conversation is getting us nowhere let's just talk tomorrow. Let me take my simple naïve ass in the house."

Shaking his head he said, "Are—"

"Stop shaking your damn head at me."

With a slight smirk on his face he continued, "Are we just friends in your eyes? Or are we more? I just have to know."

"I can't believe you had to ask me that. Xavier, yes, you are more than a friend. If you don't know that then why are we standing here going back and forth?"

Staring at her blankly he replied, "If it's okay with your brother I will call you tomorrow."

With that being said he got into his truck, closed the door, started the engine and pulled off.

Shanae stood there watching him pull off until he was out of sight. She wondered why love had to be so complicated and confusing. If two people loved each other and wanted to be together why was there so much hurting involved?

It took everything in him not to turn around as he watched her staring at him through his rearview mirror. He loved her with his entire being. He kept asking himself how he could be in love so quickly but he never came up with an answer. You just can't help who you love.

Shanae walked slowly up her driveway and into her house, her brother was anxiously waiting. When Shanae entered the house she walked into the living room he was sitting on the couch.

Looking at her demeanor Victor knew things didn't go as planned. Or, she didn't get what her spoiled ass wanted. He totally understood why this man was upset. She referred to him as just a friend. That was the worst thing a female could do to a man's ego if they were more than friends.

Vic walked over to Shanae and started singing the infamous song by Biz Markie, "Oh baby yooouuuuu—you got what I need but you say he's just a friend."

Squinting her eyes instead of slapping him she yelled, "Vic, I am so pissed at you. I'm glad you think this shit is funny."

"Sis, how many times have I told you to chill out around me? I might not like the thought of men dating my sister but I'm not going to flip out. I would be concerned if you didn't have a man. The way you guys were all over each other, I would have to say that you all are definitely more than friends."

Victor took a sip of his water and shook his head at Shanae.

Shanae couldn't believe he thought this ordeal was amusing. She looked at him and wanted to scream. She was sick of people shaking their heads at her. Narrowing her eyes she said, "I can't believe you are joking around while I am stressing. This isn't funny. And another thing, your cock blocking ass better call before you ever come over here again!"

Victor spit his water all over the carpet. He had been called many of things in his life but never a cock blocker. He couldn't regain his composure. He was bending over laughing at the top of his lungs. Before they realized it, they were both hurled over in laughter. She was laughing to keep from crying. He was honestly entertained.

After several minutes of mutual laughing Victor said, "Sis, I love you and I only stayed here because I didn't know where momma's new place was. Next time my cock-blocking ass will call before I come. But on a serious note, you might want to go get things in order with your friend."

Shanae kissed Victor on the cheek, grabbed her keys and ran out the door. Victor watched her go down the driveway, hop into her vehicle and pull off.

He continued gazing out the window and thought about how happy he was to be home. No matter how much crap he talked about Columbia there was nothing like being home. He couldn't wait to see his momma and of course he couldn't wait to surprise Jade. He decided to call it a night.

Shanae and Xavier had been seeing each other for several months but she had never been inside his house. Since she was new on the dating scene she always wanted to be on her own turf. Not that she wasn't invited to his home she just preferred to be at home. At least, that's how she felt in the beginning, but now she felt comfortable and safe to go into his home. He had just stopped asking her and figured when she was ready she would come over.

She was a little reluctant to knock on the door. Their last encounter wasn't the best and she didn't want things to get worse. There was no way in hell they were going to bed mad at each other. Shanae was standing on the outside his door contemplating whether to knock or not.

Xavier had no idea she was so close to him. He was sitting on the leather sofa nursing a beer, thinking about how hopeless Shanae looked when he drove off and left her standing in her driveway. He sat the empty bottle down and walked to the kitchen to get another one when he heard a light tap at the door. There weren't many people who stopped by to visit him.

He assumed it was Ray stopping by needing help with his woman problems.

He yelled, "Who is it?"

His loud baritone voice startled Shanae. She wanted to go back to her truck and deal with this in the morning. Instead, she replied, "It's me."

Xavier couldn't believe she came to his home. He looked around and made sure there was nothing out of place. Thank God he was an immaculate housekeeper. He was happy to hear her voice but he wasn't going to let her know it just yet. He snatched the door open with his beer in hand and walked back to the sofa. Shanae walked into the house, shut and locked the door behind her. She took a deep breath to clear her head. She knew one thing. She did not come over here to argue and fight. She wanted to get back on the right foot and make sure they were still cool.

Looking around the exquisite home she was very impressed. He actually had great taste. He had the normal bachelor pad colors, which were red and black with white accents. Everything was color coordinated and matched. She knew his momma or sisters had to have helped him with some of the décor in the home. She couldn't wait to see the remainder of the house, especially his bedroom. Xavier couldn't help but watch her as she took in every detail of his home. She was amazing.

Shanae slowly walked over to the couch Xavier was sitting on, nursing his second beer and watching television. Shanae was thinking about what she wanted to say. For God's sake if she came off simple and naïve he would stone her. She knew she had messed up and she wanted to make it right.

It took everything in him not to pull her in his arms and hold her. His head was saying that he needed to teach her lesson. His heart was saying, kiss her and give her hug. He decided to go with his head, the one on his shoulder's that is, and play hardball.

Clearing her throat she said, "May I sit down?"

Never taking his eyes off the television, he nodded his head.

Not happy with the way he was treating her, she reminded herself it's not about her. She hurt his feelings so she would have to make things better. She gently sat on the leather sofa, grabbed the remote and turned the television off. Xavier continued looking at the blank black screen.

His attention was on the television. He never looked Shanae's way. He wanted to show her how it felt to be let down and hurt. Shanae hoped she could fix things because she didn't want to lose him. She had lost many people in her life. She couldn't stand to lose another person.

Shanae thought he looked good when he was upset. She wanted to jump in his lap and give him a kiss. She quickly decided against it. As she envisioned herself getting up off the floor after he knocked her off him.

Men are so hard to understand. Shanae wanted to understand this one. She was going to do everything in her power to make things right. She didn't want him to walk out of her life because she made one slip up and called him "friend."

Xavier leaned his back against the arm of the sofa. Shanae picked his feet up and sat down. His muscular legs fell into her lap. It was hard for him not to react to her touch. There was no way in hell he could stay mad at her. Giving her the cold shoulder was something new for him and he was failing miserably.

Shanae hated the way things had turned out. She just wanted things to go back to the way they were. "Xavier, I'm sorry."

He never acknowledged her and continued looking at the television screen. Running out of options, she slowly eased herself from under his legs and on top of him. Her face was nestled in between his arm and chest. She just wanted him to say something but he continued to hit her with the silent treatment.

Again she whispered, "Baby, I am sorry."

Taking a swig of his beer, Xavier replied, "Money bags let you leave the house?"

She opted out of knocking the beer out of his hand and

decided to ignore him. She scooted closer to him and didn't say anything about his snide remark.

No matter how rude he was trying to be there was one thing he couldn't deny. He couldn't deny their love. The only thing that was on his mind was holding her closer and never letting her go. Xavier stretched his arm across her slender body and sat his beer on the table.

Shanae sensed he wasn't as upset as he was pretending so she started placing small kisses on his muscular chest and neck. He didn't stop her so she continued. After feeling his tense body relax she knew she had him where she wanted him. Eventually, his muscular arms embraced her and held her tightly. To feel his acknowledgment was all she needed. She promised herself she would start thinking before she spoke and to be considerate of others. Once you said something you could never take it back. She was truly sorry for downplaying their relationship. She was going to be sure to start empathizing with others.

Xavier raised her on top of him and kissed her passionately. In between kisses Shanae continued to apologize.

"Baby, I am so sorry. It won't happen again."

Xavier was truly in love with this complex drama magnet."

Shanae, it better not. If you want to be friends then we can. I happen to think of you as my woman and I thought I was your man. Now, if I'm wrong please put me in my place."

Shanae sat up. Now she was straddling Xavier. She looked into his sexy brown eyes and replied, "I know I made a mistake so stop rubbing it in. I love you so much."

Shanae was happy to be back in his good graces.

"Raise up, Shanae, I have to go to the bathroom."

Shanae got up and let Xavier go. She used his bathroom break as a time to call Vic and let him know she wasn't coming home. She was ending the call when she saw him standing in the hallway looking at her.

"What?"

"You checking in with your bro? Did he say it was okay for you to stay?" joked Xavier

Smiling, Shanae replied, "Yeah, I told him I was staying over my friend's house."

Shaking his head he said, "Lady, when are you ever going to learn."

He walked over to her picked her up and carried her into the bedroom.

54

Shanae and Xavier had finally patched everything up. They were talking to each other and had placed honesty at the top of their priorities list. They both realized honesty was truly the best policy. At last her life was back on track and she was happier than ever. She had kicked the drama to the curb and vowed to stir clear of drama.

Her shrink was proud of her recent improvements. She was focusing on her recovery and there was nothing holding her back but her own pride so she had decided to put her pride on the back burner and concentrate on her mental health and stability.

She proved that she could kick depression without medication. Her shrink had given her options early in the counseling sessions. Shanae was adamant on not taking medication and she was doing so much better. She'd witnessed people looking like zombies on antidepressant medications. She decided to go at it the old fashion way counseling, meditation and prayer.

Shanae was happy Victor and Xavier hit it off. After their first encounter she didn't know how it would pan out. She found out they had a lot in common. Sports being the number one thing they had in common. Shanae had much to be happy about in her life. She was happy her brother and Jade were going stronger than ever. She and Xavier were good. As a matter fact they were really good. However, the only person that needed someone was her momma.

Her momma was happier than ever. Everybody needed somebody. It made her wonder if her momma had someone. She wasn't in her business as much as she used to be. She also kept taking mini-trips to who knows where. That didn't include the disappearing acts she'd been accustomed to lately. Shanae made a mental note to run this pass Vic. Thinking about all she had accomplished over the short period of time pleased her. She figured it was time to stop the trip down memory lane.

She decided to focus on the issues at hand. The family had a late lunch scheduled at Murray's. She had a few hours to kill so she went to her home gym and ran on the treadmill. She was happy where her life was headed. There was no turning back now. She was headed to the top. She couldn't wait to get the crew together. After her brief run, Shanae had an hour before she was to meet Xavier at his house. They were going to meet the rest of them at the restaurant. She hoped lunch went well. She hadn't been her normal self and with graduation only weeks away she was scattered brain.

She had so many last minute things to do. She'd finally mailed all her announcements. It was a bittersweet occasion like every other milestone in her life. There was always the thought of what her father and Janae were doing. There was always the thought of their never being there. That weighed heavy on her heart. One day when she found them she prayed they would be a happy family. Knowing they were out there but not knowing where. The not knowing was the worst feeling she ever had. She prayed every night for God to lead her to them. Her prayers hadn't been answered. Looking on the bright side, she was thankful for the people she did have in her life.

Really not in tuned with the discussion, she heard the guys talking about sports. Jade and her momma were talking about fashion. She was too busy worrying herself silly with things she had no control over.

Joining into the conversation she said, "Y'all talking all that noise about basketball which one of y'all plays the best."

They had both been bragging on how they beat Xavier's friends at a pick me up game. She wanted to know who the better player between them was. Silence swept over the entire table. Shanae continued looking back and forth between them waiting for an answer. No one replied.

Again she asked, "Who is the better player?"

Dena couldn't believe Shanae was starting trouble between the two men.

Vic and Xavier both sized each other up and in unison replied, "I am!"

Smiling, Shanae said, "Looks like we may need a game of one on one to see who's telling the truth."

Now instead of bragging about their earlier accomplishments on the court they were debating whom the better player was.

"Shanae, now look what you started," laughed Dena.

"I was just curious," said Shanae as she winked her eye at the ladies.

Both Dena and Jade shared a laugh. The guys were starting to draw attention to them and Dena had had enough.

"Okay children! Enough is enough, agree to disagree."

Lunch ended on a high note. There was nothing like the presence of family, food and good conversation.

Shanae was taking her shoes off when Xavier walked through her bedroom door. He was so refined. It wasn't often you found a refined, educated, employed, well-mannered and lovable man. She was happy he walked into her life.

Pulling his shirt over his head he said, "For the record, I am better than your brother on the court."

Laughing, Shanae said, "I believe you, baby."

"What's so funny?"

Throwing a pillow at him that he sidestepped, Shanae laughed, "You and your ego are funny. I need you to stop worrying about basketball and get over here and handle your business."

"What business are you talking about?"

Shanae slowly and provocatively slipped out of her sundress. She was wearing a black lace thong set that fit her perfectly. Walking away from him she replied, "Maybe we don't have any business to handle."

Purposely dropping her dress, she bent over to pick it up and Xavier replied, "That business? I remember now."

55

Shanae had cased the place for weeks. She knew his

routine like the back of her hand. She had made up her mind.

Today was the day. So many times before she had chickened

out, but not today. She didn't know what she would say to him

but something had to be said. After talking to both Hasaun and

Keya, it felt refreshing. She felt lighter in spirit. It was as if her all

the stress and worry had disappeared. She figured talking to

him would benefit her recovery.

    He didn't even look the same. He looked tattered and

old. He lacked his usual debonair stance. Maybe he was

suffering after all. Did people like him suffer? Once news started

spreading around the hospital that he raped his stepdaughter,

no one wanted him near them. Eventually, he was forced to

resign. He found it easier to resign then to deal with the

pressure of people knowing what he had done.

    Approaching him, sitting on the porch, noticing the

unkempt yard, she found this was totally out of the norm. She noticed him squinting as she closed the gap between them. Shanae wasn't scared anymore. She was ready to face her demon head on.

When she was inches away from the porch he finally recognized her. You could see the anxiety spread across his face. His nervousness was an understatement. He was fidgeting and beads of sweat was scattered about his forehead. Not knowing where she got her courage, she walked on to the porch and sat in a chair adjacent to his. Maybe it was the fact he didn't intimidate her anymore. On the other hand, she had her gun in her purse. She prayed he didn't do anything that would leave him with holes in his body. Looking into his jaundice looking eyes, she no longer saw the strong man she once knew. He was broken.

Bernard hadn't seen her since he had sex with her or was it since the hospital when their daughter died. He knew it was one or the other. He wasn't sure because the cheap vodka was clouding his memory. One thing he did remember was the day they made love. She had the sweetest and tightest pussy he had ever had. He was a sex addict. He had to have it and he didn't care where he got it. With the exception that it had to be a woman, he didn't discriminate. All his life he tried to be normal. It was his uncle's fault. He molested him for years. He ruined him. He noticed she was still gorgeous and she still turned him on. If she slipped, he would most certainly have his way with her again.

Breaking the silence she asked, "Why? Why did you do it?"

She'd wanted to know this answer for years. She never saw this ever happening. There was nothing about her stepdad that screamed pedophile or pervert. Never in a million years would she think he would violate her.

Bernard didn't know what to say or do. He didn't know why. He knew he had some issues but he had never gone as far as he had with Shanae. Sex was at his fingertips. He had plenty of women, sex toys, pornography, whips, chains and many other sex toys. He even had a separate apartment where he took his women. He never had to take it. He only took it from her because she was so self-righteous. Boy, when he found out she was a virgin he lost his mind.

"You haven't been invited here. Now leave!" he demanded in an unsteady voice.

"Bernard, you owe me this. What did I ever do to you?" screamed Shanae.

He smirked at her, took a swig from his pint of vodka and laughed. His laugh was an evil laugh. The women were like trophies to Bernard. Something for him to brag about. They never did anything for him but to prove a point. The point was, that he was in control.

Furious she yelled, "I want you to know that I used to love you. I never thought you would ever bring me harm. When you took my virginity you destroyed a piece of me, I can never get that back. That dreadful event is etched in my head for life. I want you to know I am stronger because of you. What you did was less of a man. You are a sick bastard and no real man would have ever done what you did."

With that being said she stood and walked off the porch.

On wobbly legs, Bernard stood and walked into the yard. He was a man. He didn't care what she said. Hell, he was the man.

"Shanae!" yelled Bernard.

Inches from her car she heard him yelling her name. She turned around and for the first time she saw him as a weak, scrawny, pathetic man. He was running around the yard screaming and yelling trying to get his point across. It was too late. She didn't care anymore. She was laughing at him. He reminded her of "Mister" in The Color Purple, once Cellie left him, just like Mister Bernard had taking everyone for granted. Shanae never uttered another word. She just stared at him.

Bernard felt as if Shanae was staring right through him. His pride wouldn't let him apologize so instead he screamed.

"I am a man. You selfish little heifer!"

Shaking her head, she realized he was mentally ill. He

continued to spew profanities. She refused to allow him to belittle her. She hopped in her truck and yelled, "Bernard, you will never be a man!"

She backed out of his drive way and left. Looking in her rear view mirror, she saw him jumping around and screaming in the middle of the street. She couldn't believe how ignorant Bernard was acting. He was no longer the strong predator he used to be. He was a feeble creep who was most definitely reaping what he sewn.

56

She managed to graduate in the top five percent of her class and she had received several honors and accolades. She had been accepted to a slew of universities. She wanted to stay close to home so she chose the University of Chicago Law School. She decided she would spend her time in Columbia and Chicago. She anxiously waited for them to announce her name. She was beyond excited. She and Xavier were both graduating today. His family was in town and she would finally get the chance to meet all of them. They were all celebrating following graduation. She couldn't wait to get up on the stage. All her life she had waited for this moment. It was even better than she had imagined.

"Shanae Nicole Davis."

Shanae walked on stage, received her diploma and exited toward the right of the stage. All her family and friends cheered. She was elated to make so many people proud. Over all the screams and yells there was one voice that stood out the most. Shanae searched the crowd until their eyes met.

She couldn't believe her eyes. She looked beautiful and she was happy. Shanae also wanted to know who the white guy she was holding hands with was. Keya winked at Shanae and waved. Shanae smiled and winked back. Walking back to her seat, she saw Keya and her friend leaving the building. It felt good seeing Keya.

Seeing Keya had her start thinking about her family she hadn't seen in a long time. Oh, how she wished her father and Janae could have been at her graduation. She decided not to harp on that situation and to enjoy her graduation.

Seeing Xavier walk across the stage was so thrilling. When she saw him she felt warm inside. She was so proud of him. They both had accomplished something major in their lives. Someone once told her that success is any move towards a worthwhile goal. She felt super successful today.

Graduation was awe-inspiring but she knew the celebration afterwards was going to be just as awesome. Dena had gone all out for her and Xavier. Dena knew how to plan an event and you would walk away from the event talking about it for months. Shanae had many reasons to celebrate.

Xavier and Shanae were both ecstatic. All their family members were getting along and having a grand time.

This celebration is off the hook.

Xavier's parents were inspirational. They raised a special young man that had Shanae's heart. His sister's were beautiful and pleasant. She couldn't ask for a better party. She stood back and watched everyone interacting. Ma Rose, Vic, Xavier, Momma, Jade, Xavier's family and all their other friends. It was great to be surrounded by family.

Shanae continued working the crowd and mingling with everyone in attendance. Shanae noticed a lady dressed in black standing towards the back of the crowd. She never saw her before. Shanae walked in her direction. She wanted to speak and thank her for celebrating with them. As Shanae walked towards her the strange lady ran from the building. Shanae figured she walked into the wrong party.

She and Xavier were being the polite to the guests that they hadn't spent much time with each other. She noticed he was with his friends. She figured it was the perfecting timing for them to figure out their plans for the evening.

She grabbed a flute of champagne and walked towards the trio. Shanae could only imagine what Xavier, Kent and Ray were talking about.

Approaching the men she said, "Hey, guys!"

She was nice and pleasant as always. She hoped they didn't mind her stealing their friend for a brief second.

Xavier wrapped his arms around her and pulled her perfect body closer to him. Ray was still mesmerized by Shanae's

beauty. Kent couldn't believe how he gawked after her.
Taking the attention away from Ray, Kent said, "Hey, Shanae!
Congratulations. It must feel good both you and your man
graduated together."

Shanae genuinely liked Kent. However, Ray made her feel
uneasy.

"Kent, it does feel good. Thanks."

Kent could see why Xavier was head over hills for her. She
was worth keeping. "Well, I'm happy for the both of you."

Ray still hadn't said a word which made him borderline
spooky. Shanae had told Xavier on numerous occasions that he
was a creeper. Kent noticed Shanae's uneasiness and nudged
Ray.

Strutting, Ray managed to say, "Hey, what's up, Shanae?"

Hesitantly, Shanae replied, "I'm doing good. How about
yourself?"

"Oh, I can't complain. Congratulations on graduation."

Smiling Shanae said, "Can I borrow Xavier for a few
minutes?"

She didn't wait for their answer as she pulled him over to
the side and started lining up their evening plans. She was
talking a mile a minute. Xavier bent down and kissed her
delicate lips. She closed her eyes. She loved the way his lips felt
against hers.

"I needed that."

Smiling, he replied, "So did I. What's up?"

Holding on to his waist and looking into his eyes, she said, "I'm trying to figure out if you're going to be able to get away later. I will be at home."

"Then I will be there."

"Ok, can't wait to see you later." Shanae gave him on last peck on the lips and walked off.

She went over and gave Ma Rose a much-needed hug. Shanae had kept her promise and had been visiting her every week. Ma Rose had played an intricate part in her life. When she was at her lowest Ma Rose had become her motivational force.

"Shanae, I'm so proud of you. You know you're like a daughter to me. I love you so much," stated Ma Rose.

"Awe, Ma Rose, I love you too. I am so grateful for you."

Ma Rose handed Shanae and envelope. On the front it said open when you graduate from law school. Frowning, Shanae said, "What is this about?" Passing the envelope back to Ma Rose.

Shanae continued, "You can give this to me when I graduate from law school." She had done a good job of not crying all night but she felt the tears forming in her eyes.

"This is too beautiful of a day for you to be shedding tears."

Handing her some Kleenex, Ma Rose said, "Dry those tears up and keep that pretty little face together.